Faking it

MANCHESTER
UNIVERSITY PRESS

For Colin McKenzie, who provided the inspiration for this book

Faking it

Mock-documentary and the subversion of factuality

Jane Roscoe *and* Craig Hight

Manchester University Press
Manchester and New York

distributed exclusively in the USA by Palgrave

Copyright © Jane Roscoe and Craig Hight 2001

The right of Jane Roscoe and Craig Hight to be identified as the authors of this work has been asserted by them in accordance with the Copyright, Designs and Patents Act 1988.

Published by Manchester University Press
Oxford Road, Manchester M13 9NR, UK
and Room 400, 175 Fifth Avenue, New York, NY 10010, USA
www.manchesteruniversitypress.co.uk

Distributed exclusively in the USA by
Palgrave, 175 Fifth Avenue, New York,
NY 10010, USA

Distributed exclusively in Canada by
UBC Press, University of British Columbia, 2029 West Mall,
Vancouver, BC, Canada V6T 1Z2

British Library Cataloguing-in-Publication Data
A catalogue record for this book is available from the British Library

Library of Congress Cataloging-in-Publication Data applied for

ISBN 0 7190 5640 3 *hardback*
      0 7190 5641 1 *paperback*

First published 2001

10 09 09 07 06 05   10 9 8 7 6 5 4 3 2

Typeset in Minion with Rotis Semi Sans
by Northern Phototypesetting Co. Ltd, Bolton
Printed in Great Britain
by Bell & Bain Ltd, Glasgow

Contents

Illustrations

Every effort has been made to obtain permission to reproduce the images in this book. If any proper acknowledgement has not been made, copyright-holders are invited to contact the publisher.

Tables

Preface

This book is the culmination of a number of years of teaching and research on fact-fiction forms – those film and television texts which retain elements of documentary aesthetics but do not fit comfortably into most existing definitions of 'documentary'. We are very conscious that comparatively little writing has been done in the specific area of mock-documentary, and we hope that this work will serve to stimulate debate both on the nature of this form in particular, and fact-fiction forms in general. Many of the observations we make of mock-documentary are based on texts produced within the last few years, and, given the apparently increasing acceptance of this form within mainstream cinema and television (with even the American animated sitcom *The Simpsons* featuring a mock-documentary episode entitled 'Behind the Laughter'), no doubt readers will be able to add to and contest our analysis of its main textual strategies. We are in the position of attempting to create a general theoretical framework within a comparatively under-theorised area of media studies, and consequently our discussion inevitably ranges across a wide variety of areas within the study of cinema and television. We hope that readers who are more expert than us in any of these areas will grant us licence to cover their speciality in such a cursory fashion.

This book is primarily intended to introduce ideas about mock-documentary to students and academics working within media and documentary studies. For media studies students unfamiliar with work on documentary, and for the more general reader, Chapters 1 and 2 are intended to cover theoretical material that we feel is relevant to mock-documentary. We full acknowledge the difficulty of presenting a subject as complex and challenging as 'representations of the real' in such an abridged fashion, and we hope that the reader who is a novice in this area will feel inspired to pursue some of the more comprehensive theoretical texts that are available. Similarly, those readers who are already familiar with recent documentary theory are encouraged to treat these initial chapters simply as an explanation of the wider framework that we use to discuss mock-documentary.

A feature of this book which we hope will prove useful to both teachers and students is a listing of texts which we have identified as 'mock-documentaries' (contained in the first section of the Filmography). We have found many of these texts difficult to obtain, and some items of this list are films and television programmes that we know only by reputation. Please bear this in mind before expending time and expense hunting down any texts that look promising. We must also acknowledge that this list is inevitably incomplete, both because we have taken the rather arbitrary decision not to include short films within our discussion and because any number of mock-documentaries are likely to have been produced between the time that this book was written and its publication date.

Our research into mock-documentaries has proved extremely enjoyable, and there are a considerable number of our favourite scenes and pieces of dialogue from mock-documentaries which (despite our best efforts to include them) did not survive the final editing for this book. We hope that the often sober analyses contained here add another layer of appreciation to viewers' encounters with mock-documentary, and encourage readers to seek out the more classic examples of the form.

Jane Roscoe and Craig Hight

Acknowledgements

As is always the case, there are many people and institutions to thank.

We are grateful to the University of Waikato for funding this project and to our colleagues in the Department of Screen and Media Studies for their support, in particular Ann Hardy and Geoff Lealand. Students who participated in the third year Documentary Screen course in 1998 and 1999 were the early audience for the bulk of this work; their enthusiasm and criticisms have been important in the development of our ideas.

The Visible Evidence conferences of 1998 and 1999 provided a significant forum for us to develop our arguments. We are grateful to fellow participants who debated and discussed the work with us, and have shared our enthusiasm for the material.

Comments and critiques along the way from Richard Kilborn, Arild Fetveit, Patti Zimmermann, John Hess, Carl Plantinga and Janet Walker have all helped to sharpen the arguments contained within this book. Costa Botes provided invaluable materials on *Forgotten Silver*, and in many ways are responsible for us taking up the mock-documentary challenge.

A very special thanks goes to Derek Paget, who has encouraged us throughout this project. As well as being a wonderful critic of our work, he has displayed all the qualities of a good friend.

Finally, we would like to thank our families and friends for all their support, especially Michael Johnson and Cathy Coleborne.

Introduction: mock–documentary and the subversion of factuality

There are any number of fiction and non-fiction texts which challenge, articulate or reinterpret many of the central tensions within the documentary form. Of the non-fiction texts (that is, the examples of these texts that could be seen as still operating *within* the genre), the most significant have perhaps been reflexive documentaries. At the margins of documentary are also a growing body of *fictional* texts which, to varying degrees, represent a commentary on, or confusion or subversion of, factual discourse. This book addresses a particular group of these fictional texts, which are distinctive in that they appropriate documentary codes and conventions and mimic various documentary modes. In other words, we examine here those fictional texts which to varying degrees 'look' (and sound) like documentaries.

This group of texts have been labelled using a variety of terms; 'faux documentary' (Francke, 1996), 'pseudo-documentary', 'mocumentary', 'cinéma vérité with a wink' (Harrington, 1994), 'cinéma un-vérité' (Ansen, 1997), 'black comedy presented as in-your-face documentary', 'spoof documentary' and 'quasi-documentary' (Neale and Krutnik, 1990). We favour the term 'mock-documentary' (including the hyphen) for two reasons:

1 because it suggests its origins in copying a pre-existing form, in an effort to construct (or more accurately, re-construct) a screen form with which the audience is assumed to be familiar
2 because the other meaning of the word 'mock' (to subvert or ridicule by imitation) suggests something of this screen form's parodic agenda towards the documentary genre. This is an agenda which we argue is inevitably constructed (however inadvertently by some filmmakers) from mock-documentary's increasingly sophisticated appropriation of documentary codes and conventions.

It is the nature and extent of the relationship which mock-documentaries collectively construct with the documentary genre which marks these fictional texts as a distinctive screen form, and which is the primary focus of this particular study.

Before outlining the structure of this book, however, we need to be more specific about the types of texts which we do not see as falling within the category of 'mock-documentary'. Paget, for example (Paget, 1998: 87), uses the term to refer to Michael Moore's *Roger and Me* (1989), an example of a documentary where the director effectively becomes the central protagonist, as he works to construct a self-reflexive commentary on American business practices of the 1980s. And Nichols (Nichols, 1991: 56–68) has written of 'mock-documentary' in a manner which neglects to investigate the distinction between mock-documentaries and reflexive documentaries. In both these cases, the writers essentially refer to representational strategies *within* the documentary genre – to *non-fiction* texts with particular attributes (although Nichols obscures the issue by referring to both fictional and non-fiction texts in his discussion on reflexivity).

Our definition of mock-documentary is specifically limited to *fictional* texts; those which make a partial or concerted effort to appropriate documentary codes and conventions in order to represent a fictional subject. A close approximation, and one which we argue is an important precursor to the mock-documentary form (see Chapter 5), can be made to the 'tradition' of fake April Fools' Day news stories now regularly included within news bulletins. In general terms, these could be referred to as 'hoaxes' constructed by the producers of these programmes, but they are none the less deceptions which the audience is assumed to be party to, to accept and to appreciate.

That said, however, we do not include within mock-documentary the numerous recent examples of media hoaxes which have been perpetrated *against* news organisations – those instances where media professionals (within print and electronic media) have been discovered to have faked either some information or entire news stories. These are clear transgressions of journalism's own professional code, texts which are intended to operate as non-fiction and be accepted as such by their audience.

Winston has written of the controversy over these hoax documentaries, which have attracted widespread condemnation – not least from rival forms of news media (Winston, 1999). His list of the more infamous United Kingdom examples includes reconstructed and faked sequences within a number of recent docu-soaps and documentaries (such as BBC's *Driving School* and Channel 4's *Too Much Too Young: Chickens* documentary on boy prostitutes). The most interesting of these recent cases is the variety of faked footage by German filmmaker Michael Born. Because of the cult status which these texts have gained in Germany, they have become interesting examples of texts which are celebrated for their deliberate blurring of the line between fact and fiction. We place these texts in a close proximity to mock-documentary, but we do not see them as constituting examples of the form itself (in large part because they have emerged from a completely different filmmaking agenda).

Winston notes the problems which commentators have had in distinguishing between techniques which documentary filmmakers have employed since the early development of the form, and explicit violations of the documentary project. To some degree these 'faked' documentaries can be claimed as simply more recent manifestations of the tension within documentary between the need to reveal the 'truth' and typical frustrations with being able to acquire photographic evidence of that truth. Some early documentaries, for example (most notably Robert Flaherty's *Nanook of the North* (1922)), have been revealed to be the product of a much greater degree of mediation on the part of its director than was initially claimed. This is a tension which has arguably become more acute in recent years, given an increasingly commercial broadcasting environment within which documentary filmmakers are required to operate. (At times it appears that television networks view the line between fact and fiction as merely either an opportunity to engage the voyeuristic tendencies of viewers or an inconvenience to constructing dramatic television.)

Although these types of faked non-fiction texts are not included within our definition of mock-documentary, they could perhaps be described as increasing the awareness of how fragile is the adherence to the standards demanded by factual discourse. In this sense, they provide a significant part of the wider context for the acceptance of mock-documentaries, in that they represent further evidence of a destabilisation of the distanced, responsible and principled stance of documentary or news practitioners.

In seeking both to account for the increasing popularity of the mock-documentary form, and to suggest some of the theoretical implications which this form presents, we position these texts within this wider context of an increased awareness of the constructed nature of factual programmes. We also view as significant for the emergence of this form a culture in which the association between factual discourse and factual means of representation is increasingly tenuous. In fact, the documentary aesthetic (those codes and conventions associated with the various documentary modes of representation) often appears to be becoming merely one of many styles used within the fictional realm (including the realm of advertising). Within this complexity of social-political and audio-visual contexts, mock-documentary seems to be symptomatic of a subversion of the continued privileged status of documentary itself.

The majority of this book comprises chapters detailing the complexities of the mock-documentary as a textual form. The initial chapters are devoted to situating the form, both within a variety of contextual factors which appear to have supported its emergence and in relation to other texts within the fact–fiction continuum. Chapter 1 looks to define 'factual discourse' – the set of assumptions and expectations which form the basis of the documentary genre – and the particular cultural position which this discourse has enjoyed. This chapter also includes some discussion of the tensions within the genre, in particular where different codes and conventions appeal to competing, often contradictory, cultural understandings of how 'reality' can be represented. The intention here is partly to foreground the dynamic nature of documentary, but more specifically to provide also an outline of the codes and conventions which mock-documentary appropriates from the genre.

While Chapter 1 presents the traditional basis (something of an abstract ideal) of the documentary project, Chapter 2 looks to outline the nature of the more recent expansion of textual concerns and representational strategies employed by documentary filmmakers. The focus of discussion here is especially on those documentary texts which suggest a separation of the close association between documentary aesthetics and the underlying assumptions and expectations which define factual discourse (performative and reflexive documentaries). To a large extent, these are generic transformations which derive from the tensions inherent within the genre, although 'performative' and 'reflexive' are also documentary modes which reflect changes within the wider social, political and cultural context which the genre addresses. An important part of our definition of mock-documentary is that they represent an external (fictional) challenge to documentary. This chapter discusses those *non-fiction* texts which have problematised the relationship between documentary codes and conventions and factual discourse.

Mock-documentary represents only one instance of a continuum of fictional texts which are characterised by a blurring of the line between fact and fiction. This is a characteristic which this form shares with those texts grouped under the label of 'drama-documentaries'. Chapter 3 looks to compare these contrasting screen forms, concentrating especially on the nature of the distinctive relationships which they each construct towards the documentary genre.

As suggested above, a defining characteristic of mock-documentary is an (often latent) reflexive stance toward documentary – a 'mocking' of the genre's cultural status. Chapter 4 continues this effort to identify the characteristics of mock-documentary as a screen form, briefly outlining the strategy we have used for distinguishing between the variety of texts which can be defined as mock-documentary. This chapter extends the definition of mock-documentary outlined above, to suggest some of the complexities of textual concerns which have thus far typified this screen form.

We introduce here a schema of three 'degrees' of mock-documentary, in part reflecting the diversity in the nature and extent of these texts' appropriation of documentary aesthetics. A key part of our discussion within this chapter is our contention that the emergence of mock-documentary is evidence of wider changes in the relationship which audiences have with factual discourse. Our schema for studying mock-documentary is intended to acknowledge especially the degree of reflexivity towards factual discourse which individual mock-documentaries construct for their audiences. This is a discussion which necessarily draws upon an understanding of the complexity of viewers' engagement with the mock-documentary form.

Chapter 5 outlines a speculative genealogy for the mock-documentary as a distinctive screen form, suggesting various textual precedents within American and British cinematic and television traditions which have made this form acceptable for both filmmakers and audiences. This 'genealogy' is intended to provide some background for the detailed discussion of mock-documentary texts in Chapters 6, 7 and 8. Given the large, and increasing, number of texts which fall within the category of mock-documentary, we have chosen within these three chapters to focus on a number of texts which collectively suggest the complexity of the form. (See our Filmography for a fuller list of mock-documentary texts.) We need to emphasise here that we are by no means attempting a taxonomy of mock-documentary – the form is still too underdeveloped to endure any exhaustive categorisation. Instead, these discussions are intended to promote wider debates about the central issues posed by mock-documentary; the nature of its sophisticated appropriation of factual discourse, the tensions within its parodic examination of documentary, and especially the complexity of the reflexive stance towards the genre which it constructs for audiences. Finally, our concluding chapter offers some discussion of the theoretical implications of the growth of mock-documentary as a distinctive screen form.

1

Factual discourse and the cultural placing of documentary

Mock-documentary is a 'fact-fictional' form which has a close relationship to both drama and documentary. It not only uses documentary codes and conventions but constructs a particular relationship with the discourse of factuality. This chapter outlines some of the key issues for our analysis and discussion of this relationship which mock-documentary texts build with documentary and factuality discourses. It is not a comprehensive survey of the documentary theory literature but an overview of the key arguments with a view to showing how documentary positions itself as the screen form most able to portray the social world in an accurate and truthful way. 'Documentary suggests fullness and completion, knowledge and fact, explanations of the social world and its motivating mechanisms' (Nichols, 1993: 174).

Documentary holds a privileged position within society, a position maintained by documentary's claim that it can present the most accurate and truthful portrayal of the socio-historical world. Inherent to such a claim is the assumption that there is a direct relationship between the documentary image and the referent (social world). Within documentary then, the image and the record of that image are seen as being one and the same, suggesting a strong and direct connection between the cinematic record and 'reality'. It is because of such perceived connections between the recorded and the originary event that documentary continues to suggest a 'fullness and completion' in its representations. The cultural status of the documentary form is effectively challenged by the development of the mock-documentary, which is itself symptomatic of the wider challenges to documentary which we outline in the following chapter.

Things we know about documentary

There are a number of cultural assumptions, and underlying discourses, which serve to reinforce documentary's privileged position. Importantly, documentary has attempted to present itself as being engaged in a coherent project, that of objectively recording reality. It has sought to present itself as a unified discourse, yet documentary has never been able to secure such coherency. In fact, the very concept of 'documentary' is riddled with a number of competing discourses that position it as artistic, propagandist, educational, scientific and so on. These competing voices are perhaps most apparent in the numerous attempts to define documentary.

There is little consensus over how to define documentary, whether it should be considered a genre or a style, or understood in terms of the particular stance it takes towards the social world. Early documentarists Grierson and Flaherty considered the documentary to be an artistic endeavour, a creative enterprise through which raw material was transformed into meaningful narratives. For those associated with the Direct Cinema movement in the 1960s, the idea of 'creative interpretation' was rejected, and replaced by the rhetoric of naturalism, the idea that documentary could *capture reality as it unfolded*, as if the camera were absent (Winston, 1995). Such notions of documentary as 'pure' and unmediated still hold much cultural sway, and can be seen as underlying the recent resurgence in 'fly-on-the-wall' documentaries, and the emergence of the 'docu-soap' see Chapter 2.

Although some critics have unproblematically characterised documentary as a genre (Britton, 1992), Kilborn and Izod (1997) suggest that the term 'documentary' may have outlasted its critical usefulness, owing to the proliferation of actuality programming and the difficulties in pinning down the criteria by which texts can be defined and distinguished from fictional texts.

One approach to defining documentary is to consider its relationship to fictional texts. This approach is predicated on the existence of a fact/fiction dichotomy, with documentary on one side, and drama on the other. In this way documentary is regarded as factual and in direct opposition to the imaginary worlds of fiction. Although culturally this seems to be somewhat taken for granted, it is a rather unhelpful in the attempt to understand the complexity of the genre. We prefer to think about documentary as existing along a fact–fictional continuum, each text constructing relationships with both factual and fictional discourses. This takes us a little closer to understanding Nichols when he describes documentary as 'a fiction (un)like any other' (Nichols, 1991: 113). Nichols refers to the way in which documentaries, like fictional texts, construct narratives and employ similar codes and conventions (say the use of dramatic music) to construct stories about the social world. Whereas the view of documentary as a recorder of reality suggests that out of raw data stories (and therefore meaning) naturally emerge, our view acknowledges the creative work through which documentary transforms the fragments of real life into argument or story. This perspective highlights the constructed nature of documentary representations of reality – and also the subversive potential of those texts (such as mock-documentary) which play with these constructions.

Documentary does not provide an unmediated view of the world, nor can it live up to its claims to be a mirror on society. Rather, like any fictional text, it is constructed with a view to producing certain versions of the social world. However, Nichols' description, while pointing to the similarity between documentary and other fictional texts, also suggests a difference between them. Plantinga (1997) argues that this difference is expressed by the stance that documentary takes towards the social world. Even though we may agree that documentary representations are as constructed as fictional ones, the stance that documentary takes toward the social world is one that is grounded on the belief that it can access the real. Plantinga calls this an 'assertive stance' (40). Further, documentary contains a call to action in the sense that the representations on offer not only yield information about the social world but can and should alter the social world. In this way documentary has attempted to align itself with what Nichols refers to as 'the discourses of sobriety' (1991: 3); that is those non-fictional systems such as Law, Science, Medicine and Politics that have instrumental power.

The challenge which mock-documentary represents is not just to documentary itself but perhaps also to the wider cultural adherence to these 'sober' discourses. Mock-documentary looks to 'mock' central tenets of classic documentary; in particular, the beliefs in science (and scientific experts) and in the essential integrity of the referential image.

Documentary and science: a shared project of Enlightenment and progress

Documentary has been most successful in its attempts to align with the other discourses of sobriety through its association with the discourses of science. Renov (1999) has argued that documentary is intimately tied up with the scientific project and the advancement of technology. Documentary is a product of the Enlightenment in which the discourses of Science were married with a liberal-humanist view of the world and were propelled by a desire for social change and progress. Science soon replaced religion as the new paradigm and developed a variety of scientific methods and procedures to chart, map and ultimately uncover the truth about the social world. In doing so, the Enlighteners aimed to change the social world for the better of all humanity (Seidman, 1994). '[Documentary] is the domain of non-fiction that has most explicitly articulated this scientific yearning' (Renov, 1999: 85).

This 'scientific yearning' has also been propelled by a 'modern faith in facts' (Paget, 1990: 8). Science prioritised the documentation of factual information and in effect fetishised 'facts'. As science and the scientific method developed as the new dominant paradigm, so 'facts' became significant to individual lives. This was summarised by Ellul in 1971: 'Modern man needs a relation to facts, a self-justification to convince himself that by acting in a certain way he is obeying reason and proved experience' (quoted in Paget, 1990: 17).

The camera became an apparatus through which the natural world could be accurately documented and recorded and, in this way, was able to capitalise on the new thirst for facts. There is a long history of pictorial representation as a mode of scientific evidence, a tradition extended by the development of the camera as a scientific instrument. In his discussion of the development of the camera, Winston (1995) suggests that the public understanding (and acceptance) of the camera as an accurate recorder of reality was shaped by its association with other scientific apparatus such as the barometer and the thermometer. Just as these were considered tools which were able to give objective and truthful readings of the natural world, so too the camera was regarded in much the same way. It gained credibility through its association with these scientific tools. Importantly, these instruments were seen to be removed from human judgement; their credibility was linked to their perceived objectivity. 'Beyond art, beyond drama, the documentary is evidential, scientific' (Winston, 1995: 127).

Such a connection has led to a focus in documentary on facts, evidence and objectivity. It is a position which has itself also been informed by the shift in social thinking about the very concepts of 'objectivity' and 'subjectivity'. Raymond Williams (1976) discusses the development of the objective/subjective dichotomy formed in the mid nineteenth century and notes that it was at this time that the concept of 'objectivity' was explicitly linked with the concept of 'fact'. This was in opposition to the concept of 'subjectivity' which was linked with an impressionistic view of the world. Such a definition of objectivity lies at the heart of positivistic discourses and underpins the 'realist' tradition in art and film – especially the representational form eventually termed 'documentary'.

> Documentary's scientific connection is the most potent legitimation for its evidential pretensions ... To this day, documentarists can not readily avoid the scientific because the context is built into the cinematographic apparatus ... Watching 'actuality' on the screen is like watching the needles dance on the physiograph: the apparatus becomes transparent; the documentary becomes scientific inscription – evidence. (Winston, 1995: 137)

Of course, documentary has never been free from question, as Renov argues, but it has come the closest to convincing us that the camera never lies.[1] But, like the project of science, documentary has attempted to extrapolate general truths about the human condition. It has convinced us that its objective, unmediated view of the world provides the most direct route to such truths. In doing so, it explicitly offers up its representations as factual evidence. In contemporary society there is a double-edged response to such connections. On the one hand, facts and evidence are seen as constituting truth, while, on the other, there is a questioning of certain types of evidence as automatically and equally true.[2]

The very concept of 'fact' has been problematised in contemporary social discourse. Facts have tended to be conflated with the concept of truth, just as objectivity has been typically seen as interchangeable with 'facts' and 'truth'. It is useful to think about facts as having both an ontological existence, and an epistemological one. As Bhaskar (1989) argues, 'facts are real and we are not free to invent them, but they belong to the realm of epistemology and are discovered through theoretical paradigms and are historically specific social realities' (quoted in MacLennan, 1993: 26). So, for Bhaskar (and MacLennan) there is a 'reality', but that 'reality' can be accessed only through social knowledges; facts may exist but they have to be interpreted.

Within positivist discourse facts are seen to speak for themselves, to be self-evident. They are used as 'evidence' at the service of 'objective arguments' about the social world. Because they are seen to be free of subjective interpretation they are more highly valued and regarded within society (Malik, 1996). Documentary has in the past capitalised on these associations between facts and truth, by claiming that its photographic lens is capable of recording facts about the social world.

Expositional documentary itself follows the structure of a scientific experiment. In a scientific experiment the scientist tests out a hypothesis by collecting data and submitting this to a variety of experimental tests. Results produced by these test are seen as confirming or denying the original hypothesis. Similarly, the documentarist (the scientist) making an expositional documentary builds a narrative around a social problem or issue (hypothesis). The data collected, in this case various pieces of evidence and facts, are then objectively scrutinised and presented within the text (experimental process), yielding insights (results) which lead to a textual closure in the form of a solution to the problem (Silverstone, 1985).

Recording the real: the camera does not lie

The claim that documentary can present a truthful and accurate portrayal of the social world is not only validated through the association of the camera with the instruments of science but also depends upon the cultural belief that the camera does not lie. This is predicated on two things: the first is concerned with the power of the photograph, and the second with the discourses of realism and naturalism. Together these provide the basis for our strong cultural assumptions about documentary, while also allowing issues of ideology to be side-stepped in our evaluations of the form.

Bazin (1971) argued that the photograph should be understood as a phenomena of nature, and further, that the relationship between the image and the real should be seen as one and the same. The philosopher Charles Peirce (1965) argued that the photograph physically corresponds, point by point, to nature, and in doing so (as Winston notes) mistakenly described the photograph as indexical. That is, the image and the originary object are seen to be connected physically, rather than symbolically. This reinforces, and provides the basis for, the notion that the camera can capture the real. As Barthes (1981) has stated, the authenticity of a photograph outweighs or exceeds the power of representation. We assume that if a photograph exists the object must be found in the real world. Like the photograph the documentary representation is thought of as containing a trace of the real. The image is seen to make direct reference to the extra-filmic world and is thus connected in some directly physical, indexical way to that world.

This brings us to a discussion of referentiality and evidentiality, so central to the documentary project. Although the spoken word is important to the documentary form (as narration or testimony) it is the visual which has prominence. In particular, it is the visual that seems to carry so much weight when evaluating the fidelity of documentary truth claims. Cowie argues that seeing is believing and, that 'seeing is more real than knowing' (1997: 2). Documentary relies on the discourses of realism and natural- ism to maintain its referential status. Realism is associated not only with documentary but with fictional texts also. While in fiction it serves to make a plausible world seem credible and real, within documentary it works to make the arguments more believable. The discourses of realism have a second consequence within documentary, one that results in a masking of the ideological nature of their representations (Britton, 1992). Realism tends to render representations as ideologically neutral; such representations seem to appear as naturally occurring rather than con- structed. The documentary camera is conceptualised as a neutral eye, merely collecting and presenting material to the viewer. Images are taken at face value, unproblematised, unlike such images in fictional works which are more often assumed to be metaphorical and needing interpre- tation. This is summed up by Kilborn and Izod (1997):

In documentary, however, images usually function in a metonymic mode. Metonymy is the rhetorical convention in which the image represents a part of a larger whole and partakes of the same order of reality as that to which (in the case of lens based imagery) it is indexically bonded … In short, metonymy is a signif- icant part of the persuasive machinery of documentary realism. (36–7)

The materiality of documentary representations

The discussion of documentary materiality is one way in which to engage with its indexical and referential relationship with the real. Laura Marks (1999) utilises the metaphors of 'fetish' and 'fossil' to explore these relationships. 'My use of the fetish and fossil metaphors relates to the materiality of film itself as witness to an originating object: to documen- tary's indexical quality' (224). Marks uses these metaphors to explore the non-audio and non-visual sensory knowledges produced through docu- mentary; here, however, the focus will be on using these metaphors to explore documentary's relationship with the real.

   Both fetish and fossil are defined in terms of their contact with such originary objects, and as such encompass various histories and narratives of the social world. Importantly, both are seen to contain physical traces of the originary object. Fossils contain the physical traces of vegetable and animal tissue that is now 'recreated in stone' (Marks, 1999: 227). Marks quotes Deleuze (1989), who argues that fossils are not cold, stone objects, but are live, dangerous things. A fossil is an important artefact because of the stories it can tell, and those stories are valued because they are seen as directly linked to a historical material reality. Just as the fossil becomes a piece of evidence, so too documentary representations are seen as carrying a trace of the real, and that it is through such traces that we can gain access to reality, be it historical or contemporary.

While the fossil may be thought of as a natural phenomena, the fetish is most definitely a cultural one. Again the fetish is linked to an originary powerful object, and a fetish is itself given life like powers through physical contact. In this way it is not a representation but sacred in its own right.

All documentary images are fetishes, insofar as they retain some indexical trace of an originary event. However, they do not transparently reflect it ... Documentary cinema has the same materiality as any other fetish, in that it brings the multisensory character of the originary object into contact with the body of the viewer. (Marks, 1999: 240)

Both documentary and fossils need to be interpreted, as the evidence cannot speak for itself. However, a distinguishing characteristic of documentary is its continuing claim that its recordings of the social world do speak for themselves. This is an axiom which is itself partly shaped and informed by the discourses of journalism.

Standards of truth-telling: journalism, education and public service

Documentary practice, and the cultural assumptions and expectations we have of it, have been informed by the discourses of journalism. Journalism, like the broader discourses of education, is linked with documentary through its adherence to the project of the Enlightenment and its modernist tendencies. As Hartley (1996) notes, journalism has a huge investment in modernist technologies of truth. Like documentary, journalism's status relies on the cultural acceptance that it has, as a genre, a certain 'truth value' (Meadows, 1999: 45). This has developed (and been maintained) through the development of a set of professional practices, the most important of which is objectivity (Lumby, 1999). Journalism has sought to encourage political emancipation through reasoned and logical argument (Felski, 1998). These objectives, and such professional standards of truth-telling, are utilised within the documentary project for similar ends. It is interesting to note that, while postmodernist theorising has questioned the metadiscourses of (say) science, and has certainly challenged the documentary project, journalism has been slow to 'uncouple' from the notions of 'science, progress, and truth' (Hartley, 1999: 29).

The discourses of journalism tend to reiterate the role that documentary has constructed for itself as an objective commentator on society, and an educator of the masses. It continues to draw on positivist practices in order to legitimise its modes of inquiry. Further, journalism's perceived cultural weight also stems from other professional practices such as detailed and extensive research, another practice through which documentary similarly seeks to validate its claims.

Yet, like the very concept of documentary, journalism too is a fragmented field and this characterisation of journalism is only a partial rendition of a broad arena. As Lumby (1999) notes, developing parallel to such professional ethics associated with a serious press were discourses we might now describe as 'sensationalist' and 'tabloid' (30–1). Journalism's 'trivialities' tend to be overlooked, receiving a less sustained analysis (Langer, 1998). (Some of the more effective mock-documentaries involve a deconstruction of the nature of journalistic practices see especially our discussion of *Man Bites Dog* in Chapter 8.)

Both documentary and journalism are able to maintain their privileged positions because audiences continue to put faith in their professional practices and their ability to present truthful and honest accounts of the social world.

Towards a working definition of documentary: practitioners, texts and viewers

The range and diversity of documentary texts and practices, coupled with the contradictions and tensions in the underlining factual discourse, does not make documentary an easy concept to pin down and define. No one definition seems able to capture all of its complexities and variations. Unlike Kilborn and Izod, however, we believe that the term 'documentary' is still a very useful one. Following Nichols (1991) we have at least found a working definition of documentary that goes some way to capturing these complexities and allows a recognition of how documentary shifts and changes over time. Like Nichols, we take a tripartite approach to documentary and consider in the following section the production, texts and consumption of the form, in the development of a working definition. This tripartite framework is also one which we have found useful for distinguishing the mock-documentary form from others which are similarly positioned within the fact–fiction continuum (in particular, reflexive documentary and drama-documentary – see Chapters 2 and 3 respectively).

Production context

It is generally accepted that there is a community of documentary practitioners who share in common a language, a set of goals and a mandate to represent the 'real' world rather than an imaginary one. The influence of a journalistic discourse is expressed through a commitment to representing their subject in a fair and reasonable way, and to fulfil audience expectations that they will present real people, places and events. Shared assumptions include the importance of detailed and wider-ranging research, and the importance of covering both sides of the story. There is also an (implicit) acceptance of an ethical code of conduct. Documentary filmmakers seek to represent their subjects fairly and honestly, while still maintaining editorial control. A key issue for the filmmaker is to consider the impact their representations will have on the lives of the subjects after the film has been broadcast. Of course, no filmmaker can know exactly how a film may be received, but there is an attempt to consider possible outcomes and to balance these during the final editorial process.

Documentary can also be seen as constituting an informal institution. There may be institutional groupings, for example a documentary unit of a national broadcaster, or a more informal community or a cross-national one (for example, European Documentary Union). Such communities and groupings are often linked to funding strategies and distribution networks. These aspects help to mark documentary out as a specific screen form.

Texts

The texts themselves can be distinguished in terms of a range of codes, conventions and modes of representation that are regularly utilised by documentarists to build particular arguments and narratives about the social world. Although not all of these codes and conventions are unique to documentary, there are specific ways in which they are utilised in documentary that are different or distinct from their uses in fictional texts. The pro-filmic and filmic codes and conventions work towards a richer sense of 'being there' for the viewer. The objective is to sustain a sense of realism, a sense of the world that is unproblematic and needs no questioning – 'it's just the real world'. The discourse of realism is particularly important as it enables documentary to construct ideological positions, but to obscure such positions as naturally occurring under the guise of common sense.

A number of conventions can be seen as operating at different levels within the text. For example, the use of camcorder footage serves to heighten the feeling of seeing the world unfold before our eyes. This is also achieved through long takes which hold our gaze in the 'fly-on-the-wall' documentary. Naturalistic sound and lighting further support the appearance of an unmediated reality, and reinforce our feeling of being witness to the actual events.

Many documentaries use a narrator, either on- or off-screen, to guide viewers through the argument. The role of the narrator is commonly thought of as one of description – the narrator merely tells us what is happening, who people are, and relates the basic competing arguments. However, the narrator plays a crucial role in shaping the thematic structure of the text, pushing viewers towards certain readings and favouring specific arguments. The effectiveness of the role is further enhanced by staying close to the traditional authoritative voice who is likely to be middle class, white and male. Of course, not all narrators conform to this model, but it is one which is, in a sense, the benchmark, both for those making documentary and for viewers.

People play the key roles in documentaries, especially those presented as eyewitnesses and experts. The eyewitness provides viewers with a direct link to a particular event. As the eyewitness has *seen it with their own eyes*, so we as viewers gain access to the socio-historical world through their accounts. It is not so direct as *seeing the events unfold*, but, as the eyewitness addresses the camera (and viewer) directly, we have the opportunity to identify and empathise with their position and to gain unique access to their subjective point of view.

The expert is central to many of the documentary modes, and is given a privileged position within such texts. The expert draws credibility from their official position or standing (such as a lawyer, a doctor, a government official) and from their access to specialised discourses (legal, medical and parliamentary). They are expected to present us with material and knowledge we might otherwise not have access to, provide evidence to back up arguments, and help us discover and gain access to the truth.

Most documentaries will also make extensive use of photographic stills, often black and white, as well as various types of film and video footage.

As with the stills, such footage often seems to carry more authority if it is black and white. The use of black and white footage and stills is seen to be more authentic, and, given that so much contemporary material is manipulated, this material is assumed to be 'original', because manipulation is a recent phenomena associated with the development of certain digital technologies. These materials are used routinely within documentary to authenticate a story (the photograph provides 'conclusive' proof), to contextualise events and issues (newsreel footage can be used to set the scene), and to provide essential material in visual form that would take too long to provide verbally.

Such codes and conventions are so frequently used that we give them little thought. We assume that the newsreel footage and photographs are original and authentic. We do not question the status of the scientist, nor the truthfulness of his or her account. We tend to ignore evidence of skilful editing in favour of an acceptance that events have been shot in real time as they unfolded. These conventions have in themselves become part of our everyday common sense understandings of documentary. They are documentary's visual and verbal shorthand and rely on our continued acceptance and belief in them. They are part of the code of realism and naturalism, allowing documentary to continue to position itself as a mere recorder of the real, rather than actively constructing ideological accounts of the social world.

These textual conventions work towards maintaining documentary's stance as fact, rather than fiction, and as a distinct screen form. Yet there are other conventions utilised by documentary filmmakers that are drawn explicitly from fictional genres. Documentary makes frequent use of reconstructions, and in these we see the explicit use of fictional and dramatic codes. From the use of actors (rather than real people) to the use of music and lighting techniques to enhance tension or emotional identification, documentary narratives are not necessarily so far removed from fictional ones. Even if a documentary does not contain re-enactments or reconstructions, it is likely to use a musical score to cue viewers at an emotional level. Likewise certain camera techniques, such as close-ups, are used in the documentary as they would be in a fictional text, to aid identification and to manipulate emotional responses. Television documentary in particular often follows the classic three-part structure. As television documentary often has to be constructed around a number of advertisement breaks, the text has to develop turning points, cliff-hangers and even plot twists to ensure viewers return to their programme.

While documentary has developed a set of codes and conventions it can call its own, and which help to mark it out as a distinct screen form, there are many examples of convention usage that serve to complicate and blur the boundaries between fact and fiction.

Documentary utilises these codes and conventions within a number of modes of representation, modes which are mobilised in order to advance arguments about the social world and to reinforce its truth claims. Nichols (1991, 1994) has provided a useful template of five documentary modes of representation. Each uses various codes and conventions in different ways, and positions the filmmaker, subject and viewer into differing relationships within the parameters provided by factual discourse.

Expositional mode

The expositional documentary most obviously builds an argument about the social historical world. It takes shape around a problem and attempts to persuade viewers of its answer to that problem. This mode directly addresses the viewer, and presents the filmmaker as an objective outsider. Documentaries utilising this mode tend to position themselves as value-free and objective, and to draw particularly upon the discourses of journalism.

Textually, these documentaries' concerns are translated into a visual representation through the use of various experts (often scientists), photographic evidence and a narration that guides the viewer through these processes and towards the desired conclusion of the argument. This mode more explicitly marshals evidence into a coherent, rational and persuasive argument. This mode is effective because it maintains the appearance of objectivity and balance. Editing (evidentiary editing) is central to the construction of the argument. The editing serves to maintain rhetorical continuity, rather than continuity of spatial and temporal continuity (Nichols, 1991). While it clearly promotes a particular argument, it also typically allows alternative voices to be heard. For example, an oppositional voice may be presented in an interview and we are encouraged to accept that we are being presented with both sides of the argument. Of course, it is likely that the interview will be conducted in such a way as to undermine the credibility or trustworthiness of the oppositional voice, thus reinforcing the interviewer's own perspective. This mode is particularly successful in the representation of dominant ideology through its use of the discourses of naturalism, realism and objectivity, and is invariably further reinforced through the rhetoric of science.

The expositional documentary uses its subjects and evidence to build a persuasive argument, and there is little sense of a collaboration or any give and take between the filmmaker and the subjects of the documentary. Many contemporary television documentaries utilise this mode, yet it has its origins in the early documentary work by filmmakers such as Flaherty and Grierson (Kilborn and Izod, 1997).

While this mode draws validity for its truth claims from the discourses and practices of journalism, it embodies many similarities with fictional texts. For example, reconstructions are also quite common within this mode. These not only allow the viewer to see how things happened (the knowledge is treated unproblematically within this mode, Lockerbie, 1991), but also add dramatic interest.

Observational mode

Documentary's claim to capture reality is most clearly expressed through the observational mode. In Gillian Leahy's words '[T]here is a "real" relation to the real in observational films, or at least a stronger relation to it, one of more fidelity than provided by other forms' (1996: 41). Although Leahy falls short of claiming the observational film as more 'truthful' than other modes, it is often characterised as such.

The introduction of lightweight and highly portable 16mm cameras in the 1960s allowed documentary to develop new modes of representation (Corner, 1996). Contemporary observational documentary has its origins in two earlier traditions, *cinéma vérité* and Direct Cinema. *Cinéma verité* tends to be associated with the French documentary movement, and Direct Cinema usually refers to the American counterparts (Corner, 1997; Winston, 1995). Both heralded a move towards the recording and investigation of private and domestic spheres.

Nichols (1991) collapses *cinéma vérité* and Direct Cinema into his description of observational documentary. The observational documentary is marked out as different from other modes, most notably in the way in which it takes shape around an exhaustive depiction of everyday life, rather than around an argument about the social world. In this mode the filmmaker takes up a non-interventionist stance, and the text is presented as having an unfettered and unmediated access to the real world. In this way, the viewer is provided with a window on reality – an idealistic (voyeuristic) spectator position.

Observational cinema affords the viewer the opportunity to look in on and over-hear something of the lived experience of others, to gain some sense of the distinct rhythms of everyday life, to see the colors, shapes, and spatial relationships among people and their possessions, to hear the intonation, inflection, and accents that give a spoken language its 'grain' and to distinguish one native speaker from another. If there is something to be gained from an affective form of learning, observational cinema provides a vital forum for such an experience. Though still problematic in other ways, there are qualities here that no other mode of representation duplicates. (Nichols, 1991: 42)

The 'fidelity' of this mode relies on the notion that there is a direct relationship between the image and what it signifies, that the image has an indexical relationship with 'reality'. This mode most obviously draws on the notion that images are capable of 'speaking for themselves', of offering the 'truth' without any need for interpretation. This relies on the notion that the filmmaker is capable of standing outside the socio-historical world; as Hall (1998) has noted, observational filmmakers purport not to 'interview, argue or editorialize, but simply to look and to listen' (229). The observational filmmaker typically insists, as Pennebaker says of *Don't Look Back* (1967): 'You couldn't fake it in a hundred years' (quoted in Hall, 1999: 227). Of course, you can fake it, as the mock-documentary testifies, but we will return to that later.

Interactive mode

This mode takes shape around the direct encounter between the filmmaker and the subject of the documentary. It tends to stress the verbal testimony of the social actors, and it is their stories that occupy the central role in any interactive text. Because of this, the most commonly used convention is that of the 'talking head', an expert or eyewitness directly addressing the camera (and viewer). Whereas in other modes the filmmaker is absent, or takes the position of objective observer, in this mode the filmmaker is part of the action. Their questions and comments are as important as those of the participants. The insights offered through this mode are gained through those interactions. In fact, the film might actually be about that interaction, for example in *Sherman's March* (Ross McElwee, 1985). In this way the interactive documentary presents us with 'situated presence, and local knowledge' (Nichols, 1991: 44), and consequently a more subjective form of knowledge.

Interactive documentary also functions as 'oral' history, when it utilises the testimony of witnesses to bring together the past and the present, or to reconstruct a particular historical terrain. For example, Gaylene Preston's *War Stories (Our Mothers Never Told Us)* (1995), in which seven women tell of their experiences of the Second World War, is an oral history that is specifically a woman's history, and one further grounded in the experience of being a New Zealand woman.

This mode, then, does not claim to give us a direct access to the social world, as in the observational mode, but we are positioned as secondary witnesses to the historical world through the participants' stories and accounts.

Reflexive and performative modes

Of the above modes, mock-documentary tends to play with the expositional and observational modes most often. The more sophisticated mock-documentaries will also reference the interactive mode. These three modes represent the classic documentary form (what could be termed the Classic Objective Argument) which is most easily appropriated by mock-documentary. However, the reflexive and performative documentaries, the last of Nichols's five modes, are more usefully thought of as extra-textually connected or referenced to the mock-documentary, rather than of being a focus of the 'mocking'. Given the confusion between mock-documentary and reflexive documentary (not least by Nichols himself), we devote more space in the next chapter to their differentiation.

Audience

The third part of Nichols's tripartite approach is also the most interesting to discuss in relation to mock-documentary. Mock-documentary's point of departure is an audience which not only is familiar with the expectations and assumptions associated with factual codes and conventions but is ready to explore a much more complex relationship with factual discourse itself.

We, as viewers of documentary texts, share a number of assumptions about documentary and what it can offer. These assumptions serve to frame our reception of such texts, and as such may be described as a 'documentary mode of engagement' (Nichols, 1991: 25). We expect real people, places and events, rather than fictional characters and issues. To a certain extent we expect a specific type of representation, one that will give us access to new knowledges or ways of understanding the social world. In this way we assume we will be given access to facts and evidence.

Whereas in a fictional film we assume that the pro-filmic event was constructed solely for the purpose of the story, in documentary we expect that the events we see on screen *would have happened, as they happened, even if the filmmaker had not been present*. In this way, we make a direct link between the documentary representation, and the historical events it portrays. We begin viewing with this assumption, and the textual conventions reaffirm this for us. 'Our fundamental expectation of documentary is that its sounds and images bear an indexical relation to the historical world ... The literalism of documentary centres around the look of things in the world as an index of meaning' (Nichols: 1991: 27).

Documentary relies on us recognising the social-historical world in its representations. Of course our viewing of documentary is not as simple as the above might suggest. Although it is essential that we recognise and believe that documentary is concerned with the 'real' world, it also sets up a position for viewers in which we are encouraged to interact with those representations, and not necessarily accept the arguments presented. Nichols talks of viewers as oscillating 'between a recognition of historical reality and their cognition of an argument about it' (Nichols, 1991: 28). So, it is important that we believe that it is real, but we do not have to accept the argument about the real world that documentary presents.

So, although documentary has been accorded its special position on the basis of its claims to truth, documentary also includes a contradictory position for viewers in which they can argue against its truth claims. Just as the underlying discourses of documentary are contradictory rather than unified, so the expectations, assumptions and positions constructed by documentary for viewers are also more complex and complicated. Mock-documentary complicates these engagements further, by allowing audiences to enjoy a subversion of their knowledge and adherence to these already fluid subject positions. (This complexity of viewer positions, and hence potential interpretations, also necessitates a complexity in our textual analysis – see Chapter 4 for the outline of our textual framework.)

Collectively these three layers of definition (practitioners, texts and audience) allow a more complex and dynamic view of documentary, one that recognises the way in which certain discourses shape the production of documentary texts, and acknowledges the important role that the audience play in accepting and reinforcing documentary's privileged status. The three levels are brought into focus when we consider that for each documentary an implicit contract is made between the filmmaker and viewer in which the filmmaker promises to deliver a truthful and honest portrayal, and in return the viewer will not question the reality of the images presented (Leahy, 1996). The importance of this contract is highlighted in the public outcry over 'fakes' and 'hoaxes' and is central to our argument about mock-documentary.

Telling (true) stories

'Some form of 'truth' is always the receding goal of documentary film' (Williams, 1993: 20). Although documentary continues to enjoy a privileged position within society, on the basis of its claims to be able to portray the most accurate and truthful account of the 'real' world, documentary has never been a unified or coherent discourse. In practice, documentary texts operate along a continuum between fact and fiction, with the majority of documentaries being grouped at one end, but with a considerable number of others that have tested the basic tenets of factual discourse.

As the discussion of the different modes of documentary has shown, texts routinely blend or blur the boundaries of fact and fiction. The regular use of reconstructions, for example, involves the use of fictional representations where evidence is non-existent or there is no direct referent to reality. Fictional codes are used to engage audiences and to heighten the emotional qualities of that engagement.

Documentary attempts to create a position for audience in which we are encouraged to take up unproblematically the truth claims offered to us. Although we would argue that a documentary mode of engagement does mean a participation in a contract with the filmmaker through which we agree to accept the representations as 'real' and 'truthful', the process of negotiation still involves some consideration of the believability of the text.

Notes

1   Such discussions were foregrounded by the earliest documentary works. For example, *Nanook of the North* (Flaherty, 1922), considered to be a key historical starting point for documentary, mixes observational footage with reconstructions and is clearly much manipulated. Rothman (1998) argues that it is important, not only because it is claimed as part of the documentarists' inheritance but because as a film it marks a moment in documentary history before the distinction between documentary and fiction was set (24).

2   Winston (1995) here makes a connection between documentary and legalistic discourse, where 'facts' do not necessarily speak the truth.

2

Recent transformations
of the documentary genre

As we have argued in the previous chapter, the domain of documentary is problematic either to identify or to define easily. Documentary as a genre, as a concept, is inherently unstable and continuously undergoing transformations. Historically documentary has been quick to adapt to external changes, such as the emergence of television (Corner, 1996; Winston, 1996; Hughes, 1996). More recently, new broadcasting contexts and funding regimes have challenged documentary's secured status within television schedules and theatrical programmes (Kilborn, 1996; Roscoe, 1999). Media convergence and digitalisation have presented new marketing opportunities for documentary filmmakers, together with the prospect of a global audience. With this has come the increased demand from those global broadcasters for documentary to be more entertaining (Goldstein, 1996). The postmodernist critiques of metanarratives and of the concepts of 'reality' and 'truth', coupled with new digital technologies that seriously undermine the camera's ability to record accurately and honestly, have proved to be the latest and most severe challenges for documentary (Roscoe and Hughes, 1999).

In this chapter we will examine some of these recent transformations of the documentary genre and explore the ways in which documentary has responded to these various challenges. These transformations have resulted in a range of new representational strategies that have consciously opened up spaces between the (assumed distinct) entities of 'fact' and 'fiction'. In blurring these distinctions, the documentary has developed a range of styles that *potentially* challenge the very foundations of the genre.

We are interested here in the ways in which these new forms have extended the basic assumptions of documentary, and have incorporated a range of codes and conventions beyond those usually associated with the genre.

Different histories/shared futures?

Big-budget feature-length documentary has shown that it can draw large audiences to cinemas – one only has to look at the success of *Hoop Dreams* (1994), *When We Were Kings* (1996), and *Crumb* (1994) for evidence of the cinematic form's popularity. Yet for most documentarists the hope of getting sufficient funding to be engaged in projects like these is at best a slim possibility.

Although there are many similarities across documentary texts which are produced for the cinema and those developed for television, their distinctive institutional contexts have resulted in some important differences, including the development of specific traditions and styles. Unlike media-specific genres, such as *film noir* and *soap opera*, documentary has been a staple of both television and cinema since their respective inceptions. Cinema and television have been posed as opposites in a dichotomy that mirrors those of high and low culture, elite art forms and populist commercial forms, and these discourses have played some role in shaping the documentary form across the two media. To a certain extent, film and television represent two different institutional contexts for documentary production and reception.

In the early days of cinema documentary was posed as an alternative screen form, to fictional film in general and more specifically to the studio films produced by the Hollywood-based motion picture industry. In direct opposition to this form of cinema, Grierson argued that documentary should be regarded as an art form rather than a populist genre, and as a site for auteurist expression (Corner, 1996). This also had the effect of positioning the documentary form (and the documentary audience) as morally superior to Hollywood product (Hughes, 1996).

Documentary film does exhibit a strong auteurist strand which can be seen, for example, in the work of Frederick Wiseman, D. A. Pennebaker, Humphrey Jennings, Basil Wright and Grierson himself. It is a tradition that continues with filmmakers such as Errol Morris (US) Nick Broomfield (UK), Gillian Armstrong (Australia) and so on. Documentary cinema, then, is often marked by strong personal visions and a sense of professional autonomy. Feature-length documentaries are usually made with a larger budget and have a much longer research or pre-production life-span compared to their television counterparts. Cinema has allowed documentarists the time and space to develop their particular view of the world and of the issues under scrutiny within a given text.

Such a tradition is often associated with work that is politically more radical or challenging and texts that present viewpoints from marginal groups or perspectives. Documentary cinema provided a rich site for the development of feminist, and lesbian and gay filmmaking (Waldman and Walker, 1999) as well as being associated with experimental film and the avant-garde – for example the work of Stan Brakhage (Testa, 1998).

There are other aspects of the cinema release documentary that mark it out from those made for television. Documentary films are often conceptualised as having an on-going or extra-textual life beyond the initial screenings. Distribution deals may see the film playing in a number of different countries over a twelve-month time-span. In addition to this, the appearance of the film on video, rental and sell-through enables the life of the film to be extended. Documentary film, then, is imagined as having a number of lives, and consequently a number of different audiences. Although the initial audience will be smaller than that for a television documentary there is the potential for a documentary film to reach a variety of viewers, through a number of different contexts over an extended period of time. However, it is worth noting that the majority of documentary films play to very small audiences in art-house cinemas and have little chance of attracting the sort of audiences that a television documentary can reach.

While national film commissions and governments may provide state funding for documentary films under various public service or cultural heritage programmes, such funding is difficult for documentarists to obtain (particularly for those without a substantial track record in the genre). Many of the auteur documentarists are forced to do considerable commercial work in order to subsidise their documentary projects.

Television documentary is marked by a different set of aesthetic objectives and requirements (Corner, 1996). It is also true to say that television has been responsible for what some have termed a 'redefinition' of documentary (Vaughan, 1976) and has had the effect of breathing new life into the form (Kilborn and Izod, 1997).

Television documentary is less marked by the auteur, although there are examples of auteurs working in television, for example in the UK John Pilger, who continue to be able to make interesting and provocative documentaries for the main television networks. However, he is probably the exception to the rule rather than the norm. Instead, television documentaries tend to be collective projects, made by either in-house units or by independent production houses. On a day-to-day basis television documentaries tend to be shorter and cheaper and as a consequence also typically tackle 'safer' issues. Where once public service broadcasters considered documentary to be a schedule staple, it now has to compete with other genres within deregulated and competitive broadcasting environments. Broadcasters often have documentary 'slots' that they are required to fill, each slot having its own particular focus or characteristics. There is less scope for one-off documentary or for longer series with more challenging material. Although it is possible to make such longer, 'riskier' documentaries for television, the international trend suggests a move away from these traditional forms (Corner, 1996; Kilborn and Izod, 1997; Bullert, 1997).

Of course, the commercialist pressures to make documentary more engaging and entertaining and to find new ways of telling 'true stories' do not necessarily lead to bad documentary. As Corner (1996) has argued, these pressures have forced documentary filmmakers to be more inventive and to rethink their methods and techniques. Out of such critical self-examination new forms of documentary have started to emerge, many of which are capable of innovative, entertaining and challenging forms of representation (as discussed later in this chapter).

Television documentaries can reach large audiences, but they will not necessarily be able to extend their life-span beyond the initial broadcast (although off-air recording enables individual viewers to watch the programme at a later date, or for a second time). Most documentaries are screened as 'one-offs' with little expectation of a repeat screening, and only the larger budget series documentaries have the possibility of being repackaged for sell-through video.

While there are contrasting institutional factors that have shaped documentary across film and television, the future of the genre appears to promise a production environment in which there may be more convergence than divergence (FitzSimons et al., 2000). Already there are examples of documentaries which are jointly financed by both television broadcasters and film commissions and are intended for both cinematic release and television broadcast. New Zealand's *Punitive Damage* (1998) is a good example of this trend. Financed by the New Zealand Film Commission, Television New Zealand, and through independent sources, it enjoyed a cinema release which was followed by a television broadcast, and video sales.

With the advent of digital television and interactive television, and especially the potential of the internet as a site for the exhibition and distribution of documentary, we are likely to see new traditions, styles and filmmaking agendas that transcend the divergent institutional factors that have tended to shape documentary within film and television (McQuire, 1997).

What happened to 'truth' and 'reality'?

As well as institutional changes, documentary has also faced a wider
cultural challenge from postmodernist discourses. One of the most significant critiques offered by postmodernists such as Lyotard (1984) has been
the challenging of metanarratives; in particular those of science and the
discourses of the Enlightenment. Whereas the Enlightenment generated
a faith in facts and in the ability of science to solve social and individual
problems, postmodernism has questioned and undermined the authority
of such narratives. Science, then, is seen as being only one discourse
amongst many which can offer ways of making sense of the world and of our
individual social, political and historical experiences (Seidman, 1994). This
questioning of scientific authority is not merely an academic exercise, but
one which has filtered into various popular domains; for example, the fields
of alternative medicine and herbal remedies have become as common-place
as traditional medicine. Margaret Sommerville (1999) has described this as
part of a generalised loss of trust in social institutions.

This aspect of a wider postmodernist critique has a number of specific
implications for documentary. As was argued in the previous chapter,
documentary has relied on its close relationship with the discourses of
science for its continued authority. The critique of metanarratives offered
by Lyotard and other 'postmodernists' challenges the foundational discourses of documentary; if society becomes suspicious of science, to what
extent will documentary be subject to the same scrutiny?

Documentary, like science, has sought to maintain a claim to be able
to access and reveal the truth about the social world. The postmodernist
critique shows this claim to be untenable; documentary can only ever
present *a truth*, not *the Truth*. Documentary has also been linked to the
discourses of modernity through its project of enlightenment and social
progress, in particular its claim to be able to change the world rather than
merely represent it. Postmodernism argues against a blind faith in this
progressive imperative, effectively undermining the project of documentary (Seidman, 1994).

It has been argued that at the heart of postmodernism is a crisis of
representation, an implosion of meaning and a collapse of the real.
Baudrillard (1983), in introducing the notion of simulation, argues that
there is no 'gap' between media representations and the originary event or
image in the postmodern world. Both must be considered real, with the
implication that neither can be accorded the status of the authentic. Documentary's claims to the authentic are clearly disrupted by such a stance

(if not overthrown). The genre's reliance on the distinction between truth and falsity no longer holds if we accept Baudrillard's thesis, and so it would seem that documentary has the most to lose by the collapse of the 'real' in postmodernist discourse.

However, as well as undermining some of the foundational discourses that documentary draws upon, postmodernist critiques have yielded certain possibilities for documentary. One of the consequences of the critique of 'truth' and 'reality' has been the blurring of traditional boundaries between documentary and drama, and between fact and fiction. Although this has caused certain unease, particularly over ontological questions involving media texts, it has also enabled documentary to extend itself in interesting ways. One way in which it has done so is through the adoption of certain strategies or concepts that have been foregrounded in postmodernist discourse and practice. Here we look in particular at the notion of parody.

Parody

In our discussion of mock-documentaries and reflexive documentary we are drawing upon a number of key concepts derived partly from postmodernist discourses. Parody, irony and satire are concepts that have most recently been discussed in relation to debates about postmodernism, yet all are concepts that have a far longer and more detailed history than these debates typically acknowledge (Rose, 1993).

Postmodernism can be crudely characterised as being concerned with surfaces (rather than depth) and style (rather than content). Postmodern texts are characterised as being intertextual, reflexive and consumed by knowing audiences (Rose, 1993). In this context parody is often associated with pastiche, irony, burlesque and the carnivalesque,[1] and discussed in purely stylistic terms (or as being 'merely comic'). Little attention is paid to the *critical* aspects of parody. This is noted by Jameson (1984), who argues that the actual intent of parody is the generation of a critical commentary. He suggests that parody ultimately works by borrowing styles in order to mock and critique them. In other words, there is always something that the parody is working against – a normative discourse. '"Parody" can only survive so long as there is common sense, so long as there is a discourse that takes itself seriously' (Stewart, quoted in Tulloch, 1990: 261).

In postmodern relativism there is no such normative discourse to critique. Jameson argues that in postmodernism this critical potential of parody has been neglected and we are left with images that are constantly recycled and reused; in effect pastiche has replaced parody. There is also a tendency to group a number of comedic-related terms together without a consideration of the often subtle difference and implications of such terms. As Plantinga[2] notes:

The terms 'satire' and 'parody' are often used as synonyms, but have slightly different meanings. Both involve the imitation of and ironic commentary on another discourse. Yet satire implies ridicule of its target, while a parody need not devalue its object, but may range from an ethos of condemnation to one of homage and celebration. (1998: 321)

Parody can be described in terms of comic quotation, imitation and transformation and, unlike satire and the burlesque, makes its target a significant part of itself. As Margaret Rose notes, parody 'is ambivalently dependent upon the object of its criticism for its own reception' (1993: 51). Like irony, parody disrupts normal and serious communication processes through strategies of the absurd, and characteristically offers up more than one meaning. Parody texts are therefore double-edged, and any normative discourse can be both victim and model for the parodist. This marks parody out as quite different from satire, which tends to be distanced from its object of criticism.

Parody works by raising expectations around a particular text (such as the documentary) then disappoints (when we realise it is not a documentary), but still produces a non-factual text that can be engaged with in new and complex ways (the mock-documentary). Parody then, works at several levels, providing opportunities for humour, anger and critical reflection.

Parodic texts set up a number of relationships between the filmmaker, the text and viewers which reflect the possible complexities of such texts. In thinking about the relationship between the filmmaker and the (normative) text, for example, Rose (1993: 45–6) suggests a number of attitudes that the parodist might have towards the object of the parody. First, in mocking a text the parodist can be seen as being motivated by contempt for that text. A second agenda suggests a more complex relationship, with parodic imitation seen as being motivated by a sympathy for that text. In this way the parody can both reinforce and critical of its subject matter. The parodic text, then, is both object and subject of its criticism and can be read as both against the object of criticism and as sitting alongside it. In this way, we can think of parody, among all of the comedic terms listed above, as most characteristically embodying ambivalence and ambiguity.

Such ambivalence suggests that a crucial role for the audience is being constructed within parodic texts. In other words, it is the audience that turns a 'bad imitation' or the intention of the comic into a critical parody. 'Both parody and satire depend on the sophistication of the viewer, and on some familiarity with the satiric or parodic target' (Plantinga, 1998: 321). This suggests that parodic texts talk to a knowing viewer. The comic elements of parody can be appreciated only if we recognise the object being mocked. The mock-documentary can develop the complexity inherent to parody only if we are familiar with the codes and conventions of documentary, and its serious intent. Parodic texts actively construct a position for viewers through which they can take up an at least potential critical stance towards the object of the parody.

One of the ways in which we are thinking about parody and documentary is in relation to the transformation of documentary as a genre. Here we are drawing on the arguments of Cawelti (1979) who in an insightful article on Roman Polanski's *Chinatown* discusses the use of parody in the transformation of contemporary American cinema genres. He notes how parody is used to 'set the elements of a conventional popular genre in an altered context, thereby making us perceive these traditional forms and images in a new way'. The point is that these popular forms have to be highly conventionalised genres with an established and rich heritage for such a parody to work. He argues that films like *Chinatown* do more than merely draw attention to the form of the genre, but alert us to the underlying myths and ideological discourses these forms are built upon.

Parody is one of four strategies identified by Cawelti in the transformation of any genre, and one which clearly contains a critical component. He suggests that genres move through a cycle of transformation; from the initial articulation and discovery of the genre, through conscious self-awareness on behalf of both filmmaker and audience, and finally through to the exhaustion of the genre as viewers become tired of their predictability. Such exhaustion is based partly on the decline of those underlying discourses, but is also derived from a growing sophistication within audiences.

This view of parody and its relation to the development and transformation of genre can be most usefully applied to documentary. The use of parody and irony within the reflexive and performative documentary modes has resulted in a new focus on how we represent the social world, and has served to make unfamiliar those very aspects of documentary that we have taken for granted. This can be associated with a maturing of the genre and a recognition that viewers are increasingly sophisticated in their reading of the variety of documentary forms which now comprise the genre.

Changes from within

Documentary has never been a static genre, but has been continually extended and re-formed through internal transformations. The most significant recent developments have been the reflexive and performative documentary (discussed in depth in Nichols, 1991 and 1994 respectively).

Reflexive mode

In this mode, the representation of the historical world, so taken for granted in the previous modes, becomes the focus of inquiry. As Nichols notes; 'Reflexive texts are self-conscious not only about form and style, as poetic ones are, but also about strategy, structure, conventions, expectations and effects' (1991: 57). Reflexive texts such as *The Thin Blue Line*, (1987) and *Roger & Me* (1989) make use of parody, irony and satire to raise questions for the audience concerning the taken-for-grantedness of documentary's claim to truth. Such conventions tend to be used to interrupt or subvert the realism of documentary representations. This mode puts a far greater emphasis on the viewer to consider the relative value of truth claims made within documentaries. A good example in this regard is the repetition of the reconstruction of the murder in *The Thin Blue Line*. Each time the reconstruction changes slightly, giving a different perspective of the murder of a local police officer. It is the viewer, rather than the documentary, who has to decide which version may be the truth. Although this mode utilises the same pool of codes and conventions as other modes of documentary, it does so in order to foreground the constructed nature of its representations.

The reflexive documentary has extended the documentary form in key ways; through its often innovative use of fictional codes and conventions, and through its questioning of how the form represents the social world. While it disrupts the relationship which documentary claims to have with the real, the form is still based on that relationship and to some extent this has limited its potential to engage in a sustained critique of the documentary project itself. This is a constraint which we argue is a key distinction between reflexive documentary and mock-documentary.

Within recent writing on documentary, some mock-documentary texts have been described as reflexive documentaries. For example, Nichols describes *David Holzman's Diary* (1967) and *No Lies* (1973) as such (1991: 59, 70). Certainly the two forms seem to have much in common, each attempting to question critically and undermine taken-for-granted aspects of the genre. Both screen forms examine and question the validity of documentary's claims to be able to record, represent or reconstruct aspects of the social-historical world accurately and objectively.

However, there are some key differences that mark out the position which each of these screen forms takes up in relation to the documentary. The differences derive from the degree of referentiality that each constructs towards the social-historical world; reflexive documentaries are constructed from images with a *direct relationship to the real*, while mock-documentaries' content is purely fictional. In other words, reflexive documentaries deconstruct the genre from *within*, while mock-documentaries operate from *outside* of the genre. This is an obvious but important point to make. The ambivalent and complex stance which parody adopts towards its subject is a strategy which seems to be most persuasively used in fictional forms, and is central to the mock-documentary form. To work, parodic representation cannot contain a sustained indexical link to the real. Central to parody is an anti-normative convention, a built-in rejection of the referential. In other words, it is possible only for *fictional* forms to utilise truly the potential of the parodic form.

A good example of the tendencies of the reflexive mode is the Australian documentary *Cane Toads* (1988). *Cane Toads* draws on a range of codes and conventions from both documentary and drama to construct a humorous and engaging look at a non-indigenous species of toad introduced into Australia to control cane grubs, and which has subsequently become both an admired and a much-hated pest. The film parodies nature documentaries and the authority of documentary and questions the ability of science to find solutions. It is of interest here not only as a key example of a reflexive text but also because it highlights the way in which such texts open up spaces that are neither 'fact' nor 'fiction' (and as such serves as a potential 'precursor'[3] to the mock-documentary).

There are a number of sequences in this text that use parody and irony with the intention of questioning what is fact and fictional in this documentary. Together with its innovative use of dramatic codes and conventions, it shows how the reflexive mode has extended and developed the documentary genre. In addition these sequences demonstrate how the reflexive mode gives a greater role to audiences in terms of determining what is 'true' – something which the mock-documentary consciously builds upon.

Cane Toads uses dramatic music to great effect, as illustrated in its early sequences. At the beginning of the film, as the screen begins to be filled with images of the cane toad, the sound track is reminiscent of that of the fiction film *Jaws* (1975). This works to set up the cane toad as a 'monster', or at least an animal of which we should be suspicious. This notion is developed several times during the course of the film. One sequence shows a small child playing with a cane toad in a garden. Shots of the child chasing the cane toad are intercut with shots of her mother on the phone inside the house. The music once again mimics that from *Jaws,* cueing a build up of anticipation, fear and tension. A previous sequence has discussed the effect of the deadly cane toad poison which can be extracted from the toad by squeezing its glands. As we watch the young child pick up the toad we are encouraged to fear for the child's safety. Just as we expect the worst, the child's mother comes out of the house and saves the child. In a second sequence we are presented with an image that mimics the famous shower scene from Alfred Hitchcock's *Psycho* (1960). Behind the curtain we see the shadow of a man, and hear him singing about the Queensland cane toads. These images are juxtaposed with those of cane toads seen coming into the bathroom. Suddenly the shower curtain is drawn back, the man looks at the toads, then directly into the camera in mock horror.

Both of these sequences parody conventional horror films. They mimic certain aspects to engage viewers in an emotional way, but fall short of delivering 'real' horror. We recognise these sequences as parodic, a fact which is crucial for their humour to be successful. But the use of these dramatic codes and conventions also implicitly draws our attention to other issues. The exaggerated and staged nature of these sequences serves to highlight the constructed nature of documentary representations, with viewers encouraged to consider the implications of the text's casual attitude toward factual codes and conventions.

Another sequence uses parody and humour not only to highlight issues of representation but to offer a commentary on certain aspects of cultural and political life. We are offered the image of an authoritative man in a white coat working in an officious-looking lab. He tells us that Australia sent the British Royals, Charles and Diana, a wedding gift of a small book covered in the skin of several cane toads. Accompanied by the sound of *God Save the Queen,* he reads a letter supposedly sent to him by Prince Charles. Read in a stilted and mock-serious tone, the scene is somewhat hilarious. One can not help but think that there is more being parodied here than the documentary form.

Students often ask whether this film is a 'proper documentary'. This is probably because it is so humorous, it utilises many fictional codes, it is highly stylised, and many sequences have obviously been staged. In fact, although we are led to believe all the people are real – that they are playing themselves – there are times when we wonder whether the filmmakers are in fact parodying the expectations of the audience. One scene in particular comes to mind. After a discussion of the hallucinogenic properties of the cane toad poison, we are offered an interview with a cane toad 'drug abuser'. Presented to us in stereotypical fashion, his guilt is encoded in the shadowy lighting, in the focus on his hands as he rolls a cigarette (possibly containing another drug?), and in the accompanying Indian music. There is something not quite right about this character – he seems to be playing the part of the cane toad drug abuser a little too well. This is the closest that this text comes to suggesting that an interviewee himself may in fact be fictional. We are left with the feeling that it may be us, the audience, who are being taken for a ride.

Cane Toads effectively sits on the borders of documentary proper, having extended the reflexive mode in a number of ways. Although it uses parody to great effect, it maintains its connection to the real world, as we have suggested above, and consequently excludes itself from the category of mock-documentary.

Performative mode

Like the reflexive mode, the performative text puts great emphasis on viewers to decide for themselves the relative merit and truthfulness of documentary accounts of the world. Whereas the reflexive mode focuses our attention on the way in which the social-historical world is represented, this mode attempts to make a more complete break from the referential quality of documentary (Nichols, 1994: 93). A key focus becomes the prioritisation of the subjective aspects of documentary accounts of reality. These texts are heavily stylised and quite consciously blur the boundaries between fact and fiction. In his discussion of performative texts, Nichols argues that the mode clearly embodies a paradox:

[I]t generates a distinct tension between performance and document, between the personal and the typical, the embodied and the disembodied, between, in short, history and science. One draws attention to itself, the other to what it represents. One is poetic and evocative, the other evidential and referential in emphasis ... These films stress their own tone and expressive qualities while also retaining a referential claim to the historical. (Nichols, 1994: 97-8)

The performative documentary complicates notions of fact and fiction as distinct entities and challenges viewers to consider the possibilities of playing in the spaces between fact and fiction. While it rejects 'realism', it has not rejected 'Reality'; the indexical bond is subordinated, but not abandoned. Performative documentary certainly disrupts the relationship between the referent and the image, yet it still retains the remnants of the referential claim to the historical which crucially distinguishes documentary (Nichols, 1994: 98).

The reflexive and performative modes of documentary are the factual precursors for the mock-documentary. Parody, irony and various dramatic codes and conventions are utilised in order to make less familiar the documentary genre. These forms have significantly expanded the documentary repertoire, yet, crucially, while they have challenged the assumed boundaries of 'fact' and 'fiction' they have nevertheless effectively left the foundations of documentary intact.

Both the reflexive and performative mode attempt to question the ways in which documentary claims to be able to present the most truthful and accurate portrayal of reality, by making issues of representation central to their texts. By prioritising the personal and subjective over the pretence of an objective stance, these modes challenge the notion that there is only one Truth to tell, yet they are still able to retain the notion that there is some (small portion) of 'truth' to be discovered or revealed by documentary. They also give a far greater role to the audience, expecting them to be able to arrive at their own conclusions about any given issue, and to be able to determine for themselves what is 'true'. However, because these modes fail to break away from documentary's foundation discourse of actuality, the potential to provide radical critiques is limited. It is arguably the mock-documentary that has instead been able to take these potential tendencies and manifest a systematic critique of documentary and its claims to truth.

New hybrids

As we have argued, 'documentary' is a term that is used by broadcasters and audiences alike to refer to an ever-expanding body of texts. In the last ten years there have been numerous documentary spin-offs, rips-offs and cast-offs. These have extended the documentary genre in a number of ways which have collectively served to blur the boundaries between fact and fiction, and to complicate what we might consider to be the documentary project. Unlike the reflexive and performative modes, docu-soap and Reality TV, which we consider next, blur boundaries in less reflexive or critical ways. Their popularity has had an impact on the shape of contemporary television documentary and there is now considerable international trade of such formats. These forms have also opened up debates concerning documentary's access and representation of the real. As with the texts above, such discussions have provided viewers with opportunities to reflect critically on the documentary project.

Docu-soap

As the name suggests, this particular spin-off combines aspects of documentary with those of soap opera, and to date appears to have developed most successfully in the United Kingdom. Docu-soap producer Andrew Bethell (1999) has argued that the 'docu-soap has been the most significant development in recent British television' (14). The success of the British versions of this form has in turn spawned numerous copies in New Zealand, Australia and the United States.

These hybrid texts tend to take shape around an 'exposé' or 'behind the scenes' look at large institutions – especially those that have day-to-day contact with 'the public'. Their documentariness lies in their claim to present real people, places and events. Utilising the observational mode, or 'fly-on-the-wall' techniques, these programmes present a slice of 'naturally' occurring everyday life. This visual mode of spontaneous reality is undercut slightly by an often-used authoritative voice-over which guides viewers through the narrative. Unlike the documentaries of Wiseman, for example *Hospital* (1970) in which intimate portrayals of institutions are used to raise broader ideological questions, docu-soap merely makes a spectacle out of the ordinary (Izod, 1998; Mapplebeck, 1998).

These programmes gain their credibility through their association with the documentary form, but their appeal lies in the way in which their narratives are constructed along the lines of soap opera. Like the fictional serial form, these programmes usually have several narrative strands which are on-going, and although such programmes are limited to series lengths of six to twelve weeks, narrative closure is deferred as long as possible. Individual episodes usually contain a summary of the various narrative strands, allowing new viewers to catch up and regular viewers to re-visit major themes and characters. Here, an argument is only indirectly constructed, with instead a main narrative drive coming from the personal experiences of the central personalities. These programmes explicitly make 'stars' out of ordinary people, with their experiences rendered worthy of our scrutiny, an agenda which also has the interesting effect of foregrounding the performance of identity itself.

These programmes make good use of the recent lighter, smaller cameras which make observational filming less intrusive and cumbersome. Yet we are typically made acutely aware of the presence of both the camera and the crew. Very often the 'stars' of the programme will talk directly to the camera in a quasi-confessional style. Although sometimes their comments are directed more widely towards the imagined viewer, often we as viewers feel as though we are being given direct access to a private interaction between an individual and the crew.

Many of these programmes have been criticised for staging sequences, most famously scenes from *UK Driving School* (Winston, 1999). Interestingly, the realisation that the presence of the camera and crew are having an impact on the social actors and action, while implicitly pointing to the constructed nature of these texts, seems to do little to challenge the 'reality' or the 'documentariness' of the form. Having said this, it is possible to argue that through such a foregrounding of the constructed nature or 'performed' nature of such representations, a space is opened up for viewers to engage more critically and reflexively with the form. In this sense, although docu-soap does not seem to reflect the questioning stance toward documentary of either the reflexive or performative mode, it can still be grouped with those developments which work to challenge documentary proper.

Reality TV

Another hybrid documentary form is Reality TV, which is distinctive because it pairs documentary traits with fictional aesthetic devices. By this we mean that it maintains the claims for access to the real, while presenting this reality in a highly popularised and stylised manner. Reality TV, with its characteristically shaky hand-held camera, gives the impression of unmediated, spontaneous action, captured as it happens (Dovey, 1995). Yet these are also the aspects which alert us to the presence of the camera and thus the constructed nature of the representations on offer (O'Neill, 1995). Such programming seems both to extend a particular mode of documentary (the observational mode) and to reinforce its claims to give direct access to the real, yet it potentially also contains a critique of such modes and their truth claims. These new hybrid reality formats make careful attempts to 'establish their public service credentials' (Kilborn and Izod, 1997: 160) by claiming an educative role, and by arguing that such programmes encourage viewers to help solve crimes. However, they owe more to tabloid sensationalism and similarly reflect the need to entertain and retain large audiences. In ideological terms, it is significant that their investigative potential is muted and they do little to challenge the dominant order (O'Neill, 1995).

Docu-soap and Reality TV are connected to mock-documentary because they too have developed in the spaces between fact and fiction. These formats can be regarded as a response to both changing economic and broadcasting contexts, but their most interesting aspect is their apparent relation to some of the critiques offered by postmodern theorising. While docu-soap and Reality TV seem to offer very little in the way of a critique of documentary, they can be seen as representing a popularisation of a postmodern scepticism toward the expert and the professional. Both of these formats are built around lay experiences and perspectives, rather than that of the experts so central to certain documentary modes. They both reject professionalism for a more general amateurism which is seen as being more truthful or 'authentic'.

'Faking it' has never been so easy

Finally, within this discussion of recent transformations of the genre, we need to mention recent technological developments that have also impacted upon documentary in a number of ways. Advances in image construction and manipulation have allowed filmmakers a much greater latitude to mediate representations of the social-historical world (Davis, 1997; Krieg, 1997). Such technological advancements can be seen as presenting the potential to capture new audiences through new formats, while also posing a direct threat to the integrity of documentary's claims to truth.

Digital technologies perhaps present the most potent challenge to documentary's privileged truth status. These advancements in photographic and computer technology have already had an impact on journalism. Computer programmes such as Adobe Photoshop allow even the relatively unskilled to manipulate photographic stills (Becker, 1991). Extend this to the general post-production process and the implications are clear. Although documentaries are always 'constructed' to some extent, because of the need to select and structure information into textual form, these new technologies allow the referent itself to be manipulated – in other words, the basic integrity of the camera as a *recording* instrument is fundamentally undermined.

In this way, it has never been easier to 'fake it' and to be able to go as far as producing evidence, in the form of stills or film, of events, people and objects that really have no referent in the 'real world'. Feminist filmmakers have used particular stylistic strategies in order to break the direct relationship between the image and the referent, yet this was done in the knowledge that the process was highly constructed and was not necessarily meant to look natural or real. With these particular texts, we were not supposed to believe that such presentations were to replace such images of the real. However, technology now allows us to make the same breaks, to manipulate stills and film footage, without anyone being the wiser. This, more than any other development, challenges documentary's reliance on the power of referentiality.

This developing capability to play with the referential quality of documentary representation is obviously most 'dangerous' when combined with an intent to hoax. Popular documentary formats in Britain have recently been the target of media witch-hunts and of various official inquiries over fears of this very tendency. Winston (1999) notes headlines in British newspapers such as 'Can We Believe Anything We See on TV?' as typical of the panic over fakes. Documentary originally secured its privileged status as a representational form by promoting its trustworthiness. Recently, that trust has been eroded. Although it is widely acknowledged that documentary is inevitably 'constructed' to a certain extent, viewers nevertheless have trouble accepting that it may deliver images of the social world that are not true. Hence the public outcry when it was revealed that a major producer of documentaries in the UK, Carlton TV, had set subjects up and lied to audiences (Winston, 1999).

Documentary is undergoing a number of quite complex transformations in the light of recent challenges to its status and public role. As a consequence the genre has been extended and developed in new and innovative ways. This process of transformation has always been an inherent, if not always openly acknowledged, aspect of documentary and in recent years has opened up space for hybrid formats such as docu-soap and Reality TV. Mock-documentary needs to be discussed in relation to these hybrid forms because it also partly derives from and reveals a weakening of the bond between factual discourse and the codes and conventions typically associated with documentary. The following chapter extends this discussion to drama-documentary, a form which operates at the margins of the genre, and like mock-documentary occupies those spaces between 'fact' and 'fiction'.

Notes

1   See Bakhtin (1981) for a discussion of the carnivalesque and its relationship to parody, in particular the discussion of the laughter of the carnival, which like parody is directed at all, including both the participants and the carnival itself.
2   In discussing this istinction between parody and irony, Plantinga draws on the work of Linda Hutcheon. See Hutcheon, 1985: 30-49.
3   See Chapter 5.

3

A cousin for the drama-documentary: situating the mock-documentary

In the previous chapters, the discussion focused on developments within the continuum of *factual* texts which provide part of the wider context for the emergence of mock-documentary. In this chapter the intention is to position the mock-documentary form in relation to one of the *fictional* forms which similarly works to complicate any apparent divisions between fact and fiction.

We argue that part of the process of defining what mock-documentaries are by necessity involves identifying *what they are not*. Both drama-documentary and mock-documentary are fictional forms which seek to establish particular relationships with the documentary genre. Both are seen to blur the boundaries between fact and fiction, and both are seen as being (potentially) problematic for viewers who may be confused or 'tricked' by these forms. The distinctions between the two forms can be useful in illuminating the specific characteristics of mock-documentary, including both the distinct stance which the form takes towards factual discourse and especially the role which it constructs for audiences.

Defining drama-documentary, or should that be documentary-drama?[1]

'Drama-documentary is not a universal or a historical programme category, but a historically specific controversy about such categories, not so much a distinct genre as a debate about genre distinctions' (Kerr, 1990: 76). In the broad critical debate drama-documentaries are often seen as being problematic in both form and content. They are criticised for merging 'fact' and 'fiction' and for potentially misleading the viewing public. This concern over the blurring of the boundaries of documentary and drama relies on the notion of a fact/fiction dichotomy. It also relies on the idea that documentary television can deliver the 'facts' whilst drama can only deliver 'fiction'.

As practitioners such as Leslie Woodhead and Ian McBride have argued, there are as many definitions of drama-documentary as there are people making them. There are a number of terms for this particular screen form used within institutional, academic and public contexts. There has been a tendency to conflate the terms 'drama-documentary' (popular in the UK) with 'docudrama' (popular in the US). Derek Paget (1998: 82–3) has provided one of the most comprehensive attempts to define the form and to distinguish between the different configurations:

Drama-documentary[2] is best described as the form that attempts to stay closest to the actual historical event or persons. It follows the sequences of events from a real historical occurrence or situation. The perceived closeness between their presentation and the actual events underpins this version. This form uses drama to overcome any gaps in the narrative, and is intended to provoke debate about significant events. Although it tends not to employ documentary codes and conventions, if such material is utilised it is in such a way as to minimise interruption to realist narrative.

Documentary drama tends to use an invented sequence of events and individuals to illustrate features of real historical events and issues. This form does not necessarily conform to a realist narrative. If documentary elements are presented they may actively disrupt narrative, for example by being presented non-naturalistically. In this form, 'documentary' is just as likely to refer to style as to content.

Faction tends to use real world events and characters as templates around which invented stories are constructed. It requires audiences to connect to an 'out-of-story' factual template, and relies on naturalism as the major means of dramatic representation.

Dramadoc and *Docudrama* are contemporary shortened terms that describe television programmes which mainly follow drama-documentary methodology. Although common usage seems to reinforce their interchangeability, 'dramadoc' is the term more likely to be used in the UK, and 'docudrama' conventionally used within the United States, and in fact each point to quite different historical trajectories of production.

As the above definitions (condensed from Paget 1998: 82–3) illustrate, these forms (we prefer to use the term drama-documentary) tend not to make an

issue of their fictionality, rather they make claims to absolute truths
through their association with documentary. We see drama-documentary
as aligning itself with documentary through its adherence to the discourses
of factuality. Although drama-documentary openly acknowledges its presentation of information in narrative form, the stance taken toward the
projected worlds is assertive rather than fictive. Its representations of the
social world are presented as truthful and as actually having occurred
(Plantinga, 1997). They attempt then to secure a position within an
assumed fact–fiction continuum that is closer to documentary than to fiction. Mock-documentary is situated quite differently along the fact–fiction
continuum, taking instead a fictive stance toward the social world, while
utilising documentary aesthetics to 'mock' the underlining discourses
of documentary.

The discussion below is divided into sections which discuss the differences between mock-documentaries and drama-documentaries. Following
Nichols's efforts to construct a definition of documentary (1991) we utilise
his three-part model to examine the mock-documentary and drama-
documentary through distinguishing the intentions of the filmmaker, textual conventions and the position of the audience.

The intention of the filmmaker(s)

Drama-documentary

In making a drama-documentary the filmmaker's intention is to operate
within the expectations of factual discourse and to produce a text that is
historically accurate. Those who make drama-documentaries tend to
accentuate the 'documentariness' of their portrayals. For example, the
British drama-documentary *Who Bombed Birmingham?* (1990) began
with the following caption:

On the night of 21st November 1974 two Birmingham public houses were
bombed by the IRA. Twenty-one people were killed and one hundred and sixty
two injured. Six men were convicted. They have been in prison since 1974. In
1985, three journalists from the television current affairs programme, 'World in
Action', began examining the case. *Drawing on court transcripts, taped interviews
and contemporary statements, this film is a reconstruction of a three year investigation into the true story behind the bombings.* (our emphasis)

The final sentence clearly presents the material as closely associated
with the discourses of fact and associates the programme more with

documentary than drama. In doing so, the programme-makers are asking viewers to evaluate the text *as if it were documentary.*

As Kilborn and Izod (1997) argue, drama-documentaries allow for the representation of areas of human experience not covered by the documentary project, or become an option when there are no witnesses or direct records of events.

Peter Kosminsky, who made the British drama-documentary *Shoot to Kill* (1990), had planned to make a documentary about the Stalker inquiry,[3] but this was impossible given that the majority of those needing to be interviewed were either dead or unavailable. Many of those, in particular the police, could not speak because of the Official Secrets Act (Sanderson, 1990). Whilst Kosminsky saw the advantage of using drama to reach a wider audience, the focus for both himself and director Stafford-Clarke was that the documentary should come first with the drama second. 'We strove very hard to *not to sacrifice reality* to the demands of good television' (quoted in Sanderson, 1990 21). Once again, programme-makers chose to highlight the 'reality' of the text, rather than the drama, and in doing so asked viewers to consider the representations as 'truthful' rather than imaginary.

There was much public discussion as to whether the programme did provide 'the definitive account of the events that later became known as the Stalker affair' (Sanderson, 1990: 20). Newman, a documentary programme-maker, argued that 'Viewers looking for the truth about the Stalker affair will, I fear, be sorely disappointed. It takes us no further than John Stalker's own account, which left many questions unanswered, and it didn't convince me that I was watching the truth' (Newman, 1990: 21).

As these quotations show, drama-documentary is positioned by filmmakers as close to documentary and the discourses of factuality. As Lipkin notes;

Docudrama argues with the seriousness of documentary to the extent that it draws upon direct, motivated resemblances to its actual materials. As fictions, docudramas offer powerful, attractive arguments about actual subjects, depicting people, places and events that exist or have existed. ... it is on the basis of its close resemblances to actuality that docudrama argues for the validity of its metaphors. (1999: 371).

Some will claim that their representation is 'more accurate' than a documentary or that such works are able to present 'absolute' truths inaccessible through traditional documentary methods, especially in terms of the social relationships between social groups and/or protagonists. In this way drama-documentary can be seen as opening up access to spaces usually denied to documentary. For example, it can fill the emotional gaps within accepted historical narratives and map out psychological terrain to provide convincing or insightful portrayals of historical figures (Williams, 1999). However, these departures from factual material do not necessarily detract from drama-documentary's close association with the discourses of factuality.

For many filmmakers drama-documentary is still covering the same territory as documentary. 'The basic impulse behind the drama-documentary form is, I suggest, simply to tell a mass audience a real and relevant story involving real people. The basic problem is how to get it right after the event' (Woodhead, 1981, reprinted, 1999: 104). Ian McBride (1996, reprinted 1999) talks of British dramatised documentary as being 'anchored in transcript, tape recording, and eyewitness testimony' (114), again illustrating how those making drama-documentary have attempted to align themselves with documentary and the discourses of factuality over fiction and drama. As Kilborn and Izod (1997) argue, drama-documentary uses 'dramatising ploys whilst claiming a factual basis for the work' (135).

The real 'problem' with drama-documentary seems to be in terms of its *content*, often political and controversial, rather than with the *form* (Paget, 1999). Outside of critical circles, however, public debates about drama-documentary tend to focus on the form itself and the way in which documentary codes, conventions and values are used in conjunction with those of drama to blur the boundaries between fact and fiction (Kilborn, 1994).

Mock-documentary

Like drama-documentary, mock-documentaries are fictional texts, but they position themselves quite differently in relation to the discourses of fact and fiction. In sharp contrast to drama-documentary, they tend to foreground their fictionality (except in the case of deliberate hoaxes). Whereas drama-documentary attempts to align itself with documentary in order to validate its claims to truth, mock-documentary utilises the aesthetics of documentary in order to undermine such claims to truth.

In general terms, the mock-documentary filmmaker seeks to construct a particular relationship with factual discourse which often involves a reflexive stance with regard to the documentary genre. Mock-documentary's agenda is ultimately to parody the assumptions and expectations associated with factual discourse, to 'mock' the cultural status of documentary's generic codes and conventions. Deliberately appropriating documentary codes and conventions, mock-documentary filmmakers more specifically seek to offer some form of commentary on aspect(s) of contemporary culture – it may be to parody affectionately the cultural status of popular icons, or to incorporate a specific political critique, or to comment more pointedly on the nature of the documentary project itself.

Peter Duncan, who directed *Children of the Revolution* (1996),[4] has talked about why he used the codes and conventions of documentary.

What prompted you to use the quasi-documentary format?

The format is important in terms of questioning the truth of history. It was a 'gift' in this complex, dialogue driven story to have the occasional interviews with experts which could be used very economically to establish exposition, narrative elements or tone, and through archival footage, still photographs to enrich the story and create diversity.

That's why the film is in that quasi-documentary format – to say we're presenting you with alleged truth, but we all know it's manipulated. The film makes the point that the blurring of fact and fiction can be quite dangerous. (quoted in Colbert, 1996: 22).

For many who choose to make mock-documentaries, the objective is to take viewers on a journey from fact to fiction. There is an assumption that audiences will recognise the text as a spoof, and in this way the filmmakers do not intentionally seek to confuse or misguide viewers. Peter Jackson and Costa Botes (makers of *Forgotten Silver* (1996)) apparently intended that their audience would realise the joke while viewing the programme. Jackson has expressed surprise that there was a group of viewers who seemed unable, or unwilling, to move from a documentary mode of viewing to an appreciation of the filmmakers' original intention.[5] 'We wanted the audience to start out believing it and although by the time it was finished they no longer believed it they would still have had a good time.'[6] Drama-documentary filmmakers tend to accentuate the relationship with documentary, positioning their work as a journalistic endeavour. The emphasis is on the promotion of the factual and 'truthful' foundation of such texts. Mock-documentaries foreground their fictionality; their intention is to play with, undermine or challenge documentary, rather than to seek validity through an association with the genre.

The construction of the text

Both drama-documentary and mock-documentary utilise the codes and conventions of documentary, yet each uses them in different ways. Whereas mock-documentary utilises such codes in order to look like documentary, drama-documentary tends to incorporate such codes less systematically, instead using the codes and conventions of realist narrative in order to present aspects of the historical world.

Drama-documentary

Drama-documentary does not rely upon the codes and conventions of documentary. In other words it does not 'look' like a documentary, although it may include historical footage or accurate recreations or reconstructions of historical events. These are generally constructed in the form of an identifiable *narrative*, rather than more explicitly in the form of an *argument* as in documentary texts.

Paget (1998) notes some of the conventions most frequently used within the drama-documentary format. While drama-documentary does not systematically utilise the conventions of documentary in order to achieve a 'documentary look', it does co-opt certain codes for particular effect. Although it is sometimes possible to identify particular conventions within any given text, in most cases codes and conventions have been mixed as a result of the development of the form and it is often impossible to separate such conventions out in any sequence.

Drama-documentary attempts to mimic documentary with regards to the level of research, the unwritten rules of casting (which typically aim for a broad resemblance to the original social actor) and the favouring of a 'low-key' acting style (Corner, 1995, Paget, 1999). Such mimicry reinforces the relationship to the discourses of factuality, and consequently these texts' claim to truth.

Many drama-documentaries will also utilise *documentary material* such as original footage, photographic stills or news extracts. This is an important and distinctive convention by which both information and authentication of events and issues are achieved. At other times there will be simulations of documentary material or a mix of archive and library material, and acted reconstructions. As in documentary, opening, closing and linking captions are used as shorthand devices to place the film historically, to argue a representational case and to offer disclaimers as a protection against legal action. Voice-over narration, which in the past has been used to convey facts and information, now seems to function as part of dramatic *mise-en-scène*.

Such conventions work to contextualise the time and the place for the unfolding drama, and this material is strengthened through supporting camera rhetorics (Kerr, 1990). However, such conventions are always in the service of the drama, and are used for dramatic effect. Documentary codes and conventions only function actively within the drama, in such a way that the dramatic diegesis itself is never interrupted.

Most of the other conventions of drama-documentary are taken from realist drama, in particular multiple camera set-ups in realistic sets or actual locations, 'key lighting', sound recorded for maximum clarity of narrative flow, continuity editing (minimising interruptions to narrative flow) and non-diegetic music dubbed over during post-production to influence mood.

Other characteristics that mark the drama-documentary as a specific screen form include the telescoping of events and the creation of composite and fictional characters. Like other dramatic forms they focus on moments of inherent dramatic tensions and/or dramatic irony. They are more likely to present relationships between individuals and institutions than mainstream television drama, although (as discussed in Chapter 2) this has recently become the domain of the 'docu-soap'. And, because drama-documentary tends to deal with sensitive or controversial issues, there are usually a number of extra-textual events that surround such programmes – for example, continuity announcements, talk-show appearances, discussion programmes, newspaper campaigns and very often telephone helplines for those traumatised (Paget, 1998).

Mock-documentary

Mock-documentaries are fictional texts which in some form 'look' like documentaries. These texts tend to appropriate certain documentary modes, as well as the full range of documentary codes and conventions. They frequently appropriate the observational mode, (especially 'rockumentaries', themselves a sub-category of the observational form), and interactive and expositional modes of documentary. While some mock-documentaries utilise a particular mode, it is more common for them to shift between such modes to varying effects. The three modes listed here collectively provide a Classic Objective Argument as a template which mock-documentaries draw upon. However, there is often a deep ambivalence towards these modes within mock-documentary texts (as discussed

r 4, and in greater detail in Chapter 7). In part, this Classic
Argument is presented as most closely fulfilling the objectives
of the documentary project – that is, providing an accurate and unmediated view of the world – and as such these three modes collectively have a
sacred status. In a sense, this template operates in a similar fashion to the
classic realist narrative in fictional texts. However, these modes are also an
easy target for mock-documentary, most obviously because the 'look' of
their codes and conventions is easy to replicate, but importantly because
they also position themselves as morally superior in their representation
of the social world.

Mock-documentaries tend to assume an archetypal generic form rather
than recognising the complexities of the genre itself. The fact that documentary modes of representation are easily recognisable is a key factor.
The appropriation of documentary codes and conventions is used not so
much to anchor the argument in the real world or to bolster claims to
truth, but rather to offer critical commentary. Many mock-documentaries
treat the generic form as a given, while others incorporate a more explicit
degree of reflexivity within its parodic exercise, but we argue that *appropriation inherently constructs a degree of latent reflexivity* towards the genre.

The role constructed for the audience

This is perhaps the most distinctive and certainly the most interesting
difference between drama-documentaries and mock-documentaries,
and is indicative both of the contrasting relationships which each constructs with the documentary genre and of the differing implications of
these relationships.

Drama-documentary

The audience approaches drama-documentaries with similar expectations
to those of documentaries, in the sense that they are viewing a truthful (if
heightened) reality which is based on a familiarity with factual discourse
and its associated codes and conventions. This is reinforced by the stance
taken by the filmmaker, who promises to deliver a truthful account of the
events and issues. In this sense, the audience treats drama-documentaries
in much the same manner as the filmmakers, with the reliance on dramatic
context and dramatic conventions not necessarily seen as interfering with
the objective of the text – which is to represent the essential 'truth' of a

historical event or historical figure. The lack of any pretence that these texts form part of the documentary genre itself means that audiences will allow the text or filmmaker a certain degree of latitude in their representations of the historical world; that is, the narrative can be 'real' even if it is not historically accurate.

Drama-documentaries engage both documentary and fictional modes of engagement which viewers move between throughout the text (Caughie, 1980), although Petley (1996) suggests that the dramatic look is increasingly displacing the documentary look in contemporary drama-documentary. In utilising these two modes viewers effectively erase the boundaries between them but, significantly, also tend to obscure any contradictions and tensions between the assumptions and expectations which each 'trigger'. Consequently, the text is evaluated not so much on its apparent reality as on how truthful or believable is the account.

Paget (1998) argues that the expectation that drama-documentary provides a believable account comes from documentary's promise of privileged access to information, added to drama's promise of understanding through 'second-order' experience. The camera accesses two different kinds of reality; a record of external events (which still constitutes the basis of documentary's appeal) and a simulated reality of acted events which here makes claims to a larger 'more authentic' truth. 'Audiences who accept the extension of the camera's documentary showing do so increasingly within the context of dramatic suspension of disbelief' (Paget, 1998: 82).

Much of the discussion around drama-documentary has focused on whether audiences are duped by this mixing of fact and fiction and the possible implications of this. As Petley (1996) points out, this was always a weak line of argument more often than not constructed to reinforce calls for greater controls on the media. The BBC's Producers Guidelines (1993) includes statements arguing that viewers should be informed as to what exactly is factual and fictional in any one programme so as to avoid any confusion or any chance of the public being misled (26). Woodhead (1999), however, argues that viewers are more sophisticated than they are typically given credit for being; that audiences can distinguish between fact and fiction, that they will not confuse a drama for a documentary and so on. This is confirmed by the few empirical audience studies of drama-documentary (Wober, 1990; Roscoe, 1994).

Woodhead goes on to argue that drama-documentary could prompt a critical reconsideration of factual television and a 'refreshment' of the contract between filmmaker and viewers. In a similar vein, Paget argues that drama-documentary offers an intertextual relationship between drama and documentary that is provocative in audience terms. It asks, subtextually, in what ways any drama can be 'documentary' and any documentary 'drama', thus challenging an assumed fact/fiction dichotomy.

Drama-documentaries, however, do not seek to engage directly with the more fundamental assumptions inherent to factual discourse, assumptions which inevitably come with the use of documentary codes and conventions. For example, the notion that film can accurately record reality is not challenged by drama-documentaries because they do not pretend to offer an accurate representation of reality – their partiality is foregrounded. As a general rule, the closer drama-documentaries get to the genre itself, the greater is the reinforcement of factual discourse. What they can do, however, is to offer a form through which we are challenged to reconstruct our mental model of the real by means of codes both documentary and dramatic.

There is an important similarity here between reflexive documentary and drama-documentary. We have argued (in Chapter 2) that the potential for the reflexive mode to subvert the documentary form ultimately cannot overcome a paradox of referentiality – if a reflexive documentary strays too far from factual codes and conventions, it is no longer seen as documentary and its challenge to these aesthetics is consequently nullified. In a similar manner, the subversive potential of drama-documentary is also effectively limited by the audience's essential faith in the factual discourse which the form generally reinforces.

Mock-documentary

As with drama-documentaries, mock-documentaries engage both a documentary form of engagement and a fictional mode on the part of its audience. To varying degrees, the audience is expected to be conscious of the fictionality of the text; to 'get the jokes' and to appreciate the intention behind the appropriation of documentary codes and conventions. To engage with the text at this level does require the viewer to watch it 'as if it were a documentary', but, nevertheless, to do so in the full knowledge that it is a *fictional* text. The mock-documentary addresses a knowing and media-literate viewer.[7]

With mock-documentary, audiences are also asked to engage with the text, with varying degrees of reflexivity, by drawing upon a familiarity with the codes and conventions of the *documentary* genre. These are codes and conventions which obviously have attendant assumptions and expectations for the audience as well as for the filmmakers. Here the tension between these two modes of reading is, to varying degrees, reinforced and exploited. In contrast with drama-documentary (and the reflexive mode of documentary representation), it is the deliberate play between the factual and fictional modes of reading which generates reflexive potential.

With mock-documentaries, the key issue becomes the *extent* to which a text's construction encourages reflexivity towards the documentary genre (as mentioned above). We assume that any mock-documentary text, because it 'violates' the proper use of documentary codes and conventions, contains an inherent (subversive) potential to engage an audience in this way.

As with all cultural texts, the audience are assumed to have the potential to offer a critique of the text and of the documentary genre itself which may not be deliberately constructed within the text. Although a mock-documentary text in effect 'triggers' the factual discourse in using documentary conventions, it is ultimately the encounter between text and audience which determines the extent to which the latent critique of this discourse is appreciated. Such an argument rests on a complex understanding of spectatorship. The role constructed for the audience by the text offers only a preferred meaning – it does not determine the text's definitive meaning, nor necessarily the text's ultimate position in relation to factual discourse.[8] Our argument also draws upon a wider understanding of the context in which viewers engage with mock-documentary texts. We have already suggested that the popularity of the form itself is symptomatic of an increasingly complex relationship between audiences and factual discourse.

What distinguishes mock-documentaries from drama-documentaries, then, is especially the former's potential critique of factual discourse. We argue that mock-documentary contains a 'latent reflexivity'. This aspect is termed 'latent' because it is difficult to predict exactly how audiences will interpret these texts. This is further complicated by some mock-documentaries more explicitly foregrounding the reflexive potential of the form. Mock-documentaries deliberately falsify images which purport to represent the social-historical world – in effect, they ask the question 'can we really believe what we see?' In contrast to drama-documentaries, the closer that mock-documentaries get to the genre, the greater is the subversion or deconstruction of the relationship between documentary aesthetics and factual discourse.

Table 1 Situating the mock-documentary and drama–documentary

	Intentions of the filmmaker	*Construction of the text*	*Role constructed for the audience*	*Implications for factual discourse*
Documentary	To present an argument about the social-historical world, in order to inform, educate and/or entertain	Offers a rational and 'objective' argument about the social-historical world, using the codes and conventions of the documentary form	The text offers a relatively unmediated reflection of reality (complicated by the expansion of the documentary genre)	*Either* explicit reinforcement of factual discourse *or* possible expansion of the documentary genre
Drama-documentary	To construct a dramatised representation of the social-historical world	A fictional text, which offers an argument about the social-historical world in the form of a narrative	The text does not have the visual integrity of a documentary	Reinforcement of factual discourse, by allowing for forms of expression outside documentary codes and conventions
	Assume that they are able to represent reality, rather than to directly record reality	Draws upon the expectations and assumptions of factual discourse (but not the sustained appropriation of documentary codes and conventions)	Factual assumptions (accuracy, objectivity) combined with some latitude for fictional representation	
Mock-documentary	To present a fictional text, with varying degrees of intent to parody or critique an aspect of culture or the documentary genre itself	A fictional text, which offers a dramatic narrative presented in the form of an argument	Tension between factual expectations (documentary) and suspension of disbelief (fictional text)	(See Conclusion)
		Appropriates documentary codes and conventions	Degree of reflexivity, either latent within, or activated by, the text	
		Draws upon the expectations and assumptions of factual discourse with varying degrees of reflexivity		
Fictional text	To construct a dramatic story which focuses on fictional characters and events, primarily for the purposes of entertainment	Primarily uses classic realist narrative, with conventions of character and action, and drawing upon a variety of cultural and intertextual resources	Suspension of disbelief, with the assumption that the parameters of reality are determined by the text itself	Implicit reinforcement of fact/fiction dichotomy

Situating the mock-documentary and drama-documentary

In the remainder of this chapter, we look at examples of drama-documentaries which could be mistaken for mock-documentaries. These are texts which incorporate aspects of documentary codes and conventions, but quite differently from those texts we identify as mock-documentaries. These examples will be used to illustrate our arguments outlined above, and to distinguish further between these two types of screen texts.

The Battle of Algiers (1965) and *The War Game* (1966)

The Battle of Algiers (Gillo Pontecorvo, 1965) is a text which has been specifically described by some writers as a 'mock-documentary' (McNeil, 1993). It is a reconstruction of French colonial defeat and disgrace in Algeria, covering the pivotal years of 1954–7 in the Algerian struggle for independence. It is a partly fictionalised account of real and representational events that took place during the National Liberation Front's guerrilla war, but although it makes extensive use of documentary aesthetics we argue that it is clearly identifiable as a drama-documentary.

Making extensive use of a *cinéma vérité* style utilising hand-held camera footage which was becoming 'fashionable' in the mid-1960s, Pontecorvo's method is 'simulated documentary' (qualified by the film's opening credits which contain a message stating that 'not one foot' of actual newsreel had been used in making of the picture). As Lorenz (1984) notes in her review of the film, by drawing on actual people (with the exception of Jean Martin as 'Colonel Mathieu') and events as the basis for its story, and with the adoption of a convincing documentary style, it presents a believable account of this historical incident.

The film is characterised by dynamic cutting, dramatic juxtaposition, hand-held, mobile camera, over-exposure and shooting against the light to give the effect of on-the-spot reportage, a commentary briskly interpolating chronology, facts and figures, and brief biographies. As such it has a 'newsreel authenticity' captured by Marcello Gatti's grainy, black and white photography (Wilson 1971: 160).

Pontecorvo has said that the main challenge he faced was 'that of coming as close as possible to the truth' (Wilson, 1971: 160). For Pontecorvo this 'truth' is centred on the film's political objective of a presentation of an anti-imperialist statement. In other words, here 'truth' has a political basis, rather than an evidential or referential basis. The film contains various 'representative events' (such as a fictional scene of a central character's harassment by a group of arrogant young Frenchmen), as well as manipulating the historical chronology. The use of documentary codes and conventions is clearly seen by Pontecorvo as a way of validating such 'truths'. In other words, he is anxious to attach the legitimacy of the documentary project to his film, positioned like other drama-documentaries in a close alignment with the discourses of factuality.

As has been the case with many drama-documentaries, this partial appropriation of documentary codes and conventions has provoked both praise and condemnation, with some critics expressing admiration for the film's aesthetic achievement and others questioning the ethics of filming a partly fictional scenario in such strikingly realistic terms.

The position constructed for the audience is one of in which viewers are encouraged to take the political message as a 'reality' or 'truth', with the use of documentary codes and conventions encouraging a belief in the account presented. The film does not present a challenge to documentary, nor to the discourses of factuality. Insead it uses them to validate and give credibility to this historical account. *The Battle of Algiers* may be politically reflexive in the sense that it presents a radical perspective on the events it depicts, but it does not require or ask us to question the broader discourses of factuality.

As suggested earlier, the differences between mock-documentary and drama-documentary are not merely a matter of how a film looks but rather a complex interaction of the intentions of the filmmaker, the textual strategies, and the role constructed for the audience.

In a similar vein to The *Battle of Algiers* is *The War Game* (Peter Watkins, 1966). In 1965 Watkins was commissioned by the BBC to make a fictional film about the effects of a nuclear attack on Britain. The BBC found the portrayal so harrowing and disturbing that it was not shown on British television until 1985. This film also utilises many documentary codes and conventions, most notably an authoritative voice-over, black and white footage, and the use of 'purely' informational insert of statistics and graphs and so on (Paget, 1990). Paget argues that the film systematically and consistently offers a documentary look. Its *vérité* camera, quasi-academic footnoting and the visual bibliography which ends the film all work to convince us we are watching an accurate version of real events. Although the voice-over begins with the implicit disclaimer '*Should Britain …*', the images work with 'an apparent reality' and we are discouraged from reading the film as portraying a hypothetical event (Paget, 1990: 102).

The film uses an amateur cast, with the Kent Fire Service playing themselves in the film. The interviews and representations retain a sense of spontaneity and seem unmediated, which once again serves to reinforce the 'reality' of the film. The film is positioned as being a prediction of what *could* happen, yet at times the narration moves to mimic news bulletins, by changing to the present tense. In this way, the film shifts from dramatic mode to documentary mode (Paget, 1990: 104).

In a similar way to *The Battle of Algiers*, *The War Game* is 'documentary' in its intention. The codes and conventions reinforce the seriousness and reality of what could happen during a nuclear attack. Watkins intended the film to be informative and instructional, and a position is constructed for the viewer which focuses on education and knowledge, as in documentary proper. Consequently, this film too can clearly be characterised as drama-documentary, rather than mock-documentary.

Schindler's List (1993)

A final example we would like to look at in this chapter is Steven Spielberg's *Schindler's List* (1993), which offers a more complex use of documentary aesthetics than the examples above, and is a text which has enjoyed more popular appeal for mainstream audiences than any of the fact/fiction texts discussed above. *Schindler's List* was seen as being able to provide the popular imagination with a master narrative about the Holocaust (Loshitzky, 1997: 2). It was received virtually unproblematically, a reflection perhaps of the fact that there is a popular consensus on accounts of the Holocaust and because it is seen as being safely in the past. However, its mixing of fact and fiction did attract some controversy from a number of critics, and prompted some heated debate concerning the role of popular culture in the construction of collective memories.[9]

We think it is useful to go through the film in terms of Nichols's definitional breakdown of documentary, the intentions of the filmmaker, the construction of the text and the role constructed for the audience – in order to explore its position as a drama-documentary and to consider the relationship it has to documentary.

Intentions of the filmmaker
The film looks to construct a specific relationship with the social-historical world, one which explicitly aligns with that of documentary. Spielberg has stated that his intention was to draw upon the truth objectives of the documentary project.

I felt more of a journalist than a director of this movie. I feel like I'm reporting more than creating. These events, this character of Oskar Schindler, and the good deeds he did at a terrible time weren't created by me, they were created by history. I'm sort of interpreting history, trying to find a way of communicating that history to people, but I'm not really using the strengths that I usually use to entertain, to keep the audience interested – not to bore anybody. (Spielberg, quoted in Palowski, 1998: 172)

The film clearly makes certain truth claims about the Holocaust. It was seen as significant that even Spielberg had to fight to make the film, suggesting a weight and importance of subject matter unusual for a Hollywood film. Importantly, part of the film's promotional material claimed that the producers never expected to make a profit, leading some critics to note that Hollywood had now performed its 'public service' role, and that there is unlikely to be a film such as this again (Baxter, 1996).

Spielberg's positioning of himself as a 'journalist' is interesting because the writer Keneally, in presenting the book upon which the film is based, himself sought to describe his account as that of a reporter rather than a novelist (Slavin, 1994). By positioning the account in the realms of journalism the film is itself constructed as more factual and closer to documentary than drama. Again, these aspects reinforce claims to be presenting a realistic and truthful account of the Holocaust.

I think we all feel that we are making a contribution – not just to the movies – but we're making a contribution toward the world remembering the Holocaust. I think everybody realises that this isn't just another movie. We hope people view this film, but even if they do not see it, it will become part of the record – the public record – about the deeds of the Nazis between 1936 and 1945. In that sense we have all bonded in an effort to communicate something that we feel is of great importance. (Spielberg, quoted in Slavin, 1994: 173).

Clearly Spielberg saw *Schindler's List* as being very different from his other feature films. As he says in the above quotation, this wasn't just 'another movie'. This call to action, to communicate and to make a public record is very similar to the ways in which documentary asks for its arguments about the social world to be taken up by viewers. One cannot merely turn away and say 'it's just a movie'. '[*Schindler's List*] has attained the status of historical document, the final and undeniable proof of the ultimate catastrophe endured by the Jewish people' (Loshitzky, 1997: 7). This statement clearly positions the film as having constructed a close relationship with the discourses of factuality, and reflects the effect Spielberg intended the film to have with its audience.

Textual representations

Central to the film's reinforcement and legitimation was its utilisation of a range of documentary codes and conventions. The film incorporates documentary aesthetics and builds these into the fabric of the fictional narrative. The effect of this is to construct a text which looks realistic (and therefore more believable), but does not sacrifice any narrative tension or drama. In this way, the film uses a complex combination of filmmaking techniques and integrates them into a conventional form of fictional narrative (Loshitzky, 1997). As discussed below, this approach brought both praise and harsh criticism for Spielberg.

In shooting the film, Spielberg avoided as much as possible all post war advances in technique and told his cameraman (Janusz Kaminski) to work towards a naturalistic look. The objective was for the text to look as if were filmed in Krakow during the Second World War, with small cameras, without lights and favouring long lenses and many hand-held shots (Baxter, 1996). The film was shot entirely in Poland, with a Polish cameraman (Kaminski) and Polish line producer, Branko Lustig, himself an Auschwitz survivor. Its referential power is further reinforced by examples such as the faithfully reconstructed set of the Auschwitz camp. Although Spielberg was not allowed to film there, he constructed a mirror image of the real camp which shared the entrance gate. Such attention to detail provided important reference points for the evaluation of the film's reality.

Historical film and docudrama assert authenticity on the basis of factual accuracy and verisimilitude, and, as Horowitz (1997) states, this is why the reconstructions and location shooting were so important to the film's success in constructing a definitive account of the Holocaust. They reinforced the significance of the film's referential aspect.

Loshitzky (1997) argues that *Schindler's List*'s broad postmodernist aesthetics are a pastiche of cinematic styles incorporating a visually spectacular and multi-layered film, quoting from styles as diverse as film noir, German Expressionism, Italian Neorealism, Second World War newsreel and CNN news coverage. Spielberg is to a certain extent also drawing on an 'aesthetic of imperfect cinema' in which he is consciously renouncing Hollywood products by resorting to low-quality (but highly authentic) images of newsreels and television news. In doing so, the seriousness of the film is more heavily weighted textually against the entertainment or dramatic intentions of the film. The film moves between styles yet, as Loshitzky argues, the final product does not contain contradictions; its transitions from style to style are invisible, with the film never calling attention to itself as a complex constructed text.

Horowitz (1997) suggest that the utilisation of a 'pseudo-documentary' look for many scenes conveys both the impersonality of history and an intimacy with its key players, yet conversely these scenes are also more staged and obviously played more for emotional manipulation than for the sake of verisimilitude. While there is much to say about the way in which the film attempts to construct a documentary look and to align itself with the documentary project, it also works in opposition to such a project. Although the black and white footage and the 'realism' of the film might work towards a call to action, there are numerous examples within the film which illustrate the way in which we are drawn away from the bigger conclusions and issues. The film consistently draws our attention away from wider scenes of brutality, atrocity and genocide – for example when we see someone saved, the film does not dwell on those millions who are left behind. In a climactic scene where Schindler saves a number of female workers from Auschwitz, the text does not explicitly recognise that their shipment will be replaced by another. Similarly, when Schindler has a train stopped to save his accountant Stern, there is no recognition that the rest of the train's occupants have not been saved, instead the tension in the scene is relaxed, with the focus exclusively on Stern thanking Schindler. In these examples we can see how the codes and conventions of documentary are appropriated without necessarily being able to take up the implications of the documentary look.

As well as more general concerns over the merging of factual and fictional styles within the film, there have been more specific complaints from some film critics that the film integrates the trauma of the Holocaust into a narrative structure which is favourable towards the perpetrators rather than the victims, and that the Holocaust is used as a mere backdrop to a story of beauty, wealth, glamour and survival (Gelley, 1997). As part of a wider complaint that the film seems to present itself as the 'whole' or 'complete' representation of the Holocaust, these critics argue that the film uses documentary codes and conventions to validate its claims to truth while moving beyond the moral and ethical framework provided by documentary to build a drama out of real events. In this way, the film maintains a complex relationship with documentary and the discourses of factuality and sits comfortably alongside other drama-documentary texts.

As mentioned above, while in mock-documentary the key debates are set up around issues of representation, cultural icons and institutions, and the relationship with the discourses of factuality, drama-documentary tends to take shape around debates over content. Weissman (1995) makes some interesting points concerning perceived absences in the film. He notes that there are a number of events that Spielberg chose not to film, chiefly for reasons of obscenity; for example, instances in which the SS were reported to have thrown babies from windows. He goes on to conclude that in not showing these images they may in fact disappear from the public consciousness about the Holocaust. Such a discussion is based on the notion that the filmic representation is directly linked to the actual events and issues, and that the film plays the role of history teacher in contemporary society.

The debate over *Schindler's List* has tended to focus on whether it was a truthful account of the Holocaust, and the extent to which filmic representations are ever able to capture the whole truth. While much effort was made to locate the film within a non-fiction arena, there was still debate among commentators over the ethics of representing the Holocaust within a fictional narrative (which gave rise in particular to comparisons with the much-acclaimed Holocaust documentary *Shoah* (1985)).[10]

Audience

The manner in which *Schindler's List* addresses the audience is a key aspect which most clearly distinguishes the film as a drama-documentary. The film was received in virtually reverential fashion by most of its audience (apart from its banning in countries such as Malaysia). There is a marked contrast between the film's popular status as a historical 'document' of the Holocaust – bringing the historical significance of the event to the mainstream of American cinema – and those critics who have especially sought to distinguish (and contrast) *Schindler's List* historical account with documentary approaches to the Holocaust (such as *Shoah*). These critics, like members of any audience for the film, have been encouraged to view and evaluate the film essentially as though it were a documentary.

In the viewing of this film, certain expectations and associations usually associated with a documentary mode of engagement are foregrounded. These textual representations push viewers towards an understanding of the film as a realistic and truthful account of the Holocaust. It takes an assertive stance toward the social world and we are encouraged to accept this.

The context of viewing *Schindler's List* is also of crucial importance. The film's publicity and the extra-textual discussions foregrounded the status of the film as factually based. It was framed as a historical document, rather than a work wholly fictional. Before audiences even saw the film, there was encouragement to discuss the film in relation to other non-fictional texts about the Holocaust. In a sense, the film does contain a degree of reflexivity towards historical representations (particularly of the Holocaust) but this is a reflexivity which has been activated by a comparatively minor, and elite, portion of the film's audience.

At all times the films was positioned as a serious cultural and historical work – a status not usually conferred on Hollywood fiction. For example, Baxter (1996) notes that many cinemas distributed a 'Code of Conduct' suggesting, amongst other things, that eating popcorn would not be appropriate. Likewise, Weissberg (1997) talks about the opening of the film in Germany and how it was positioned as one of the most significant cultural and political events in recent history. As Paget (1998) argues, at a functional level the drama-documentary and the documentary proper share territory rather than dispute it. Drama-documentary is an *inherently indexical form* and it points more insistently towards its origins in the real world than other kinds of drama. This is exactly the intention of *Schindler's List*, and how it addresses its audience.

Schindler's List is a good example of a drama-documentary which makes extensive use of factual aesthetics, but which nevertheless cannot be confused with mock-documentary. It is a fictional work that utilises the codes and conventions of documentary for sustained periods within a complex aesthetic style, but does so only in order to construct a strong relationship with the discourses of factuality. This text illustrates the key arguments of this chapter. Both drama-documentary and mock-documentary occupy similar positions along the fact–fiction continuum. Both problematise the truth status of those codes and conventions typically associated with the documentary. The distinction of mock-documentary as a screen form here is that it appropriates these codes and conventions, not in the service of historical representation (as does drama-documentary) but from a more complex and inherently subversive relationship with factual discourse.

Notes

1 For more detailed discussions of the drama-documentary form see Paget (1998) and Rosenthal (1999).
2 See also Corner (1996: 34), and his discussion of dramatised documentary and documentary-drama.
3 In 1982 John Stalker (Greater Manchester Deputy Chief Constable) was asked

to lead an investigation into six civilian killings by undercover units of the RUC. See Stalker (1989) for further discussion.

4 Although this text does appropriate documentary aesthetics, it does so rather inconsistently. For this reason we see it as located on the margins of mock-documentary.

5 See Chapter 7.

6 Interview with Peter Jackson (1996) *Midwest Art Magazine* 10: 23.

7 As discussed in Chapter 2, it is no coincidence that mock-documentary has emerged into the cinematic and television mainstream at a time when the documentary genre has itself perhaps reached a point of saturation for audiences. And, just as documentary proper is becoming increasingly fractured, for a variety of reasons, so too is the mock-documentary form developing an increasing complexity and sophistication in its parody of the genre.

8 This discussion is developed further in Chapter 4.

9 See Barbie Zelizer, 'Once in a While', in Loshitzky (1997: 18-41), for a fuller discussion of some of these tensions and debates.

10 See Loshitzky (1997) for a wide-ranging discussion of these issues.

4

Building a mock-documentary schema

This chapter will outline the framework which we use to differentiate mock-documentary texts from each other, and which forms the basis of the discussions contained within the following chapters. Our approach essentially involves identifying three main 'degrees' of 'mock-docness' within the texts we have analysed, degrees which are derived especially from the type of relationship which a text constructs with factual discourse. Before outlining our mock-documentary schema, we need to mention a number of qualifications for the interpretative framework which we propose.

Firstly, it needs to be stressed that the model outlined below is not intended to provide comprehensive or fixed categories. The degrees which we propose cannot be considered ideal or 'pure' forms, but are instead suggestive of groupings of textual tendencies. The mock-documentary form is a complex one, incorporating as it does a variety of filmmakers' intentions and a range of appropriations of documentary aesthetics, and encouraging layered interpretations from audiences. Our aim here is especially to promote discussion on mock-documentaries which acknowledges the evident complexity of the form, and especially the degree of *reflexivity* which these texts construct towards the documentary genre.

Secondly, our approach draws upon the range of audience research traditions which have emerged particularly from the post-structuralist developments within sociological theory.[1] The essential common insight within post-structuralist approaches is that the meanings associated with any text are assumed to be generated through interaction with an audience (Philo, 1990; Ang, 1991, 1996; Fiske, 1992; Jancovich, 1992; Morley, 1992).

This is an insight which is also increasingly accepted within the established audience research traditions which have tended to dominate this form of qualitative research. Jensen and Rosengren (1990) provide a summary of five such traditions and they conclude that there is an increasingly complex theoretical basis to each of these traditions, and within audience research in general. In particular, audience members are increasingly assumed to play an active and selective role in the use and interpretation of mass-media messages. What has developed within these various audience research paradigms to date is a continuum of models of reception operating between two poles; those that assume viewers' readings from textual analysis, and those that dissolve the text itself into a potentially infinite number of audience re-constructions.

Post-structuralist approaches to audience research typically construct a comprehensive understanding of the significance of a variety of social, political and historical contexts for audience readings of a text. The reading which any viewer makes of a programme or film is 'unstable' in the sense that meaning is never fixed but is constantly being reconstructed, (Dahlgren, 1992). Any text still has a degree of determination in the 'fixing' of its meaning, to the extent that the effect of its construction is to work to constrain, or at least shape, the range of possible interpretations which an audience can make. The specific objective of audience research, then, is to explore the variety and nature of such interpretations.

Individuals who make up the audience are understood to be first of all social beings, able to draw upon a number of different social and political knowledges in order to make sense of a text. The social locations (such as those associated with class, ethnicity or gender) of each individual audience member determines the social and cultural contexts within which she/he is immersed. These contexts shape such aspects of social experience as subjectivity, individuality and an individual's membership in social groups, all of which are 'constructed, defined and articulated' through discourse (Wetherell and Potter, 1992: 59). In other words, each of us inevitably (and often largely subconsciously) draws upon a discursive field which serves to shape our interpretations of media texts.

Within this theoretical framework the viewing experience itself is seen primarily as a discursive encounter, one which involves a complex interaction between the narrative constructs of the text, the field of discourses accessed by members of the audience, and the constraints on discourse generated by the immediate viewing context (Philo, 1990; Ang, 1991, 1996; Fiske, 1992; Jancovich, 1992; Morley, 1992). It is important to note that these are not one-way relationships; each individual is involved in fluid, complex, dynamic and dialectical relationships with both immediate and wider social-political contexts (Fiske, 1989; Ang, 1989, 1991; Hoijer, 1990; Dahlgren, 1992; Roscoe et al., 1995). In this sense, audience interpretations are inherently fluid and unstable; they are not fixed but are part of a constant process of mediation. (Dahlgren, 1992: 206) The ways in which individuals discuss and understand a media text not only change over time are, but shaped by a myriad of factors such as immediate social relationships and physical surroundings. Within any such context, each individual's social experiences (especially those based on differences in such socio-demographic factors as gender, age, class and ethnicity) provide for rich and varied discursive resources which have the potential to shape the nature of such social interactions.

A more complex understanding of any viewer's interpretation would need to consider the specific circumstances in which an individual or group response to a text is formed; that is, the specific historical and socio-political contexts which framed that particular audience's encounter with a given text. Ideally, this would incorporate a detailed assessment of the role played by factors such as the medium through which the text is accessed by an audience (whether it is seen as a broadcast, fractured by advertising, on video and so on), and the variety of social factors which come into play in any given viewing environment (such as whether a viewer is alone or part of a group, the level of conversation among viewers, or any other types of distractions).

Within this general understanding of the heavily contextualised and discursive nature of spectatorship, Roscoe et al.'s simplified schema of ways of conceiving of viewers' interpretations of media messages becomes a useful interpretative tool (Roscoe et al., 1995) These writers suggest that within audience research there are three common constructions of viewers' responses to media texts: 'social', 'active' and 'critical'. The term 'social' draws upon the same ideas regarding the place of the individual within various discursive systems as is discussed above,[2] while the term 'active' refers to the ways a viewer's reading of a text involves him/her drawing upon, and actively engaging with, pre-existing frames of reference in order to produce 'meaningful interpretations'. Viewers, then, are assumed to be involved in a continual process of negotiation with the text, either accepting, contesting or critiquing the information it offers. Viewers may also be 'reflexive', in the sense that they are capable of drawing upon wider social, political and/or economic debates associated with any given event or issue, in making sense of a text.

Within this general theoretical model, audience research itself emerges as a social and discursive practice, one in which the researcher brings his/her own conceptual frameworks to the task of re-constructing audience interpretations of media texts (Ang, 1996). As Ang has correctly observed, there is no objective, scientific knowledge which can be gained from the study of the reception of cultural texts (Ang, 1989: 105) – the 'social world of actual audiences' is too complex and fluid a field of practices and experiences to be incorporated into any discourse on reception (Ang, 1991: 155). At the same time, as Fiske has noted, such analysis should not incorporate the assumption that notions of 'text' and 'audience' have no practical relevance, that only the process of viewing itself is worthy of study (Fiske, 1989: 57).

These broad assumptions concerning the nature of the engagement which audiences make with any text shape the nature of the schema used here to differentiate between various mock-documentary texts. We argue that an integral part of the 'mock-docness' of a text is the extent to which it encourages audiences to acknowledge the reflexivity inherent to any appropriation of the documentary form. Much depends on the ability of viewers to recognise, acknowledge and appreciate the *fictional* nature of mock-documentary texts, and the typically parodic nature of the appropriation of factual codes and conventions. A text may be explicitly reflexive for a particular audience, but not engage other viewers in this manner. Consequently, it needs to be emphasised that our degrees are fluid groupings. They are not mutually exclusive; individual texts may activate different degrees of reflexivity with different audiences, and individual viewers may engage in a variety of interpretations while viewing mock-documentaries. *Forgotten Silver* (1995) is an obvious example known to the authors which seemed to encourage a number of readings amongst New Zealand audiences during its initial broadcast on New Zealand television.

The framework of analysis which we develop here is not intended to suggest the full extent of interpretations which any audience may make of mock-documentaries. Our analysis is indicative of the variety of relationships which the appropriation of documentary aesthetics entails, and particularly those strategies of appropriation pursued by mock-documentary filmmakers. In other words, we are dealing, both here and in the following chapters, with the writers' assessment of the *preferred reading* of such texts. As stated previously, our intention with this study is to provide an overview of the mock-documentary form, one which could ideally be subsequently explored by audience researchers.

We suggest an initial schema of three degrees, a model which approaches mock-documentaries according to the intersection between the intention of the filmmakers, the nature and degree of the text's appropriation of documentary codes and conventions, and the degree of reflexivity consequently encouraged for their audience.

Degree 1: parody

This degree includes those fictional texts which involve what could be termed the 'benevolent' (or not deliberately reflexive) use of documentary codes and conventions. Generally, these texts feature the consistent and sustained appropriation of documentary codes and conventions in the creation of a fictional milieu. The intention of these texts is generally to parody some aspect of popular culture. These are fictional texts which both make obvious their fictionality (the audience is expected to appreciate the text's comic elements) and are comparatively muted in their challenge to the nature of the documentary project itself. While the appropriation of documentary codes and conventions by these fictional texts is *inherently* reflexive, this is not an issue which the filmmakers themselves explicitly explore.

Here documentary aesthetics are appropriated largely for stylistic reasons. These tend to be texts where humour is emphasised by having a rational or deadpan face present, examine and investigate openly fictional figures and events. The Classic Objective Argument – that is, the generic form which collectively relies upon expositional, interactive and observational modes of documentary representation[3] – is constructed largely as a prop, a cultural reference point of sobriety and rationality. The humour in these texts, then, comes in part from the contrast between the rational and irrational, between a sober form and an absurd or comic subject.

It is a significant tendency within this degree for texts to offer a conservative perspective on aspects of culture, in the sense that the ultimate intention and effect of these 'documentary' examinations of a subject are often their ultimate reinforcement as cultural reference points. One key aspect of parody is that it often comments upon cultural forms which are 'easy targets'; their cultural currency is typically exhausted and they are ripe for mocking. The mock-documentary texts which we group in degree 1, however, tend not to carry their parodic intent through to a detailed and explicit critique of their subject. Instead, many of this group of mock-documentaries adopt a strong frame of nostalgia in their presentation of fictional representatives of an era or cultural idiom – such as the love of Beatles mythology which underlies *The Rutles* (1978), the sense of loss of the 'innocent' America of the 1920s which frames *Zelig* (1983) and the appeal to cultural myths which made *Forgotten Silver* popular with its New Zealand audience.

Perhaps unsurprisingly, it is the fictional subjects of texts within this degree which are most often celebrated by audiences. Some viewers of key mock-documentaries such as *The Rutles* and *This Is Spinal Tap* (1984) have adopted their musical subjects in virtually the same way they would an actual musical group – both of these 'bands' have released albums, both have their own official internet websites and Spinal Tap have even conducted an (unconventional) rock tour in America. And the actor who played the political candidate who is the subject of *Man with a Plan* (1996) has developed a political career, of sorts, based on his character's appeal. These are aspects of the extra-textual impact of these texts which open up the interesting issue of the deliberate confusion of their ontological status by audiences.

While documentary proper typically involves a 'call to action' – an implicit demand for some form of social or political response to the knowledges which the form reveals – these mock-documentaries construct a more varied and complex relationship with their audience. In some sense, these fictional constructs have developed a 'real' existence – not because they are convincing as simulations of reality, but precisely because viewers appreciate their commentary on actual cultural figures. Here audiences are able to actively aid in the obscuring of the fictional nature of their subjects, although not to the extent that they explicitly engage with mock-documentary's inherent reflexivity towards factual discourse.

The Return of Spinal Tap (1993), for example, is a sequel which features the concert revival of a fictional band. The film portrays the real performance of a fictional band, a contradiction which perfectly illustrates the complexities of interpretation typically demanded of the mock-documentary form. The audience, both within and outside the text, are encouraged to enjoy this contradiction, as part of a parodic stance toward cultural practices of which both they and the band are part. The result is that these audiences participate in a commentary on their own status as consumers of popular culture. As suggested above, however, this and other examples of degree 1 mock-documentary do not look to extend this reflexive interpretation into an open deconstruction of factual discourse itself.

Degree 2: critique

Like degree 1 texts, degree 2 mock-documentaries feature some degree of acceptance of the assumptions and expectations of factual discourse – or at the very least a recognition of the cultural status of the codes and conventions associated with factual discourse. However, this group of texts also includes those instances of mock-documentaries where the appropriation of documentary aesthetics could be termed 'ambivalent'. Here the Classic Objective Argument provides a familiar legalistic or investigative stance that the text adopts in order to offer a parodic critique of those aspects of popular culture which a character and/or event is seen to represent. The documentary form is typically used to confer a legitimacy on to both the subject and the conclusions which the text provides; it represents a familiar social-political stance which validates both the argument and its construction of evidence.

These texts' appropriation of the documentary form is termed 'ambivalent' because they generally also incorporate a partial or muted critique of media practices themselves (and especially documentary as a mode of inquiry, investigation and examination). In other words, the manner in which media representations are themselves constructed also typically forms part of the subject matter of degree 2 mock-documentaries. A consequent intention of these mock-documentaries is to open more space for an audience to recognise the problematic nature of any appropriation of documentary codes and conventions. In this sense, these are mock-documentaries distinguished from degree 1 texts in that, to varying degrees, they begin to engage more explicitly with the mock-documentary form's latent reflexivity towards factual codes and conventions. While the intention is not to engage the audience in a thorough critique of the documentary form, to some extent the practices of the factual media become the subject of the text (even if this is often only implicitly expressed).

For example, the 1997 series premiere episode of *ER* contains a critique of what could be termed one of the 'bastardised' forms of the genre: Reality TV shows, and their assumed failure to adhere to the ethical standards of documentary texts. However, the series as a whole also characteristically makes extensive use of, and perhaps relies upon, a *cinéma vérité* type of representation, in effect reinforcing these aspects of the observational documentary form. As discussed in Chapter 7, there is an interesting implicit tension between these tendencies within this particular episode.

Another key text we position within this degree is *Bad News Tour* (1983), a half-hour television parody of rockumentaries in a similar vein to *Spinal Tap*. Unlike its predecessor, however, *Bad News Tour* more directly explores the tensions and contradictions inherent to any collaboration between a documentary filmmaker and his/her subject. Much of the humour in this mock-documentary stems from the repeated failures of the heavy metal band ('Bad News') to collaborate with their documentary crew in the construction of an appropriate rock myth. Here the tension between the band and crew effectively undermines the pretence that a documentary filmmaker necessarily adopts a neutral and non-interventionist stance toward his/her subject.

A second textual concern we have identified within degree 2 are mock-documentary texts which deal explicitly with a *political subject*. Here we assume that there is a political aspect to documentary aesthetics; that the rational, objective ideology articulated by factual discourse itself is associated with the social-political status quo. In other words, the effort to remain 'balanced', 'objective' and 'fair' inevitably involves an acceptance of a particular vision of society, one which implicitly tends to support existing institutions and political interests. This is an adopted political stance which underpins the supposedly 'apolitical' nature of journalistic practice (Ericson et al., 1987, 1991). It is also a stance which forms a significant part of the ideology which links documentary to notions of citizenship and public service objectives. Any intention to 'document' and prescribe solutions for some kind of social, economic or political failure typically draws upon a similar vision of society, and constructs a particular social-political role for the documentary filmmaker.

One potential effect of the appropriation of the codes and conventions of factual discourse is an (even if partial) subversion of this political agenda. The mock-documentaries which we group within this tendency of degree 2 are those which begin to engage with this underlying documentary agenda; these are mock-documentaries which develop the *satiric* possibilities of the form in order to critique an aspect of popular culture.

A key text within degree 2 mock-documentaries is *Bob Roberts* (1992), where both an ambivalence toward, factual discourse and a rare satiric intent are combined. This film uses the documentary form to comment specifically upon modern political processes, especially the selection of political candidates, within the American system. It is a coherently-argued political satire which (like documentary) encourages political action from its audience, rather than operating simply as a self-contained piece of humour. Although this is an example of sustained political commentary in the form of entertainment, it also includes pointed suggestions that any form of representation contains an inherent political agenda. *Bob Roberts* incorporates a satiric commentary on the factual media as an integral part of its critique of a wider political system. As with *ER*, there is a real complexity in the way the text operates towards the documentary genre. A critique of the media and of media personnel is constructed within a text which none the less offers an implicit acceptance of

fundamental aspects of factual discourse. In *Bob Roberts* the revelation
that an assassination can be successfully faked is revealed by a British
(BBC-styled) journalist who is able to present convincingly evidence of
this deception. However, this demonstration of the investigative possibilities of the documentary approach is directly contrasted with the film's
overall pessimism toward the trivial, sensationalist form of journalism
provided by the American news media.

Hoaxes

Included within this chapter on degree 2 texts are those mock-
documentaries which deliberately look to create confusion within
audiences over their factual status, and especially those which effectively
perpetrate a *hoax*. These mock-documentaries, while not necessarily containing messages which are deliberately intended to be reflexive towards
factual discourse, still trigger reflexive interpretations among viewers
because of the subsequent uncovering of their fictional status. Audiences
are initially encouraged, by the text itself and extra-textual events to adopt
a factual mode of reading toward the text – the question of the ontological status of the text is left to the deliberation of viewers.

The key texts discussed here are *Alien Abduction* (1998) and *Forgotten
Silver*. Both are television 'documentaries' and represent instances in
which broadcast institutions supported their deception as factual programmes, a fact disturbing for a significant proportion of their audiences.
These texts' reflexive potential, then, derives from the success of their
fakery, and in particular from the context created for their reception,
including the extra-textual cues deliberately created by filmmakers and
broadcasting institutions.

Degree 3: deconstruction

This group of mock-documentary texts demonstrate what could be
termed the 'hostile' appropriation of documentary aesthetics. Their central distinguishing characteristic is that even if they focus on other subjects
their real intention is to engage in a sustained critique of the set of assumptions and expectations which support the classic modes of documentary.
The documentary project itself, then, is ultimately their true subject. They
critique assumptions such as the notion that filmed images have a direct,
unmediated relationship with reality, that a documentary text is based

Table 2 Degrees of mock–documentary

	Intentions of the filmmaker	Construction of the text	Role constructed for the audience
Degree 1 Parody	To parody, and implicitly reinforce, an aspect of popular culture	The 'benevolent' or 'innocent' appropriation of documentary aesthetics The Classic Objective Argument accepted as a signifier of rationality and objectivity	Appreciation of the parody of popular culture, and the reinforcement of popular myth Nostalgia for traditional forms of documentary The more critical viewers are able to explore the form's latent reflexivity
Degree 2 Critique	To use the documentary form to engage in a parody or satire of an aspect of popular culture	The ambivalent appropriation of documentary aesthetics A tension between an explicit critique of documentary practices and practitioners and an implicit acceptance of the generic codes and conventions	Appreciation of parody / satire of popular culture Varying degrees of reflexivity toward aspects of the documentary genre
Degree 3 Deconstruction	To critique an aspect of popular culture To examine, subvert and deconstruct factual discourse and its relationship with documentary codes and conventions	The 'hostile' appropriation of documentary aesthetics Documentary as representative of a mythical and problematic social-political stance toward the social-historical world	Reflexive appreciation of parody or satire of popular culture An openly reflexive stance towards factual discourse and its associated codes and conventions

upon a specific ethical relationship between the filmmaker and subject, and that the filmmaker is capable of adopting an objective, balanced, non-interventionist stance toward his/her subject. Degree 3 texts, then, bring to fruition the latent reflexivity which is inherent to, and which in large part distinguishes, mock-documentaries as a screen form.

 David Holzman's Diary (1967) is an early example of a text which directly critiques documentary modes of inquiry in this way. Its apparent story is of a filmmaker seeking to discover himself, but its real subject is the level of expectations associated with the camera and its perceived ability to record 'truths'. The prime example discussed in relation to degree 3 is *Man Bites Dog* (1992), which looks to deconstruct the political-ethical role performed by documentary filmmakers, the censorship and discursive limitations inherent to documentary texts, and the value system constructed by audience expectations of such texts. This text, in other words, seeks to deconstruct the documentary genre at a variety of levels.

To date, most mock-documentaries can be grouped in degrees 1 and 2 – the potential subversion of documentary inherent to all mock-documentaries but most explicit in degree 3 texts seems to be a less commonly engaged concern of filmmakers than an effort to use the form for the purposes of various forms of parody, satire and critique. The open attack on the ethical and apolitical stance adopted by documentarists seen in *Man Bites Dog* is still comparatively rare. However, we would argue that even openly parodic examples of the form are becoming sophisticated enough to generate an increasingly subtle form of subversion of factual discourse.

Our schema outlines a variety of wider trends which characterise the growth of the mock-documentary form (within the texts which we have studied). There is an increasing complexity in the appropriation of documentary codes and conventions within the mock-documentary form. These texts' appropriation of documentary form are, in a sense, becoming more convincing, derived from both an explosion of the technical possibilities for the manipulation of images and from an increased range of approaches adopted by mock-documentary filmmakers.

In some sense, our schema of degree 1, 2 and 3 mock-documentary texts also looks to chart the increasing maturity of mock-documentary as a distinctive screen form. Filmmakers are exploring a wider range of subjects and agendas using this form, incorporating various levels of parody, political intent and reflexivity towards the documentary genre itself – often within the same text. In other words, mock-documentary texts can seek to engage all three degrees, to activate a complex range of interpretations from audiences. In part, this has meant a developing tendency to place upon the viewer the task of determining which aspects of the texts are fictional. Some of these texts, despite incorporating cues to their fictionality, apparently confuse and even convince audience of their status as non-fiction documents. The development of the mock-documentary form has arguably been both symptom and cause in the construction of an increasingly reflexive position, for the viewer, in relation to factual discourse.

Although it seems that mock-documentariy is becoming more sophisticated and complex in its use of documentary aesthetics, it is difficult to determine the *origins* of this screen form. The tendency towards mock-documentary, whether or not this has been identified as such, seems to have developed in large part from the sporadic appropriation of elements of the documentary form within individual fictional texts, and not least from the preoccupations of individual filmmakers. It is perhaps only recently that the form has developed in number and variety to the extent that it can be said to constitute an identifiable and distinctive group of texts. Chapter 2 looked to outline those significant trends within the documentary genre which provided the context for the emergence of mock-documentary, and the specific relationship which the form constructs with the genre. The following chapter looks to speculate on the variety of textual trends within the *fictional* realm which have led to the development and acceptance of mock-documentary.

Notes

1   A useful summary of the origins of the post-structuralist challenge to sociology can be found in Seidman (1994).
2   This involves the assumption that each individual brings a variety of knowledges and experiences to his/her interpretation of a text, which derive from his/her membership in various social groups. The term also implies that the process of interpretation is 'social' in the narrower sense that it is framed by the immediate social context of viewing.
3   See Chapter 1, and Nichols (1991).

5

A suggested genealogy

In previous chapters we have looked to outline something of the wider context for the emergence of mock-documentary, and in particular to position the form in relation to the recent transformation of the documentary genre, and to other texts within the fact–fiction continuum (that is, drama-documentaries). Together with a brief discussion of factual discourse and the development of the documentary genre, we have examined the mock-documentary in relation to the subversive intent of the reflexive mode of documentary representation. And, most importantly, we have continued our argument of the significance of the audience's changing relationship with factual discourse that mock-documentary exploits.

In this chapter we suggest possible 'precursors' of the mock-documentary form, those (fictional) cinematic and television texts which have served as precedents for the texts discussed in the following chapters. Nichols has used the term 'genealogical precursors' to suggest the origins of the topography for a group of texts (Nichols, 1994: 102). Obviously each mock-documentary has the potential to influence the creation of others (*This Is Spinal Tap*, for example, is often cited by directors of more recent mock-documentaries as a direct source). There are a number of early examples of mock-documentary – such as *David Holzman's Diary* (1967) and *Take the Money and Run* (1969) and later *The Rutles* (1978) and a variety of other television mock-documentaries, all shaped by different intentions on the part of their filmmakers – and to varying degrees these early examples of mock-documentaries have served as precedents for later examples of the form.

Within this chapter, however, we are looking outside these early texts, to outline a number of the significant strands within cinematic and television media, in the United States and Britain in particular, which have fostered the creation and continued growth of the mock-documentary

form. It needs to be emphasised that this is very much a speculative chapter. We have not been able to trace the origins of the term 'mock-documentary' itself,[1] and the objective here is particularly to outline the
increased range and complexity of fictional forms of representation
within film and television media, which we argue have collectively led to
the development of this distinctive type of text.

Listed below are television and cinematic fictional texts which appear
to be early examples of the appropriation of documentary aesthetics: texts
which have arguably served as precedents not only for filmmakers but for
audiences. These examples represent a range of filmmaker agendas which
collectively share an approach encouraging a sporadic but nevertheless
significant appropriation of documentary codes and conventions. As
such, and perhaps more crucially for mock-documentary, they can be
said to have allowed for audiences' acceptance of the widening range of
filmmaking techniques used to construct mainstream fictional cinema
and television.

We are looking here at specific textual precursors, but it is important to
acknowledge that these have emerged from changes within wider social,
political and institutional contexts, just as have the recent transformations of the documentary genre. The accelerating transformation of the
entertainment industries in the later half of the twentieth century has
created a variety of tendencies within both factual and fictional media
forms. In fictional media, the increasing importance of entertainment as
a part of cultural life, the explosion of media outlets and the consequent
increase in competition for audiences are social and institutional topics
which are unfortunately too complex to address properly here.

What these wider contextual changes have created, however, are a
number of often contradictory tendencies within fictional media. In part
there is an increasing reliance on existing forms and genres and an unwill-
ingness to experiment beyond proven audience favourites. There is also,
however, a number of competing tendencies driven by the same institutional demands. There is the effort to reinvigorate exhausted genres, often
through hybridity and intertextual borrowing of existing generic forms,
but also through the introduction of parody and irony. In his article on
generic transformation, Cawelti has presented the idea that when a genre
exhausts itself it can take on a number of different modes, one of which is
'the use of traditional generic structures as a means of demythologisation'
(Cawelti, 1979: 194).[2]

There has also been a widespread mining of 'classic' media texts, and
the occasional appropriation of avant-garde and experimental forms

(with perhaps MTV in the United States being the most obvious example of this latter tendency). Typically these experimental forms, when they appear within mainstream media, are drained of much of their politically or socially subversive potential.

There are obvious differences in the ways in which the mainstream television and cinema industries have dealt with the transformation of their media,[3] but for our purposes perhaps the most significant common aspect of contemporary popular media is a 'knowing' audience. As suggested above, viewers of mainstream television and cinema are becoming increasingly more 'sophisticated'; we are more aware of the constructed nature of all media forms and we are more willing to allow transgression across genres (including those which violate the 'boundary' between fact and fiction, such as mock-documentary). Within both television and cinema (and in particular the British and American examples which we consider here) a factual aesthetic is increasingly becoming tied to dramatic ends, and this is a tendency which has become more acceptable to mainstream audiences.

The radio precursor: *War of the Worlds*

Before considering the television and cinematic precursors of mock-documentary, due mention must be made of a radio text which in many ways set the template for the form. The 1938 Orson Welles radio broadcast of *War of the Worlds* offers an early archetype of the electronic media hoax, one which contains significant elements of what later would emerge as mock-documentary. Welles helped to write and broadcast an innovative radio version of the 1897 H. G. Wells novel on 30 October 1938 (Halloween Eve), constructed as a series of live news broadcasts and interviews with panicked eyewitnesses of a supposed Martian invasion. Unfortunately, the performance of Welles and his cast was so convincing for many listeners that a nation-wide panic, centred on the eastern coast of the United States, led to numerous calls to local police asking if the broadcast was real and headlines in national and international newspapers the next day. Welles was forced to give a press conference the following day to apologise to the nation. He argued that there were sufficient cues during the broadcast for the audience to recognise that it was a piece of fiction (the dates in the play were wrong, it was performed in a regular drama slot, and there were two explicit disclaimers during the broadcast) and suggested that in any case the notion of a Martian invasion was an established popular fantasy (Brady, 1990: 173).

Welles's *War of the Worlds* broadcast is a significant precursor to audio-visual mock-documentaries for a number of reasons. Firstly, it used a format comprised of news bulletins 'interrupting' a dramatic programme. This was a format apparently chosen by Welles and his company for purely dramatic reasons; as an effort to create an innovative piece of drama for their regular radio audiences. In other words, it was an unintentional hoax, one in which the role of the listeners itself was crucial to the sensation and controversy which the broadcast created.

A 1940 study of the panic caused by the broadcast (Cantril 1940) notes that listeners were confused by the fact that radio was at the time an accepted vehicle for important announcements, by the quality of the performance itself, the fact that Welles had included a number of actual towns as targets for invasion, and because many listeners tuned in late and missed the (first) disclaimer which immediately preceded the broadcast. Some listeners apparently believed that news broadcasts themselves were *interrupting* the dramatic play that they had expected. Among the more potent factors underlying the susceptibility of this audience was an apparently taken-for-granted set of beliefs in the factual nature of the codes and conventions appropriated by Welles. A significant section of the audience, despite the obvious cues, uncritically accepted the information dramatised by the cast precisely because it was in a form more typically associated with radio news bulletins.

The 1938 *War of the Worlds* radio play is an interesting example of the role which wider cultural context plays in shaping interpretations of viewers/listeners. In this sense, the audience reception of the Welles broadcast leads directly to mock-documentary texts such as *Forgotten Silver* (1995) and *Alien Abduction* (1998),[4] which are both examples of media hoaxes (with *Forgotten Silver* being another interesting example of an apparently unintentional hoax which overestimated the sophistication of its audience).

Television precursors

Monty Python's Flying Circus and television comedy

This category of precursors includes television series such as *Monty Python's Flying Circus* (Britain) and *Saturday Night Live* (United States). *Monty Python's Flying Circus* was initially broadcast in Britain in the late

1960s to early 1970s and popularised a number of innovations in television comedy. The general *raison d'être* of the series involved the application of a simple comedic formula: to begin with an incongruous situation and take it to its logical conclusion, no matter how absurd the result. A significant target of the show was documentary codes and conventions, if only because they offered an immediately recognisable television form. Neale and Krutnik argue that a major theme which resulted from the parodying of television forms such as these was the 'laying bare of conventional devices', the effective subversion of conventional means of representation by drawing attention to their construction (Neale and Krutnik, 1990: 201).

The series used the visual and aural style of the BBC model of factual discourse, parodying that model in order to undermine the cultural assumptions behind their acceptance with British audiences. Often a BBC-styled presenter (in person or voice-over) sought to interview completely absurd characters, in effect creating humour out of the collision between the rigidly rational stance adopted by the presenter and the lunacy of the people and activities which he[5] was attempting to cover. These formats might include presenters sitting at desks in the middle of a field, vox-pox interviews with people 'in the street', or simulations of black and white Pathé Gazette newsreels. Another common comedic device was for authority figures (such as military officers, police, judges, Conservative politicians, BBC news announcers and even God) to take their characters to extremes by suddenly spouting complete nonsense – or experts would be interviewed who could offer perfectly rational-sounding explanations for absurd behaviour or phenomena. Often sketches would interrupt or offer various forms of commentary on each other using these same kinds of characters.

Neale and Krutnik note that the use of these types of formats created a significant degree of self-reflexivity which marked the series out from other forms of fictional television of their era.

The *Python* programmes, then, combine a comic foregrounding of the conventions of television, with a comic foregounding of the conventions of comic forms themselves. It is this *combination* that produces the particular density of construction and self-reference that constitutes the hallmark of their style. (Neale and Krutnik, 1990: 205)

The authors locate the origins of the *MPFC* style partly within the specific influences of radio's *The Goon Show* and Spike Milligan's television work, the intellectual and educational backgrounds of the performers themselves and a wider exhaustion of traditional British theatrical variety forms. Interestingly, they also note the importance of wider social, cultural and political factors such as the audience's assumed familiarity with television codes and conventions (and their consequent readiness to accept a parody of those forms), and the wider climate of irreverence toward authoritative institutions which characterised the 1960s (Neale and Krutnik, 1990: 205–7).

The original *Monty Python's Flying Circus* television series, and the longer-running American *Saturday Night Live* staple series, offer important precedents for the more consistent and sustained appropriation of factual codes and conventions which characterises the mock-documentary form. Both series should also be seen as examples of the ways in which television comedy generally has often served as a significant site for the *popularising* (if not always the originating) of a complex mixture of fictional and non-fictional means of representation. As mentioned above, these television examples also suggest the significance of wider cultural factors (including the 1960s challenge to authoritative and institution-alised practices) which made the questioning of conventional television forms acceptable to some audiences.

The influence of *MPFC* and *SNL* on mock-documentaries is also more directly obvious in *The Rutles*, which includes regular cast members from both series, and perhaps in the more absurd elements of mock-documentaries such as *This Is Spinal Tap* (1984) (which features a running joke in which drummers in the band expire in increasingly out-rageous ways, including spontaneous combustion on-stage).

Hill Street Blues and the *vérité* style

American network television during the 1980s produced a number of dramatic series which effectively offered the template for a new style of fictional representation, one characterised by techniques directly derived from observational modes of documentary representation. The original style was pioneered by *Hill Street Blues*, a dramatic police drama about a fictional police precinct set in the ghetto of a large city, but it has been copied by more recent dramatic series such as *ER* and *NYPD Blue*, and been extended especially by *Homicide: Life on the Street* (and increasingly by other national television networks, such as the short-lived British series *This Life*, among others).

The *Hill Street Blues* series created a distinctive style deliberately pat-terned after an ABC documentary called *The Police Tapes*, which covered

the activities of a police precinct in Fort Apache, South Bronx. The documentary itself was filmed in black and white, and *Hill Street Blues*
producer Steven Bochco has stated that he considered repeating this for
the series. Although this notion was abandoned, the fictional series
included a number of features which are of interest as precursors of a
mock-documentary style.

As described by Thompson (1996: 67–70), each episode opened with a
scene of a morning roll call at the Hill Street station which directly mim-
icked that of a similar scene from *The Police Tapes*. These opening
sequences aimed for the look of low-budget documentary, using hand-
held cameras and shots that incorporated obvious changes in focus.
These scenes featured a soundtrack with overlapping and chaotic conversations between characters[6] and an unusual absence of music. The rest of
the series conformed to a more conventional visual style, although with a
greater use of hand-held cameras, and scenes which incorporated jump
cuts or shots in which characters momentarily blocked the sight of the
camera. The style was developed by director Robert Butler and producer
Bochco over the first five episodes, and was chosen especially to enhance
the 'reality' of the series by creating the illusion that the events being
filmed were random, and by generating a sense of dramatic tension
through an increase in the visual pacing of typical police drama. The style
pioneered by *Hill Street Blues* was also partly developed to provide a visual
accompaniment to the increased complexity of the series' narrative structure, which incorporated significant elements of the serial narrative more
typically associated with soap opera.

This series, together with the many descendants of dramatic television
series which it inspired, represents an interesting development in the range
of techniques used within television fictional drama. In part, they have
effectively ensured the acceptance within television audiences of a style
which has increasingly become associated with 'realism' and 'immediacy'
– to the extent that the style itself almost seems the dominant means of
representation for fast-paced dramatic television forms. Two of the television mock-documentaries covered by this study (episodes from *ER*[7] and
The Practice) are both from dramatic series which are characterised by
variations on this fictional *vérité* style. Both of these episodes have stories
in which a (fictional) documentary crew attempts to cover the activities of
the regular characters, and it is interesting that, in some sense, the mock-
documentary forms used in each are almost a 'natural' extension of the
existing stylistic tendencies adopted by these series as a whole.

April Fools' Day news stories

Perhaps the most interesting television precursors for mock-documentary are the now almost traditional 1 April television news reports. In a sense, these offer an encapsulation of the mock-documentary format; they invariably use the same codes and conventions of the television news programmes within which they are couched. These April Fools' Day stories are increasingly becoming a seasonal staple of otherwise serious news programmes. This increasing popularity of the format suggests not only that news professionals themselves are becoming more comfortable with such fake or comic inserts, but, perhaps more significantly, that audiences are willing to accept this 'transgression' of factual discourse *within the very programmes* which are typically expected to exclude any suggestion of parody or irony.

These faked reports represent an opportunity for news professionals to deliberately abandon the demands of factual discourse while retaining the news form, but it needs to be acknowledged that they do this with the expectation that they enjoy the full complicity of the audience. These stories are invariably flagged for viewers, either by the news presenter reiterating the date for viewers or by placing these stories at the end of news bulletins, where viewers have come to expect a light entertainment or human interest piece. (And this is perhaps a segment of news programmes which does occasionally allow for elements of parody and ironic commentary.)

This trend derives from the same commercial pressures that are behind the explosion of Reality-TV-style programming; the demand for more entertaining forms of factual programming and the continual drift towards 'infotainment' in news and current affairs genres. In this sense, both April Fools' Day news reports and mock-documentaries could be said to be symptomatic of both the maturity (exhaustion) of factual genres, and of the increasingly competitive commercial environments in which broadcasting institutions must survive.[8]

The implications of these 'in-house' 1 April transgressions, however, are more problematic for factual programming. In a brief discussion on '*faux* documentary' texts, Lizzie Francke offers the example of the reception of a 1994 documentary called *Einstein's Brain*. The documentary represented a serious look at the attempt by a Japanese professor to locate the famous organ, but the initial television screening of the programme was accompanied by claims from tabloid newspapers that it was fake – purely on the grounds that it was screened on 1 April, and that it seemed to include unlikely subject matter (Francke, 1996: 338–9). Francke's example suggests that to some extent news and documentary pro- grammes now need to be even more careful in cueing audiences to the factual status of stories on that date.

Cinematic precursors

Stanley Kubrick's *Dr Strangelove (Or How I Learned to Stop Worrying and Love the Bomb)* (1963)

Dr Strangelove might appear to be an obscure choice to include within this list of genealogical precursors for mock-documentary, but we include it here because it features elements of style and rhetoric which reappear within the mock-documentary form. This text combines a sporadic use of documentary codes and conventions with a satiric distinctive treat- ment of its subject (a satiric style which appears to draw from the same cultural sources as the *Monty Python* tradition).

The film is a satire which targets the social and political implications of the nuclear balance of power between the United States and the Soviet Union. Released during the early 1960s, it represents a particular critique of the military and political practices which largely defined the relationship between the two superpowers. The overall theme of the film (the irra- tionality of the military and political institutional logic which defines nuclear deterrence) is represented through a specific combination of stylistic tendencies which is particularly suited to the manner in which Kubrick approaches his subject (Kolker, 1988: 110–14, has a detailed and convincing argument along these lines). Walker quotes the director as arguing that a man in an office reacting to a nuclear alarm is documentary, a man reacting to the alarm in his living room is drama, while a man react- ing in a lavatory is comedy (1971: 216). With this film, Kubrick combines the first and last of these styles, creating a sharp political satire.

Dr Strangelove includes many scenes which carefully outline military and political procedures in the event of a nuclear emergency between the two superpowers. The 'rationality' of these procedures is then thrown into comic relief in two ways. Either these procedures is 'infected' with an element of lunacy (such as the madness of Colonel Ripper as he decides to initiate nuclear war with the Soviet Union) or these scenes are contrasted with more openly comic situations in which the central characters struggle to cope with the implications of the procedures once they are set towards their logical conclusion (nuclear annihilation).

The use of documentary codes and conventions is not consistently applied by Kubrick, but they are none the less central to his detailing of these military procedures. The film itself is in black and white, a stylistic choice which partly draws upon connotations of realism (but is also suggestive of the satiric style of political cartoons; Walker, 1971: 176). The opening scenes feature a conventional expositional narrator describing the normal practices and safeguards which are associated with the nuclear bomber force under the US Strategic Air Command (as a voice-over for stock footage of B-52 bombers in flight). Scenes inside one of these B-52 bombers (commanded by Major Kong (Slim Pickens)) are filmed in mock-observational style, with naturalistic lighting, a hand-held camera and close-quarter shots of the crew in action (when a Soviet missile explodes near the plane, the camera shakes as if it is part of the action).

The most convincing of these mock-observational scenes are the extended sequences portraying the assault on Colonel Ripper's Burpelson Air Force Base, which are a sophisticated simulation of Robert Capa's Second World War combat films. These sequences use hand-held cameras and combine point of view shots through binoculars, over gun barrels and behind troops as they fire their weapons, together with rapid pans and jump cuts suggesting cameras caught in combat. These scenes also use grainy film stock which is noticeably different from that of the rest of the film.

These scenes are all then immediately capped by gags, typically with Kubrick presenting them using a stable, 'objective', distanced camera. The opening voice-over narration, for example, is capped by a cut to Major Kong reading *Playboy* and his communications officer playing with a deck of cards (Kolker, 1988: 104). The most interesting of these serious-gag constructions is the intercutting between the assault on Burpelson and Ripper explaining his paranoiac conspiracy theories to Group-Captain Lionel Mandrake of the Royal Air Force (Peter Sellers). Kubrick's specific intention in colliding these types of scenes is to 'document' realistically the nuclear machine, then to detail that machine breaking down (Palmer, 1987: 192–3). The political commentary the film generates is perhaps most explicit in the final shots of the film where he uses actual footage of a series of nuclear explosions, set in ironic contrast to the sound of Vera Lynn's 'We'll Meet Again'.

Dr Strangelove is included in this list of genealogical precursors as a representative of a style of cinematic satire which is an important element within the mock-documentary form. Kubrick's adoption of a rational discourse (Kolker, 1988: 113) here (in his use of both mock-observational scenes and a more general distanced camera style) is only one step removed from the explicit construction of a documentary filmmaker as the central character or narrator for a film. His use of documentary aesthetics is also suggestive of the tendency towards social critique which is an important, if typically under realised, element of the mock-documentary agenda (particularly in films such as *Bob Roberts* (1992) and *Man Bites Dog* (1992)).

Orson Welles's *F for Fake (Vérités et mensonges)* (1974)

Orson Welles appears within this list of genealogical precursors not only for his 1938 radio broadcast of *War of the Worlds* but for this film, which does not sit easily in the categories of either documentary or fiction film. This text is included here because, although it takes as its starting point the representation of actual historical figures, Welles eventually reveals that the final half-hour is an exercise in fantasy. *F for Fake* is a self-reflexive 'documentary' which starts by offering an account of Elmyr de Hory, art forger, and Clifford Irving, Hughes 'biographer', both famous (or infamous) examples of people who have fooled cultural 'experts' (the film originated as a film essay on Hory by Francois Reichenbach for a French television series on forgers; Combs, 1996: 222). Under Welles's direction the film takes a number of tangents, as he ruminates on the nature of art and creative genius (including his own) and the cultural and economic status of famous artists. Welles never disguises the fact that his own 'magic' is at centre stage (he first appears as a magician performing for a small crowd at a railway station, and there are extended sequences where Welles demonstrates his mastery of editing). And one of his tangents involves playful references to both *Citizen Kane* (1941) (with its opening recreation of a *March of Time* newsreel) and the reaction to his *War of the Worlds* broadcast. One of Welles's apologies for such transgressions is the suggestion that in some way every form of story is a lie, which is as good a rationale for mock-documentary as anything offered by the filmmakers featured in the following chapters.

The cinematic work of Robert Altman

The cinema of American director Robert Altman, and particularly his work in the 1970s, offers an example of an auteur who has explored, challenged and extended the range of representational techniques within American cinema – and in the process created a number of inspirations for mock-documentary filmmakers.

Throughout Altman's career he has focused on a number of stylistic tendencies, and although they have not been consistently applied in all of his films over the course of his more than two decades of filmmaking, collectively they represent a disruption to Hollywood realist narrative story-telling traditions. His 1970s films in particular – such as *M.A.S.H.* (1970), *McCabe and Mrs Miller* (1971), *The Long Goodbye* (1973), *Nashville* (1975), *Buffalo Bill and the Indians, or Sitting Bull's History Lesson* (1976), and *Health* (1979) – all offer elements of a distinctive approach to fictional filmmaking.[9]

Altman's innovations have included experimenting with non-linear narrative structures (Self, 1982: 33), character improvisation (Rosenbaum, 1975: 90–5) and overlapping sound (especially dialogue). These are typically incorporated into a particular visual style which Altman uses to create an impression of spontaneity and arbitrary observation. Kolker makes the key observation that this approach explicitly suggests that the conventional American film 'with its steady and precise development of story and character, appears to Altman to be itself a dislocation and distortion' (Kolker, 1988: 320). Instead of developing a linear narrative centred on a small number of central characters, he often approaches the narrative centre of his films from the peripheries (Kolker, 1988: 307–8). His representational style favours the creation of a visual and aural denseness within the screen, a style which places more demands on the audience than is normal for a mainstream Hollywood film (Kolker, 1988: 312–16).[10] In Altman's films 'the more random fragments of faces, figures and conversation that are given, the more coherent the space becomes' (Kolker, 1988: 315). Altman's style is one which succeeds in offering an impression of an 'overheard' and 'indirectly glimpsed' reality, and which at times is extremely close to the simulations of the observational style of representation later constructed within many mock-documentaries.

Altman also plays a more explicitly influential role in the development of the mock-documentary form as the director of a rare example of a mock-documentary series – *Tanner '88* (1988), which provided a model for Tim Robbin's *Bob Roberts*.[11] The series was broadcast during the 1988 presidential elections, and featured an actor (Michael Murphy) playing a candidate (Tanner) interacting with real political candidates.[12] Altman has stated that with *Tanner* 'I think that broke into new form. We used a mix of drama and comedy and reality and satire, fiction and non-fiction'

(Smith and Jameson, 1992: 30). The preoccupation with mixing fact and fiction which distinguished this television series provided the inspiration for some of Altman's more recent films, such as *The Player* (1992) and *Prêt-à-Porter* (1994), which both include a number of real public figures appearing as themselves.[13]

Mainstream American cinema: Scorsese, Stone and Spielberg

The three cinematic examples outlined above represent the work of auteurs (Kubrick, Welles, Altman) who have been to varying degrees isolated from the mainstream of American and British cinema. Their challenge to the range of representational styles typically used within Hollywood realist narrative has generally operated from the margins of the film industry (with the exceptions of *Dr Strangelove* and Altman's *M.A.S.H* and *The Player*, these films have not achieved widespread popular success). Although they all offer various precedents for the elements of the mock-documentary form, they could also be said to have served more particularly as influences for a community of *filmmakers* to investigate an expanded range of representational techniques in fictional filmmaking.

The filmmakers discussed below, in contrast, are included here as representatives of the more readily accepted and established mainstream directors who have popularised, for *audiences*, representational styles which appropriate elements of documentary aesthetics. These three directors are intended to represent differing degrees of preoccupations within mainstream Hollywood cinema. Each has produced highly successful forms of entertainment which to varying degrees all contain sporadic elements of representational styles more commonly associated with documentary. In this sense, these directors have all (intentionally or not) provided texts which expand upon the classic realist narrative style.

Martin Scorsese
It is impossible to do justice here to the complexity and breadth of this director's work, but with films such as *Mean Streets* (1973), *Taxi Driver* (1976), *Raging Bull* (1980) and *Goodfellas* (1990) Scorsese serves as an interesting example of an American filmmaker who appears to have deliberately and self-consciously sought to disrupt the conventional Hollywood realist style. He has helped to introduce a more dynamic and kinetic filmic style to the mainstream, in ways which offer interesting pointers to the development of the mock-documentary form.

Kolker argues that in most of his films Scorsese 'creates a tension between two opposing cinematic conventions, the documentary and the fictional'. The director has had experience making documentaries,[14] and seems to draw upon this familiarity with documentary technique to construct a cinematic style which develops from the same dramatic intentions as the *vérité* style of the dramatic television series mentioned above – although Scorsese characteristically offers a more thorough exploration of this style, and he uses it in a more complex, intelligent and measured fashion.

Scorsese is extremely proficient in the use of a fast-moving camera technique which gives the impression of 'catching' people on the streets or in natural conversation. Scorsese's camera work in *Mean Streets*, for example, incorporates a high degree of hand-held shots, which he has suggested were chosen partly to create the 'sense of anxiety and urgency' which suited the film's explorations into the life of Italian-American small-time criminals in New York (Thompson and Christie, 1990: 47). (Scorsese has also admitted that the style also partly reflected the need to shoot quickly on a tight budget (Keyser, 1992: 39).) The manner in which Scorsese uses dialogue in this film also bears interesting similarities to the impression of improvisation which is such a distinctive feature of Altman's work.

Kolker argues that the director does not just recreate documentary aesthetics but deliberately establishes a tension between these and more expressionist elements, a tension which becomes a key part of the narrative structure of the film (Kolker, 1988: 165–6). *Raging Bull*, an account of the life and career of 1949 middleweight champion Jake La Motta, contains significant elements of documentary codes and conventions. The decision to film in black and white seems to reflect an effect to project a gritty realism, and Scorsese makes frequent use of captions to establish the locations and dates for scenes. The fight scenes within this film, in direct counterpoint, are heavily stylised, and designed to purely represent Jake's perspective of his encounters in the ring.[15] Where Kubrick, in *Dr Strangelove*, uses a contrast between the rational and irrational to construct a satiric commentary, here Scorsese collides 'objective' and expressionist styles to document both La Motta's masochistic machismo and the effect it has on his family.

Scorsese has demonstrated throughout his career a willingness to incorporate a *vérité* aesthetic. In a more recent example of the director's work, *Goodfellas*, based on the life of mobster Henry Hill (Ray Liotta), at least part of the dramatic effect of the film derives from the apparent intention to mimic a documentary approach toward the subject. In Scorsese's words, he wanted to film to look 'as if you had a 16 mm camera with these guys for 20, 25 years' and filmed what you could (Keyser, 1992: 197).

Oliver Stone

While Scorsese is one of the more deliberate and self-conscious (and kinetic) stylists within popular American cinema, Oliver Stone's career is representative of a different and perhaps more conventional filmmaking orientation. The camerawork in such films as *Salvador* (1986), *Platoon* (1986), *Wall Street* (1987), *Born on the Fourth of July* (1989), *JFK* (1991) and *Nixon* (1995) suggests that Stone also recognises the dramatic potential of the *vérité* style. *Salvador*, for example, is a dramatised account of the experiences of an American journalist in the Salvadoran civil war. Here the *vérité* style is used to generate a sense of tension associated with the possibility of random violence, to increase the impression of vulnerability of the main characters and to heighten the dramatic tension within the film's recreations of battle scenes from the war (and of the assassination of Oscar Romero that was such a key point in the history of the Central American nation). The film also uses other documentary elements – it opens with film newsreel footage (in both black and white and colour, with a news presenter's voice-over) of Salvadoran police's violent quelling of political protest. Throughout the narrative Stone uses detailed captions to introduce the main protagonists in the Salvadoran civil war and key locations in the conflict.

It is significant that these stylistic devices are often associated (by audiences, and some critics) with the portrayal of historical accuracy, a 'more realistic' approach to a subject – or at least the accurate representation of experience. The *vérité* style and other use of documentary conventions is apparently a deliberate choice by the director to create just such an impression. With *JFK*, Stone's investigation of the Kennedy assassination, the director went to great lengths both to recreate the event itself and later to defend publicly the accuracy of his perspective. The most complex of the film's sequences is its opening, which blends the Zapruder home movie of the assassination with elements of the *vérité* style (using simulations of black and white observational footage, and even *black and white* reconstructions of the *colour* Zapruder film (Beaver, 1994: 174)) and more expressionist techniques.

Stone, however, offers a more simplistic, and less controlled and certainly less aesthetically successful, representational style than Scorsese, and often seems to rely too heavily on sequences comprising almost completely hand-held shots and an extremely fast cutting style.[16] The approach is intended to draw the viewer into the narrative, to allow audiences to share vicariously the experiences of a film's characters, and Stone's work has been both praised and criticised on these grounds. *Time* magazine's reaction to *Platoon* included the following approving comment:

More than any other film, *Platoon* gives the sense – all five senses – of fighting in Viet Nam. You can wilt from the claustrophobia heat of this Rousseauvian jungle; feel the sting of the leeches as they snack on Chris's flesh; hear all at once the chorus of insects, an enemy's approaching footsteps on the green carpet and Chris' heartbeat on night patrol. The film does not glamorize or trivialize death with grotesque special effects. But it jolts the viewer alive to the sensuousness of danger, fear and war lust. All senses must be alert when your life is at stake, and Oliver Stone is an artist-showman who can make movies seem a matter of life and death. (Corliss, 1986: 40–47)

In contrast, Beaver criticises Stone's reliance on a presentational style which he suggests is part of a simplistic rhetorical stance readily adopted within mainstream American cinema.

What most resembled the newer style of factually based filming was the sense of drama supplied by a constantly moving camera, one that probes fictionalized space in an apparent search for the truth within the event it explores. The frenetic camera supplants verbal investigation within the visual rhetoric of innuendo and ambiguity. Mystery resonates the information being conveyed, proving the technique a compelling one, even though little, in the end, may be clarified. (Beaver, 1994: 186)

Steven Spielberg

Steven Spielberg has offered significant additions to the development of this cinematic tradition. His *Schindler's List* (1993) can be termed a drama-documentary,[17] while *Saving Private Ryan* (1998) is more closely associated with the generic traditions of war films. As Doherty notes, *Saving Private Ryan* has been greeted with the same rhetoric concerning the 'realism' of its depictions of combat that previously accompanied other examples of the genre such as *The Big Parade* (1925), *All Quiet on the Western Front* (1930), *A Walk in the Sun* (1945), *The Steel Helmet* (1951), *Patton* (1969) and Stone's *Platoon* (1986). Doherty's description of the twenty-seven-minute recreation of the Omaha beach landing at Normandy which appears early in the film is worth repeating:

Robert Capa *mise-en-scene* and Army Signal Corp. eyelines clash in a barrage of kaleidoscopic flashes: the blurry D-Day images of the famous combat photographer spliced into the handheld combat camerawork of burly noncoms hefting

35mm Mitchels, whose lenses peer out from behind parapets and through the slits of pillboxes. Newsreel memories are evoked by angle of sight, jump-cut action, and subtle shifts in film grain, but the newsreels spooled nothing like this. (Doherty, 68-71)

Spielberg is a popular filmmaker who has tended to use a wide variety of cinematic styles over the course of his career, but the complex and detailed representations which he has constructed in both *Schindler's List* and *Saving Private Ryan* are indicative of the degree of sophistication with which the *vérité* style is being used, and of its ready acceptance, within contemporary Hollywood realist narrative.

Alternative cinematic traditions

The majority of precursors considered within this chapter are taken from American and British film and television. In large part this is because these media have historically tended to place a greater emphasis on maintaining a distinction between fictional and non-fictional forms of representation. The cinema created within other national traditions, however, has produced a more complex intertwining of representational styles. Unfortunately, there is not the space here to do justice to the influence of these traditions on the development of the mock-documentary form. At the very least, a fuller examination of the role which these various cinematic movements have had would need to consider Italian Neo realism, the films of the French New Wave and many of the revolutionary films which have emerged in the last twenty years from Latin American filmmakers. To some extent these movements have all represented external challenges to the realist narrative model promoted by mainstream American cinema.

Recent examples of a European filmmaker working with these aesthetic concerns could be Lars von Trier's *The Kingdom* (1994) and *Breaking the Waves* (1996), both of which make extensive use of hand-held camera work, with the later film especially relying on naturalistic lighting and location shooting. *Breaking the Waves* was constructed using long, unstructured takes built around the improvisation of the main actors, and Trier has stated that he deliberately aimed for a documentary feel throughout the film in order to contrast and counteract the strong romanticism of its story (Björkman, 1996). (This emphasis on capturing an impression of spontaneity and 'naturalness' is echoed in Woody Allen's explanation of his choice of techniques for his mock-documentary *Husbands and Wives* (1992).) Trier's film *The Idiots* (1998) offers a tenuous link to mock-documentary in its use of interviews with fictional characters (see below).

Together with fellow directors Christian Levring, Thomas Vinterberg and Soren Kragh-Jacobsen, Trier has formed Dogme 95, a filmmaking collective which vows to combat auteurism, reinvigorate New Wave aesthetics and subvert the illusions of mainstream cinema. *The Idiots* is part of the stable of films the group intends to produce. Dogme 95 is of interest within this suggested genealogy because it champions natural lighting, hand-held camerawork, natural locations and an absence of post-production polishing – resulting in a *vérité* style which closely parallels that of the dramatic television series discussed above.

News bulletin conventions in mainstream narrative

The use of fictional interviews and faked news broadcasts, within mainstream American cinema in particular, is much more widespread than the deliberate appropriation of documentary aesthetics undertaken by the filmmakers listed above. These factual conventions are used sporadically throughout fictional narratives, most commonly as part of an effort to ground a text within the social-historical world. Within these sporadic appropriations, however, there are also interesting examples of the parodic treatment of factual codes and conventions.

Fictional interviews

There are a diverse number of examples of this dramatic device. In general, this is a technique which serves as a substitute for a character's direct address to the camera. As with direct address, the intention is to allow for the audience to gain an insight into the psychological motivations of characters. In this sense, these 'interviews' tend to be integrated into these fictional texts in an unproblematic way; they are able to draw upon the (documentary) notion that interviews can give access to the testimony from eyewitnesses and participants of an event but without rupturing the integrity of the film's diegesis.

For example, *When Harry Met Sally* (1989) is a romantic comedy which has six elderly 'documentary couples' giving accounts of where they met and the length of their relationships. The couples are all played by actors, and these interviews provide an impression of the variety of relationships between men and women, and the theme of enduring love. They mark the divisions in scenes between the long-term developing relationship between Harry Burns (Billy Crystal) and Sally Allbright

(Meg Ryan), as they move from being friends to falling in love. At the end of the movie Harry and Sally are the seventh and final couple who explain how they met and describe their wedding.

Warren Beatty's *Reds* (1981) is a fictionalised account of the experiences of John Reed, an American eyewitness to the 1917 Russian Revolution. The film features 'interviews' with elderly leftists who provide background and insights to Reed's tale. Unlike the film above, here characters are interviewed as if they were real people, as social actors within the social-historical world. They offer conflicting memories especially of the relationship between lead characters Reed (Warren Beatty) and fellow activist journalists Louise Bryant (Diane Keaton). (The film's survey of experts and historical figures is directly parodied in Woody Allen's mock-documentary *Zelig* (1983).)

A more complex example of the use of interviews within a fictional film is *Blue in the Face* (1995). A sequel to the more conventional *Smoke* (1995), this has an unstructured narrative, centred on scenes set in and around a cigar store in Brooklyn staffed by Auggie (played by Harvey Keitel). The cigar store features constant traffic, meetings and conversations between various local characters in the neighbourhood. These fictional scenes are interspersed with a variety of interviews with actual Brooklyn locals (including celebrities such as Lou Reed, vox-pox interviews with people on the street and the direct-to-camera presentation of statistics on ethnic and national groups within the New York suburb, apparently by Brooklyn locals). At various points there are also extracts of newsreel footage featuring events in Brooklyn history (such as the emergence of Jackie Robinson as the first African-American player, within the Dodgers baseball franchise, the loss of the Dodgers to California and the transformation of their home ballpark into apartment buildings). This complex combination of actual interviews, faked interviews, direct addresses and sampling of archival newsreels provides a distinctive perspective on Brooklyn, and more specifically serves to ground the film's fictional characters within a recognisable social-historical milieu.

Faked news broadcasts

There are any number of such examples of this textual device. The *March of Time* newsreel which opens Orson Welles's *Citizen Kane* (1941) is an early example which serves a number of purposes within the text. It introduces the central character, both announcing his death and providing a brief biography of his life. The sequence also establishes he central mystery of the narrative (the meaning of Kane's final words) by effectively revealing the lack of real public insights into Kane's character and the motivations which lead to his public achievements. (Interestingly, this fictionalised version of a newsreel seems to provide a direct model for a similar sequence in *Zelig*.)

An example of the satiric use of fictional news broadcasts is the televised civil defence announcements, and breaking news stories involving local and national authorities, from *Night of the Living Dead* (1968). Here the device is used to parody the authoritative voice of the police and government bureaucracy; the bulletins provide the latest information on the origins and spread of flesh-eating zombies, and suggestions on how to dispose of the menace most efficiently and safely.

Another interesting example is the complex role which television 'factual' broadcasts serve within the narrative of *Independence Day* (1996), an otherwise conventional mainstream film. The story details an alien invasion of Earth and its eventual repulsion by combined Earth forces, and television news and information bulletins appear frequently throughout the film. The US president and his advisers gain visual confirmation of the first appearance of the alien spacecraft by watching a 'Live Sky News' report, and they eventually make an emergency presidential address to the nation through television. Emergency civil defence procedures and guidelines for treating aliens are broadcast on local television channels, and there are brief snippets from news broadcasts which feature maps showing the global location of arriving ships, the panic in major cities, interviews with alien abductees and alien fans (one woman exclaims: 'God I hope they bring back Elvis!'), coverage of the first attempts to communicate with alien spacecraft and reports of the build-up of the Earth's military forces as they prepare to retaliate against the invasion.

These various television broadcasts serve a number of purposes within the film's narrative. In part, these constructions 'ground' the text in a recognisable social-historical context, in the process offering a subtle commentary on the tabloid approach which the film suggests the media community would naturally have towards such a historic occasion. (The journalists are shown reacting in often trivial and sensationalist ways to these events, and failing to grasp the historical significance of first contact with an alien race.) On a different level, these devices also function to affirm the significance of visual media within the American social-political system. The nation (including ordinary people, armed forces personnel and even the White House administration) are all seen to use television as their primary source of information, and in particular to gain visual confirmation of events and a sense of the scale of the alien invasion. And, thirdly, in common with much contemporary science fiction, these segments are also used as part of a wider narrative strategy to suture the audience (both within and outside the film) into roles as voyeurs to the spectacle of alien invasion and human fightback.

Home movies

Closely related to the above examples is the inclusion of sequences of home movies for a variety of purposes within fictional narratives. Erens provides a useful summary of the ways in which home footage is briefly used briefly in movies such as *Raging Bull* and *Paris, Texas* (1984), *The Falcon and the Snowman* (1985) and, in a much more complex way, *Peeping Tom* (1960): 'home movies have been utilized to denote past tense, to provide insight into fictional characters, to indicate a higher truth, to serve as a Rorschach for the emotional states of the protagonists, to offer visual contrast, and to constitute an extended metaphor for the entire work' (Erens, 1985: 101). These kinds of sequences typically use jump cuts, light flashes, tilt shots, over-exposed lighting and shaky camera movements (Erens, 1986: 99) to construct documents of characters' past lives. In this sense they provide domestic versions of the more public 'documents' constructed through other simulated factual forms such as fictional news reports and (to a lesser extent) interviews. In many cases home movies are used as a more realistic substitute for flashbacks; providing 'objective' evidence of the psychological motivations of characters (such as the happy early domestic life of Natassja Kinski and Harry Dean Stanton in *Paris, Texas*).

In *Raging Bull*, in contrast, they are more problematically used both to provide a nostalgic sense of the passage of time and to suggest the distance between public and private appearances. Here the colour home movies showing a happy couple posing for the camera represent an idealised image of domesticity, and stand in stark contrast to the (literally) black and white reality of Jake and wife Vickie's domestic life which dominates the film.[18] In this example, then, the director (Scorsese) manages to draw upon the conventional cinematic construction of home movies (as documents of domesticity), but also allows the more interesting insight that these 'documents' should be recognised as incomplete bearers of truth.

An even more complex example is provided by the classic *Peeping Tom*. As Erens notes, home movies occupy a much more integral position within this film's narrative. The amateur footage of the tortured childhood of serial killer Mark Lewis provides an explanation for his psychosis, and also serves as the most potent case study of the film's examination of the psychological motivations of filmmakers and the distancing effect of operating behind a camera lens. (This is also a film which is significant here as a direct inspiration for Jim McBride's mock-documentary *David Holzman's Diary*.[19])

Digital imaging

Finally, within this speculative list of genealogical precursors for mock-documentary, there is a need to acknowledge the potential of fictional cinematic texts to take advantage of the variety of technological innovations offered by digital imaging. This is obviously a topic too large to properly address here,[20] but among the more relevant of these developments for mock-documentary is the ability to construct convincing reconstructions of documentary footage, or to integrate fictional characters into historical images.

Forrest Gump (1994), the comic-dramatic biography of an Everyman whose life story intersects with many of the significant social, political and cultural events in American history, is notable for its demonstration of the developing sophistication with which special-effects technology allows for the manipulation of audio-visual recordings of historical events.[21] This film features a variety of sequences which offer an effective subversion of the legitimacy of any historical 'evidence' provided by audio-visual texts. For example, the fictional character of Forrest appears within black and white archival footage of the 1948 confrontation between Governor George Wallace and General Graham (commander of the local National Guard) on the steps of the University of Alabama, over the enforced desegregation of the campus. This footage is spliced virtually seamlessly into a detailed colour reconstruction of the event, effectively problematising this document's status as an historical record.

By erasing the line between past and present, between social actors and fictional characters, such sequences demonstrate a significant ambivalence in their treatment of documentary images. Through a recognition of the historical significance of the events and figures which they represent, these scenes partly reinforce the status of the documents themselves as remnants of an historical period. However, by also effectively demonstrating the ease with which the images themselves can be manipulated, these scenes also undermine what remains of their status as objective, unmediated recordings of history. In *Forrest Gump*, this same ambivalence underlies the sequences used to represent Forrest's encounters with US Presidents Kennedy, Johnson and Nixon and his appearance on the Dick Cavett show with 'fellow guest' John Lennon.

The tendency to revisit and subvert historical images has obvious links with *Zelig* – although there is not the same degree of direct manipulation or doctoring of historical documents in this mock-documentary as with *Forrest Gump*. *Zelig* relies more upon the seamless editing together of faked and actual footage for its effect. In contrast, *Forgotten Silver* (with director Peter Jackson at the vanguard of the use of digital imaging in fictional narrative) is a mock-documentary which uses a complex variety of cinematic techniques, including those which suggest the potential of computer-imaging technology to create a credible social-historical landscape.

Notes

1 As suggested in the Introduction, the mock-documentary form has been acknowledged with a variety of labels, although these have largely reflected how writers have positioned the form within the fact–fiction continuum.
2 As mentioned in Chapter 2, an aspect of Cawelti's argument which is of particular interest to the discussion of mock-documentary is the suggestion that as an audience become more familiar with a particular form of representation, that audience is prepared to accept transformations which can include the deconstructing of the myths and assumptions on which the original form is based.
3 In part these differences reflect the contrasting modes of address that television and cinema media necessarily adopt towards their audiences. Television has always had to develop alternative strategies of address, to compete not only with multiple channels but with other domestic social activities and fragmented viewing patterns within typical television viewing contexts.
4 See Chapter 7.
5 A curious feature of the series was how rarely it used female actors – often female roles were taken by the male cast themselves.
6 Thompson suggests that this feature was derived especially from the films of Robert Altman – these are discussed below.
7 This is discussed in Chapter 7.
8 As discussed in Chapter 2.
9 Kolker has an excellent discussion on the development of the Altman approach to realist narrative, and he argues that Altman's work of the 1980s does not have the same consistency and focus as his best films from the 1970s. See the chapter on Altman entitled 'Radical Surfaces' in Kolker, 1988: 303–82.
10 This perhaps partly explains the comparative lack of recognition which Altman has enjoyed within the United States.
11 See Chapter 7.
12 Unfortunately the authors have been unable to track down a copy of this series.

13 Reportedly there are sixty-three actors appearing as themselves in *The Player*, which has been termed a 'docusatire of presentday Hollywood' (Smith and Jameson, 1992: 20).

14 Including *The Last Waltz* (1978), which served as unintended inspiration for *This Is Spinal Tap* (1984).

15 Both this film and *Mean Streets* are interesting also in their contrasting use of home movie footage at key points in the narrative – this is discussed below.

16 Interestingly, this tendency of Stone to over-use a particular representational style is almost elevated to a self-parodic level in *Natural Born Killers* (1994), which looks to challenge the simplicity of the conventional style of Holly-wood action movies by assaulting the viewer with as many alternatives as Stone can construct.

17 This film was discussed, in terms of the similarities and differences between drama-documentaries and mock-documentaries, in Chapter 4.

18 With *Mean Streets*, in contrast, Scorsese opens the film with actual home movies, before beginning the fictional narrative which 'documents' the lives of characters from a similar neighbourhood.

19 This text is discussed in Chapter 8.

20 *Premiere* magazine has suggested a timeline of the most significant milestones in the development of digital imaging within film, from the motion-controlled cameras of *Star Wars* (1977), through *Young Sherlock Holmes* (1985), *The Abyss* (1989), the morphing technology of *Terminator 2: Judgment Day* (1991), the animated *Beauty and the Beast* (1991), the mixing of animatronic and CG dinosaurs in *Jurassic Park* (1993), *Forrest Gump* (1994), *Dragonheart* (1996), to *Titanic* (1997) which combined CG with almost every type of effect technol-ogy (Horn, 1999: 87–8). George Lucas has also claimed that his *Star Wars: Episode I – The Phantom Menace* (1999) is the first film to have digital charac-ters (synthespians) interacting with real actors (Lucas, 1999: 58–60).

21 The film also features a number of television news reports and magazine covers of Forrest, which are used together with the sequences above to locate and establish this fictional character within an arguably sanitised and revi-sionist version of American post war history (Walker, 1994; Hampton, 1994; Chumo, 1995; Leitch, 1997).

6

Degree 1: parody

The mock-documentaries discussed in this chapter are those which we have tentatively labelled as degree 1 examples of the mock-documentary form. These are texts which collectively demonstrate a specific use of factual aesthetics, and consequently encourage a particular reading from their audiences. They make obvious their 'fictionality', using documentary codes and conventions in some form in order to parody an aspect of popular culture. These texts feature what could be termed the 'innocent' appropriation of these codes and conventions; their filmmakers do not intend to make explicit the inherent reflexivity of the mock-documentary form.

As outlined in Chapter 4, the textual analysis which follows is intended more to suggest the diversity of possible readings of mock-documentaries than to fix particular texts within a taxonomy of mock-documentary. Unlike the other, perhaps more complex examples of the form which are discussed in the following chapters, audiences of degree 1 texts are not explicitly encouraged or confronted with a need to reflect on the factual means of representation themselves. As we have already argued, the appropriation of documentary aesthetics for parodic intent *inherently* contains the potential for reflexive interpretation – the texts we identify below are those which tend also to foreground their fictionality and hence contain this potential to a comparatively lesser degree.

Within the discussion below, we further position texts according to three general textual tendencies; a nostalgic frame directed towards a fictional subject; the group of texts which could be termed 'mock-rockumentaries'; and a third group which we have termed 'mock-docu-soap'.

Nostalgia pieces

The first of the degree 1 'nostalgic' texts is an early effort at mock-
documentary, and interesting especially as an example which is not
consistent in its construction of the mock-documentary form. In other
words, it is both openly fictional and does not attempt a consistent and
sustained appropriation of documentary codes and conventions. However, it still contains important characteristics of the form which reappear
in later mock-documentary texts.

The Rutles (1978)

The Rutles follows the parodic model of the *Monty Python's Flying Circus*
television series,[1] and it features both Python regulars and *Saturday Night
Live* comics. The film uses the mock-documentary form to present the
story of the Rutles, a detailed parody of the mythology of the British
musical group the Beatles. As with similar sketches from the *MPFC* series,
most of the film's humour stems from a basic organising principle of a
meeting between the rational and irrational, between the 'straight face' of
a BBC-styled reporter (Eric Idle) and the absurdity of the Rutles' take on
the legend of the Beatles. Also like the series, this is a binary dramatic
structure which is not consistently held to throughout the film, with the
presenter also engaging in nonsense speech at different points.

The film uses a classic expository mode of documentary as its departure
point. It has a narrator, and uses interviews, archival footage, extensive use
of captions to identify locations and dates of 'archival material', and cultural artefacts (albums, music, films) as evidence to present a historical
narrative. The film's opening suggests the frame for the text. After the main
title, scrolling text is read by an authoritative male voice:

The Rutles story is a legend. A living legend, a legend that will live long after lots
of other living legends have died.

Tonight, we are extremely proud to present the semi-legendary life story of the
prefab four: Dirk, Nasty, Stig and Barry, who made the sixties what they are today.
The fabulous Rutles.

The most telling line from this opening caption is probably 'the group
who made the sixties what they are today', which carries the suggestion
that the sixties are typically reconstructed through a familiar series of
icons. The objective of the mock-documentary form here is to parody the
(at the time of the film, recent) establishment of the legend of the Beatles.

One of the early sequences in the film is a virtual reconstruction of a Pathé News item on the Beatles, here called 'Pathetique News'. In fact, most of the sequences in the film represent close re-constructions of well-known public moments from the Beatles' history; virtual re-creations of their television appearances, films, press conferences and so on. There are also montages of close simulations of Beatles album covers, with the Rutles members in the place of the Beatles, and reconstructions of well-known photographic images of the Beatles with figures such as Muhammad Ali and Khrushchev.

All of the Rutles songs featured within the film also virtually repeat the music of the Beatles. The lyrics themselves are changed, but in most cases they use the same themes and language and there is little attempt to deconstruct the qualities of the music themselves. The lyrics are changed just enough for Beatles fans to recognise the difference, but do not attempt an explicit commentary on the band itself – for example, 'All You Need Is Love' becomes 'Love Life' with the same sentiments simply expressed in a more humorous way.

The effect of the film is to parody this popular narrative, but not to deconstruct it. The film only deals with the public exploits of the Beatles as a cultural phenomena, and there is no real attempt to examine the way in which this legend was deliberately constructed both by the group and its management, and by the wider British and American musical industries. There is never, for example, any attempt to present 'discovered' footage, or even home movies of any of the Rutles, which might suggest that they are anything other than they appear to be. The film only re-creates a familiar series of iconic references, the historical evidence which underlies the Beatles mythology. The popular narrative of the Beatles and their music is effectively reinforced as an effortless, spontaneous expression by natural pop geniuses.

The mock-documentary form is used within this film, then, effectively to *recreate* an audience's public experience of the group, to parody the *mediation* of a myth, rather than to uncover its origins. The dominant frame adopted by this text is one of nostalgia. Interestingly, one of the final scenes in the film implicitly acknowledges the relationship which the film has with Beatle mythology. The presenter attempts to interview a woman on the street in New York ('Mrs Emily Pules' played by Gilda Radner) about her memories of the Rutles. She is reluctant, but he badgers her, grabs her and slaps her, until she finally takes the microphone out of his hand and launches into a pat summary of the band's career – one that mimics the popular narrative associated with the Beatles.

1 and 2 These images from the promotional material associated with the mock-documentary *The Rutles* illustrate the careful attention to detail which is at the centre of the film's affectionate parody of Beatle mythology.

3 and 4 One of the more durable mock-documentaries, *This Is Spinal Tap* has developed an interesting presence both online and within the rock market that it parodies. The first image is taken from the original official website; the second from an actual live performance by the mock group.

5 Christopher Guest holds a special place in mock-documentary for his roles as Nigel Tuffnel, lead guitarist for Spinal Tap, and as Corky St Clair, here in repose at his memorabilia store at the end of *Waiting for Guffman*.

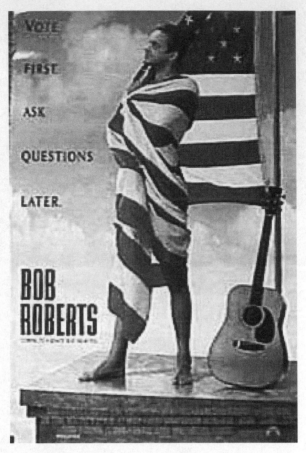

6 A carefully crafted deconstruction of American political discourse from the 1980s, *Bob Roberts* is a rare example of a mock-documentary that fully explores the form's satiric potential.

7 The Belgian mock-documentary *Man Bites Dog* disturbed many with its apparent casual acceptance of a serial killer's immorality – a quite deliberate provocation of its viewers which is suggested by this promotional poster for the film.

8 Colin McKenzie, the long-lost filmmaker that *Forgotten Silver* claimed to have rediscovered. The prospect of a cinematic pioneer on a par with Griffith and Einstein thrilled those New Zealand viewers who overlooked the film's more subtle mocking of national icons.

'The Rutles were a moptop English pop quartet of the sixties who set the foot of the world tapping with their catchy melodies, their wacky Liverpool humour and their zany, off-the-wall antics. Epitomised in such movies as *A Hard Days Rut* and *Ouch!*, Dirk and Nasty, the acknowledged leaders of the group were perfectly complemented by Stig, the quiet one, and Barry, the noisy one, to form a heart-warming, cheeky, loveable, talented, non-Jewish group who gladdened the hearts of the world ...'
[the presenter tries to take microphone back off her]

'... In 1962, they played the Cavern. After that they played several months in Hamburg. Then in 1962 they released their first single "Twist and Rut"...'
[the presenter eventually grabs his microphone and tells her to shut up]

The moment is amusing because she is so easily able to fulfil the narrator's role, a role which is effectively made irrelevant because everyone in the audience is assumed to recognise already the (public) story of the Beatles.

A more complex narrative is hinted at, but also deliberately left unexplored, such as the notion that the British music invasion gained its inspiration from almost forgotten forms of American music (blues, and rhythm and blues). Here *The Rutles* draws upon the more complex established historical narrative of popular rock music which suggests that there has typically been an underlying and wholesale appropriation of African-American forms of music by white rock stars. In an interview in New Orleans with 'Blind Lemon Pye', the reporter attempts to discover his place in the development of the 'authentic' music of the blues. Instead, Pye insists that he was a railroad worker until he heard the Rutles, when he decided to become a musician and has 'been starving ever since'. Pye directs the reporter next door, to his neighbour Rutting Orange Peel. Peel claims: 'Yessir I originated the Rutles, they got it all from me, every single bit of it', that 'four guys from Liverpool came here and took everything I ever written'. His wife immediately objects and reveals to the reporter that Peel 'every time there's a documentary on white music around here, he claims he started it all', that Peel has already claimed that he created the music of 'the Everly Brothers, Frank Sinatra and Lawrence Welk'. Here the film calls attention to the importance of African-American musicians in rock history, but does not use this to question the validity of the Rutles (Beatles) as musical prodigies.

The film's indirect, and ultimately passive, commentary on Beatles mythology is best illustrated by its treatment of the role which drugs played in the creative leaps made by the group. Instead of marijuana or LSD, the Rutles are said to have had their consciousness raised by tea. A sequence details how the substance inspired them to create their greatest work: 'Sgt. Rutters Only Darts Club Band', an album which 'contributed greatly to an idyllic summer of flowers, bells and tea drinking. Its music led thousands to experiment with tea.' The reporter explains that 'eventually even the press found out', and states that they 'grabbed the wrong end of the stick and started to beat around the bush with it'. This is followed by a montage of the front pages of tabloid newspapers (with headlines such as 'Mad Rutles Tea Party: Police Dogs Called In', 'Wild Tea Parties: Rutles cause sensation', 'Vicar admits: Yes I have taken tea too 'and 'Stones Arrested: Nude Girl and Teapot'), scenes of the arrest of Rutles members, and the beginning of 'The Campaign for the Legalisation of Tea'. By replacing substances such as LSD and marijuana with an accepted and naturalised form of narcotic the film offers the potential to showcase the hypocrisy of conservative attacks on popular culture during the 1960s, but this is a critique which is left implicit. Instead, the controversy over drugs is here simply another familiar reference point from the period. Similarly, the audience is able to make a critique of tabloid newspapers, but it is a critique left unexplored by the text. (This is in stark contrast to the savage attack on journalist ethics which is presented to the audience in *Man Bites Dog*, a text we suggest has a degree 3 level of reflexivity towards documentary – see Chapter 8.)

As with the *MPFC* series, there are some attempts to highlight the constructed nature of the conventional documentary. The narrator makes a great point of visiting the historical locations of events, often failing to gain access or the knowledge that he expects to find. He also attempts to interview 'experts' on the historical importance of the Rutles – one refuses to answer (literally closing the door on the camera), the other speaks in indecipherable academic language. And there are also a number of criticisms of the news media for their harassment and exploitation of the Rutles (although the text never acknowledges that all of the images it is parodying are themselves gleaned from the popular media).

The 'documentary' features rock stars and popular figures from the era itself (Ron Wood as a Hells Angels member, Mick Jagger as a 'Rock Star', Bianca Jagger as a French actress, Paul Simon as himself) and even includes one of the Beatles (George Harrison, badly disguised as a television news reporter asking about the bankruptcy rumours surrounding 'Rutle Corps'). In this sense, the text almost serves as an in-joke for industry insiders,[2] and an extension of the Beatles' refusal to take themselves or their cultural position seriously. Ultimately, then, *The Rutles* presents characters who are little more than signifiers for the public figures they parody.

Zelig (1983)

This mock-documentary text offers a more seamless simulation of documentary form than either *The Rutles*, or Woody Allen's early effort at mock-documentary, *Take the Money and Run* (1969). *Zelig* is the mock-biography of a man who lived in America during the 1920s, named Leonard Zelig (Woody Allen), who has the chameleon-like ability to transform himself in appearance to resemble whoever he is with. Once discovered by the American media, Zelig becomes a national celebrity, suffers from both the highs and lows of fame and eventually finds love, and a cure, with psychiatrist Dr Louise Fletcher (Mia Farrow).

As with *Take the Money and Run*, this film uses a heavily expositional form of narrative, with the films structured around a traditional male, voice-over narrator (one with correct English – almost in the style of a 1920s narrator but with a slightly more knowing edge). Except for 'contemporary interviews', the film is completely in black and white, the effect of which is to render the text overall with a heavy sense of nostalgia.[3] The film makes an exhaustive attempt to 'visit' all of the cultural, and many political, reference points of the 1920s, and incorporates a variety of audio-visual material from the period. The director has described how the film's specific appropriation of documentary aesthetics was achieved largely through clever editing and the intercutting of manufactured scenes with archival footage (Björkman, 1994: 137–40).

Zelig exhibits a contradictory attitude towards these historical documents,[4] partly treating them as valuable remnants of a rich period of American history, and partly as images which can be 'lived in'. In some sense, Allen seeks to place himself into these documents, not just as a visual joke but to recreate the history which they represent – effectively offering a commentary upon his main character within a nostalgic frame. The film also incorporates a variety of sequences designed as re-constructions of conventional documentary forms of representation, sequences which are all treated as cultural artefacts and evidence of Zelig's existence. There are colour interviews with intellectuals and cultural commentators, simulations of newspaper headlines and articles covering Zelig's life, re-creations of press conferences and other events covered by newsreels,[5] footage of main characters (especially Fletcher the psychiatrist) that has the appearance of having been filmed by a colleague, home movie footage of Fletcher and Zelig's eventual marriage,[6] black and white photos of Zelig with famous people from the 1920s, an interesting sequence from a fictional Hollywood film based on Zelig's exploits in Nazi

Germany called *The Changing Man*, and the variety of songs and other merchandise constructed for the film.[7]

A significant element of these sequences is a parody of the language and status of professional experts (especially academic and medical experts) – one which is more explicit and sustained in this film than in *Take the Money and Run*. These experts are all expected to be able to account for Zelig's condition, to place him within his social and historical context, and to speculate on his cultural meaning, but instead they all disagree, offering widely divergent views. It is interesting that the intellectuals (Susan Sontag, Irving Howe, Saul Bellow, Bricktop, Dr Bruno Bettelheim, Professor John Morton Blum) all play themselves.[8] In effect, their participation in the film allows them to parody their own rhetorical styles (Perlmutter, 1991: 211). This is a recurring feature of the mock-documentary form – such as George Harrison appearing in *The Rutles*, or Melvyn Bragg parodying the arts programme (*The South Bank Show*) with which he is most closely associated (in *Norbert Smith: A Life* (1989)).

The character of Zelig serves to illustrate a variety of themes. He is the ultimate comic impersonator,[9] who perfectly adopts all of the stereotypical attributes of a whole series of people of various religion, ethnicity, class and politics.[10] One of the film's 'experts' suggests that Zelig is the ultimate conformist, that he represents the effort to conform to social rules in order to receive all the benefits of 'fitting in'. As is distinctive of most of Allen's films, Zelig is a pathetic character, barely aware of his fate and too neurotic to be able to cope with any situation – one of Allen's passive and fearful immature characters who can be dominated by anyone. Zelig's character is in some ways the Allen archetype taken to extremes, with his efforts to please his peers justified at the level of biology. Zelig cannot help transforming himself; his body does it for him, although, as always, there is a neurosis at the heart of all his problems.

Another suggestion is that Zelig's life illustrates perfectly the Jewish immigrant experience: a desperate need to assimilate into a hostile culture. Allen here is perhaps hinting at the enormous cultural contribution which Jews have made in America – such as in Hollywood (the centre for image manipulation itself), and, less obviously in this film, in leftist political movements of the 1930s and 1940s. Allen even has Zelig re-enact the Jewish flight from prewar Germany. He becomes the archetypal Jewish immigrant who brings his talents to an America which is incapable of appreciating him (there is almost a sense of bitter irony here, in that anti-Semitism kept most Jews from becoming the adored hero figures which Zelig immediately becomes).

A significant theme of the film is the suggestion that Zelig's ability to disappear into society represents the attractiveness of fascism. This is most explicit towards the end, when Zelig escapes America to seek the safety, comfort and anonymity of fascist Germany. Here the film's uneasiness with conformity takes on a muted critique of the people who followed Hitler (although the link between conformity and fascism, for example, is never made in relation to *American* society). In some sense, however, the film represents Allen's distrust of the mass impulses of the American public. This is an element even of the way in which Zelig is for a time the ultimate fad, with all of the inevitable merchandise that is generated. It is interesting that the American public are rarely personified throughout the film. They are reduced to the adoring crowds who follow his exploits in the press, dance to the songs created to cash in on his novelty value, and are quick to both reject him as a charlatan and forgive him as a heroic refugee from Nazi Germany.

Perhaps the main theme of *Zelig* is the issue of whether individual subjectivity consists of more than a collection of personality traits expected by other people. Blake suggests that the basis of the Zelig character is that 'he is merely the sum of impressions he makes on the varied others who form their own perception of him, and who of course shape him into their own subjective image' (Blake, 1995: 100). One interesting sequence in the film consists of extended footage from the psychiatric sessions which Fletcher sets up between herself and Zelig, sessions which eventually lead to the breakthrough for his cure. The legitimacy of this scientific observational footage is carefully established within the film. A statement at the beginning of the film includes an acknowledgement to Fletcher's fictional cameraman, Paul Deghuee, and there is an unusually long sequence supposedly 'documenting' the set-up for the filming of these 'White Room' sessions. A colour interview with an elderly Deghuee has him describing Fletcher's wish to make a record of Zelig's case 'for future generations and for science', then there is detailed footage of the set-up of the room used for filming, accompanied by the narrator's careful listing of all of the features of the room.

These are perhaps the film's most explicit attempts to draw upon the notion that documentary is able to use the camera as a scientific recording instrument. As briefly outlined in Chapter 1, this is one of the fundamental pillars supporting the privileged cultural status of the documentary form. In *Zelig*, however, there is an interesting tension between these appropriations and the suggestion that even the camera cannot discover the reality of Zelig – because he physically changes according to every social context, the camera is largely negated as an instrument to record his characteristics (Blake, 1995: 109). It is this underlying tension between the film's thematic structure and its use of the mock-documentary form which perhaps offers the most potential for a reflexive stance towards documentary itself.

Man with a Plan (1996)

This third example of a degree 1 text is a comparatively subtle political parody using the mock-documentary form. The film features the congressional campaign of Fred Tuttle, a seventy-seven-year-old retired dairy farmer from Tunbridge, Vermont. Man with a Plan is structured around the expositional narration of a political journalist (Bryan Pfeiffer) as he covers Fred's campaign against long-term incumbent Bill Blachly. One of the interesting features of the film is that all of the people who appear in it play themselves,[11] and it has an amateur look – with O'Brien effectively making a low-budget independent film with some of his fellow Vermonters. The film works to highlight its fictionality, with several scenes taking on an almost Expressionist feel (such as when Blachly has a nightmare about Fred's campaign, or when Fred's dog opens the camera of 'a sleazy free-lancer snoop' journalist to steal incriminating photos of Fred's rendezvous with nymphets). Most of the film offers tongue-in-cheek constructions of observational footage of Tuttle, interspersed with interviews with Fred, his father, and members of his campaign team. Mock news broadcasts, covering the campaign tactics of Tuttle and Blachly and presenting the latest poll results, provide much of the pacing for the film and these become more frequent as the election itself nears its climax.

The media, including narrator Pfeiffer (together with various farm and pet animals), act as bemused observers of the battle between the Machiavellian political campaign of Blachly and the hometown values of honesty and common sense of Tuttle and his campaign. Director John O'Brien intended the film to be 'a throwback to American silent comedies', rather than an explicit political mock-documentary (Graham 1998), and in fact the film's theme offers some parallels to that of Frank Capra's Mr Smith Goes to Washington (1939). The film as a whole works as a nostalgic fantasy of the possibility of the victory of a political underdog who is able to succeed against all the odds with a simplistic and often incoherent political platform,[12] hard work and a virtually non-existent campaign budget. Tuttle essentially represents a naturalised conservative political figure within an apolitical package (Fred is an independent from the Regressive Party, and at the end of the film Fred literally sits down with his packed lunch in a park, ready to apply his common-sense approach to balancing the entire budget of the US government).

This is a significant example of a mock-documentary which has created something of a 'confusion' about the factual status for its subject. However, this is a confusion which is not so much a product of the *text* as an example of an *audience* extra-textual participation with the text's main character. Both director O'Brien and Tuttle himself have developed political careers because of the popularity of the film. In effect, some viewers have looked to extend the playful, and subversive, agenda of the Tuttle campaign. Vermont voters have written Tuttle's name into ballot papers on local elections (presumably as a protest vote),[13] and in 1998 he beat millionaire Jack McMullen (a transplanted Boston businessman) to win the Republican nomination for US Senate seat in Vermont. O'Brien himself has won office as Democratic candidate for justice of the peace in Tunbridge.

Forgotten Silver (1995)

As mentioned in Chapter 4, *Forgotten Silver* serves as an important example of the fluidity of the degrees of mock-documentary, and particularly of the role of the audience in determining the status of these texts. This film was intended as a parody of aspects of cinematic history and especially of various cultural myths within New Zealand society. Its success in convincing a large proportion of its audience of the accuracy and significance of its historical account, however, placed it into the category of a hoax on a par with Orson Welles's radio broadcast of *War of the Worlds*. This aspect of the film is a significant pointer to the potential reflexivity inherent to the mock-documentary form in general (and is discussed in detail in Chapter 7). The discussion below introduces this antipodean text and outlines the parodic constructions which suggest a first degree mock-documentary agenda on the parts of its makers.[14]

The film details the apparent 'discovery' of the work of a previously unknown pioneering New Zealand filmmaker, 'Colin McKenzie'. The writers and directors of the film, Peter Jackson and Costa Botes, appear as discoverers and celebrants of McKenzie's assumed legacy. They outline the significance of the discovery, present extracts from McKenzie's films, and suggest his importance within the history of international cinema. The success which *Forgotten Silver* had in convincing its audience of its claim for documentary status reveals the complexity and sophistication with which it appropriated the language, practices and conventions that define documentary as a specific screen form. In a very accomplished way, Jackson and Botes utilise all the codes and conventions of documentary to turn a *fiction* into an authentic and plausible *truth*.

Forgotten Silver utilises the expositional mode of documentary, beginning with director Jackson in his backyard, locating him, and the story of McKenzie, in real and identifiable surroundings. As Jackson tells of his role in the story and the initial discovery of the forgotten films, Polaroid snapshots of the film canisters fill the screen. Documentary has used such photographic evidence to the point where it has become a cliche. An interesting difference here is that the photographs are colour shots, in direct contrast to the 'original' and 'authentic' black and white photographs seen later in the programme.

Before the listing of the title credits the audience is presented with a line-up of clearly labelled experts; Jonathan Morris, New Zealand film archivist, Costa Botes, filmmaker, Harvey Weinstein of Miramax films and film historian Leonard Maltin. All make claims regarding the historic importance of the films found and of the place of McKenzie himself as a pioneer in the history of film. They all play the role of film experts and as such their testimonies serve both to 'authenticate' the find and, importantly, to give credibility to *Forgotten Silver* itself. Throughout the film we return to these experts, with their interviews being used to reinforce the arguments presented by Jackson.

Another key player in the documentary is McKenzie's 'widow' Hannah. She plays the role of 'eyewitness' whose testimony serves as a complement to the sobriety of the other, more expert, testimonies. As the film progresses she reveals vital clues which help Jackson and viewers piece McKenzie's story together. However, true to the expositional style, the programme builds tension and drama by pacing these revelations at regular intervals.

The rhetoric of science, and in particular of scientific discovery, is utilised throughout the film to further enhance the objectivity of Jackson's findings.[15] The revelatory nature of scientific discovery is used as the basis for much of the narrative of the film itself, and, more overtly, in the manner in which various forms of evidence are presented. Examples could be when describing McKenzie's early inventions, such as the experiments with egg whites which he supposedly used to develop film stock, or his complex attempts to develop colour film.[16] These inventions are authenticated by the 'experts' who explain the chemical reactions or the technological aspects of these various inventions. As discussed in Chapter 1, scientific rhetoric is a fundamental resource for the documentary genre, and without specialised access to scientific discourses such claims are difficult to reject outright.

These events in the McKenzie story are constantly being validated by the use of authenticating material, such as the black and white photographs which show McKenzie as a young man, with his family and with his inventions. These 'documents' provide external validation for the argument promoted. They have the appearance of being 'real' and 'original', and, as mentioned earlier, photographs of this sort are used so often within documentaries that we take them for granted. There are also stills taken from old newspapers which chart McKenzie's progress in the filmmaking business. Taken together, these 'documents' provide a seeming wealth of authenticating material to support Jackson's claims for the significance of McKenzie's accomplishments.

Perhaps most convincing are the extracts from McKenzie's own films, both his fictional work (*Salome*) and his 'reportage' films of Gallipoli[17] and of the Spanish Civil War. The latter films are of particular importance to the argument of *Forgotten Silver* because they ground its rhetoric in the real world. In a sense, these references to historical events and McKenzie's footage work to reinforce each other. The programme offers McKenzie's films as further documentation of historical events, which in turn helps to establish McKenzie's presence at these points in history.

Forgotten Silver also features Jackson and Botes organising an expedition into the West Coast bush in an attempt to find the location of the filming for McKenzie's masterpiece, *Salome*. Here history is almost treated as an accessible realm, in the sense that it has left tangible remnants which can be used in its reconstruction. The journey of Jackson and Botes into the New Zealand landscape deliberately mirrors that of McKenzie. These are the same conventions which historical documentary relies on (Rosen 1993). In utilising the codes and conventions of the genre and in inviting viewers join in a documentary mode of engagement, Jackson and Botes have succeeded in presenting a film with the appearance of an authentic historical reality, a 'true' story. Like *Zelig*, *Forgotten Silver* consistently looks and operates like any other documentary.

One of the more interesting aspects of *Forgotten Silver* is its relationship to myth, and to New Zealand myths in particular. A perhaps central part of the effectiveness of the programme with New Zealand audiences is the subtlety and variety of ways in which its filmmakers exploited cultural stereotypes and accepted notions concerning the nature of New Zealand history and society. This is combined with the more general conventions of documentary-making, forms of representation which, as discussed above, in themselves draw upon naturalised myths concerning notions of 'objectivity' and 'truth'. Outside of the use of outside experts (such as film historian Leonard Maltin) and scientific knowledge to validate the claims made by witnesses and the historical record, a second and more interesting feature, in terms of myth, has Jackson as a reporter performing the roles of both detective and tourist for the audience.[18]

Jackson operates as a detective in the sense that he presents a number of mysteries to the audience, which are then solved by Jackson and Botes throughout the course of the programme. The mystery of why Colin McKenzie remained unknown until discovered by the filmmakers serves as perhaps the dominant narrative device of *Forgotten Silver*. Much of the narrative structure of the programme serves to unfold the story of McKenzie's life, presenting a biography with references to a number of actual historical events (such as the two World Wars). How McKenzie died is one of a number of smaller puzzles solved as this story unfolds.

A central part of the solving of the over-arching mystery of why McKenzie remained undiscovered involves the search for a huge set supposedly built by the filmmaker in the West Coast bush for his masterpiece *Salome*. This search, which forms the second major part of *Forgotten Silver*'s narrative (regularly and expertly intercut with McKenzie's biography) allows Jackson and his colleagues also to perform the role of reporter as tourist. In terms of myth, here the filmmakers act as representatives of the audience on a journey into the unknown, in terms of both space (into the 'jungles' of the New Zealand bush landscape) and time (into the past to establish the authenticity of McKenzie's achievements and hence his legacy to cinema history) (Campbell, 1991: 280–7).

This journey into the New Zealand bush is one of the more important ways in which *Forgotten Silver* draws specifically on New Zealand myths to make its narrative so compelling. In New Zealand popular culture the native bush and its associated landscape plays something of a similar function as the Western frontier does in American folklore. Here it is the bush which served as a frontier for early European colonialists, and as the place where the more admired aspects of a supposed New Zealand character were forged. The resilience, independence and persistence of McKenzie in the face of the natural obstacles provided by the West Coast bush appeal to such well-established stereotypes in New Zealand culture.

Other aspects of McKenzie's character also draw upon stereotypes established by the colonial period of New Zealand history. He is one of the legendary backyard inventors supposedly at the heart of New Zealand's development, and both he and his brother Brooke serve as soldiers in the various conflicts claimed to have forged the beginnings of the nation itself. It is Brooke, with a camera built by his brother, who provides the first footage from the very cradle of the nation itself: Gallipoli. *Forgotten Silver* succeeds here by not just appealing to an important myth of the origin of the birth of the nation but reinforcing this myth by providing the first 'documentary' (and hence 'real' and concrete) evidence of the hardships suffered by New Zealand soldiers.

Above all, the character of McKenzie is the epitome of the dogged inventor-genius who perseveres despite a wealth of natural, personal, financial and political hardships. Although McKenzie's endeavours are in vain in terms of recognition for himself during his lifetime, they serve as a kind of historical lesson for the audience of the way things *should* have happened. In doing so, the narrative of *Forgotten Silver* both draws on and subverts some of the more basic value systems inherent to New Zealand mythology.[19]

Mock-rockumentary

The second textual tendency we have identified in degree 1 mock-documentaries are illustrated by a group of texts which could be termed 'mock-rockumentaries'. Rockumentaries are a popular form of documentary. They are comparatively cheap to produce and conform easily to the promotional needs of the music recording industry. They tend to be distinguished by a sympathetic perspective of the filmmaker or presenter towards the subject – they represent an effort to present the breadth of a musical artist's talent, comparatively uncritical portrayals of their performances and the nature of their appeal to audiences. In some sense, they are a recognisable 'subgenre' within documentary, and mock-rockumentaries provide an opportunity to parody this specific type of documentary text, without (as with other degree 1 texts) necessarily deconstructing the wider genre itself.

Sarchett notes that the classic rockumentaries (such as *Monterey Pop* (1968), *Woodstock* (1970) and *Gimme Shelter* (1970)) have tended to operate largely within the observational mode of documentary – these are all texts which have been instrumental in establishing and popularising the assumptions and expectations associated with this mode (as discussed in Chapter 1). They are constructed in order to capture the immediacy and 'realism' of a past event. He argues that: 'For the typical rockumentary transparency of style exploits the audience's wish to return, to repeat, and to regain an original event. That is, the rockumentary, like most documentary, is an inherently nostalgic genre which posits a retrieval of the pretextual' (Sarchett, 1994: 31).

The rockumentary films of D. A. Pennebaker (including *Monterey Pop* and *Woodstock*, and especially *Don't Look Back* (1967)) are interesting to discuss in terms of the claims by filmmakers which have accompanied some of these examples of observational documentaries. *Don't Look Back* chronicles Bob Dylan's triumphant 1965 tour of England to promote his third album *The Times They Are A-Changin'* (1964). This film is significant here, firstly, because it is an archetypal rockumentary which is directly quoted in mock-documentary films such *This Is Spinal Tap* (1984) and *Bob Roberts* (1992). *Don't Look Back* is also interesting because of the claims of its director. Hall has provided a detailed analysis of the film, and especially a critique of Pennebaker's denial of any mediation in his representation of Bob Dylan. Her argument is that the film is a skilful construction of the myth that the *cinéma vérité* style is the one mode which is most capable of telling the 'truth', of being able to provide an accurate record of an event or personality. This is a key aspect of the justification for rockumentaries; most of these films tend to follow this pattern, insisting that they present an accurate portrayal of musical performance, and denying that they are complicit in the performer's construction of rock myth.

A significant feature of rockumentaries, which complicates this naturalist argument, is that they are recording events which are themselves constructed theatrical performances. In other words, these documentaries do not necessarily attempt to gain a 'slice-of-life' perspective on an artist but instead record the creation and presentation of a personalised mythology. This places mock-rockumentaries in an interesting position of offering a parody or satire of an event or band or persona which is, to some extent, already acknowledged as a fictional construct. This is an aspect of this type of mock-documentary which is of particular relevance to *This Is Spinal Tap*, an archetypal and influential mock-documentary and the original model of a 'mock-rockumentary'.

This Is Spinal Tap (1984)

Like *The Rutles* this film uses the mock-documentary mode to generate a commentary on a specific part of popular music, in this case the heavy metal mythology of America[20] (and, indirectly, of Britain, as Spinal Tap are supposedly an English band). *This Is Spinal Tap* is something of a landmark

within the mock-documentary form. It is often cited by filmmakers working in the form as a key reference point and influence on their own efforts.
In part this is because it is extremely successful in creating a credible social
world for the fictional heavy metal band Spinal Tap. It is easy for a viewer
to believe both that this is a real documentary and that the band is totally
inept. According to Plantinga, the film's early screenings featured at least
some members of the audience wondering aloud why anyone bothered to
make a rockumentary about such a pathetic band. As he notes, the assumptions of the text's ontological status made by the audience depended very
much on the level of sophistication and critical interpretation that individual viewers brought to the screening (Plantinga, 1998: 320).

Spinal Tap attempts to be a pointed critique of heavy metal, but like *The
Rutles* it still retains an underlying affection for the band itself. Unlike that
early mock-documentary, however, *Spinal Tap* is able to develop the
members of the band as identifiable and credible characters, outside of
their comedic function as signifiers for a specific mythology – they are
pathetic losers but are also sympathetic figures despite or because of that.
In this sense, *Spinal Tap* is the ideal text to demonstrate the ambivalence
towards its subject which is such a key aspect of parody.

Spinal Tap's parody of rockumentaries[21] centres on the agenda of filmmakers who ignore the limitations of their subject, and the film is interesting partly because it successfully re-creates the nostalgic frame which
seems to be inherent to this agenda. The opening address to camera, by
Marty Di Bergi[22] introduces 'Britain's now legendary Spinal Tap', and outlines the seventeen-year, fifteen-album career of the band. Di Bergi
describes his first encounter with the band in 1966, explains that the film
records the 1982 US tour undertaken by the band to promote a new
album called *Smell the Glove*, and says that he 'wanted to capture the
sights, sounds, and smells of a hard working rock band on the road'. His
address is followed by the main title: 'This Is Spinal Tap: A Rockumentary
by Martin Di Bergi', then a series of scenes which closely reconstruct the
archetypal opening sequences to rockumentary films – intercutting
between vox-pox interviews with fans,[23] the band itself arriving at an
American airport, backstage preparations for a concert, then footage of a
concert performance. The concert footage freezes on each member of the
band in turn, as captions introduce them as 'David St. Hubbins – Lead
guitar', 'Nigel Tuffnel – Lead Guitar', 'Derek Smalls – Bass', 'Mick Shrimp-
ton – Drums' and 'Viv Savage – Keyboards'.

As is characteristic of rockumentaries, this opening sequence establishes the status of the band (the level of excitement and social traits of

their fans), the musical genre they are part of and their performance style. The film then presents the first of a series of interviews with band members conducted by Di Bergi. These interviews, together with concert footage and especially observational sequences, provide the bulk of the film's narrative.[24] The film also appropriates other standard documentary conventions, including black and white photos of the childhood of David and Nigel (played by Michael McKean and Christopher Guest), and captions both to show the locations of concerts (together with conventional establishing shots of various theatres) and to identify (fictional) figures within the recording industry that they deal with.

There are also a couple of sequences which parody archival material, as they detail the transition of the band from a mid-1960s beat group (on a 1965 British television show called *Pop, Look and Listen*, dressed in matching suits and singing 'Gimme Some Money') through to their psychedelic phase (with 1967 American television footage captioned *Jamboreebop* featuring the band in stereotypical psychedelic costumes and stage-set, with go-go dancers in miniskirts, and Nigel playing a guitar break on a double-necked guitar that sounds like a sitar).[25] These sequences are a key part of the film's suggestion that heavy metal is simply one amongst many rock styles that have been appropriated by a musical group who do not have enough talent to develop their own sound.[26]

As suggested above, most of the film consists of mock sequences of typical rockumentary observational material. There are some hilarious sequences where the crew simply follow and record the ineptitude of the band. The best of these is where the band, backstage at the 'Xanadu Star Theater – Cleveland, Ohio', get lost and increasingly frustrated in a maze of corridors on their way to the stage (David remarks 'this looks familiar' as they turn down yet another passage).[27] Di Bergi's interviews provide insights into the true feelings that they have for each other, and the delusions that the band has as a whole, as they attempt to articulate heavy metal mythology.

The film attacks just about every aspect of heavy metal mythology (and in some cases rock music as a whole) that has quickly become a cliché of the genre. Nigel adopts the pretensions of heavy metal guitarists toward the status of 'virtuoso', at times suggesting the natural affinity with classical music which is typically claimed by metal guitarists. At one point, in one of the rare scenes in which Di Bergi seems to critique the band, Nigel proudly shows the director his guitar collection. The collection includes a guitar which he refuses to let Di Bergi touch, point to or even look at, and a Marshall amp which is 'very special, because the numbers all go to

11' (most amps, Nigel insists, are inferior because their dials only go up to 10). This sequence is a perfect summation of the electric guitar-as-phallus culture of most heavy rock.

The adolescent nature of the band members (and by extension their audience) is unselfconsciously acknowledged by both Nigel (who says that he and David 'feel like children much of the time, even when we're playing') and later by the band's manager as he quits and complains bitterly about their adolescent fantasy world. Ian, the manager, represents the seedier side of the rock industry. He is ruthless when he sees the need (carrying a cricket bat for persuasion) and appears perfectly at home within the jungle atmosphere of rock promoters – and has some of the better lines in the film (when Di Bergi notes that the band seems to be attracting smaller audiences and asks if their popularity is waning, Ian replies that it is just that 'their appeal is becoming more selective').

Plantinga (1998) has a detailed discussion of the film's satire of heavy metal discourse on masculinity, and provides a critique of the sexual politics of the film. He notes that *Spinal Tap*'s satire comes from the deliberate contradiction between the mythology of male power which the band is attempting to live up to, and the pathetic situations into which the tour descends. Over the course of the film, tensions between David and Nigel (the group's Lennon and McCartney) lead the group to gradually disintegrate. By the end of the tour, a journalist (in a direct reference to Scorsese's *The Last Waltz*) asks David if this is 'the Last Waltz', if this is the end of Spinal Tap or are they 'going to try to milk it for a few more years in Europe?'

One of the more fascinating aspects of *This Is Spinal Tap* is that the band Spinal Tap to some extent also seems to have an existence outside of the film. They have performed in concert in the United States, and on *Saturday Night Live*, released albums and music videos, have an official website, and can be said to have an actual audience of some form. As Plantinga suggests, this confuses the ontological status of the band; when they are on-stage are they playing themselves, or fictional characters in a real band, or is the audience and the band simply collaborating in a parodic ritual of rock performance? As with *Man with a Plan*, there is some question over how the audience views the fictional status of the subject of the film. Just as some Vermonters have used Fred Tuttle's name on ballot papers apparently to register a protest vote against the quality of the political candidates they are asked to choose between, perhaps the band's fans can enjoy the attitude of an openly fictional band as an antidote to the pretensions of real rock bands that take themselves too seriously.

The ontological status of the band becomes a key issue when discussing the 1993 sequel to the film: *The Return of Spinal Tap*. This sequel is a less complex film than the original. Instead of the 'on the road' narrative of *Spinal Tap*, it is mostly a recording of a 1992 reunion concert (with an audience of real fans) at the Albert Hall, London – to promote the release of their (real) album *Break Like the Wind*. There are regular inserts of interviews with the band members and other characters from the original film (including Marty Di Bergi), who provide 'where are they now?' updates on their associations with the band. In addition to these interviews, there are also numerous references to the earlier film, including an explicit on-stage reference from David to their disastrous 1982 'tour'. There is also some linking between the band's performance and filmed material which is played on a screen suspended over the stage.

Outside of these elements of the film, however, there is an interesting tension between the attempts of the band to produce a parodic performance, and the conventional manner in which the concert is filmed. There is an extensive use of crane shots, the capturing of a full lighting show, and stereotypical close-ups of Nigel's guitar 'prowess'. Apart from the content of the performance, the actual form of the concert footage is virtually identical to that of similar sequences from conventional rockumentaries. In a couple of instances there are shots of David, or other band members, which are superimposed over shots of a waving and adoring crowd – a standard code for the reinforcing of rock mythology (the band are both united with the audience, and are its focus of attention and adulation). The role played by the audience itself at this performance is fascinating. There are what seem to be tongue-in-cheek banners in the crowd proclaiming the greatness of the band, and there are obviously a significant number of audience members who know the lyrics to the majority of the songs (the audience cheers in recognition when songs begin). At other points, Derek and Nigel can be seen enjoying the joke with people in front of the stage. Perhaps the best example of how this sequel treads a fine line between fact and fiction occurs at the beginning of the film, when Bob Geldof appears on-stage to introduce the band, and immediately declares that his presence does not mean that there is a deeper meaning for the evening.

This Is Spinal Tap is significant within the development of mock-documentary as a specific template or popular model which has inspired other filmmakers to pursue the form. There are also a number of direct descendants to *Spinal Tap*, mock-documentary texts which could also be termed 'mock-rockumentaries'.[28] These include *Fear of a Black Hat* (1993) and *Hard Core Logo* (1997) which are respectively rap and punk versions of *Spinal Tap*, and lesser television examples such as *Unauthorized Biography: Milo – Death of a Supermodel* (1997)[29] and an episode from the cartoon series *South Park* entitled *Chef: Behind the Menu* (1998).[30]

Of this group of films, *Fear of a Black Hat* is an example which surpasses *Spinal Tap* in terms of caricature, critique and social commentary. It presents an in-depth look at a fictional rap group called Niggerz With Hats, and overall it offers a complex parody of the music industry[31] which incorporates a variety of comments about race relations and rap culture in the United States.[32] This film includes explicit references to the 1991 beating of Rodney King at the hands of Los Angeles police, to the racism of the American music industry and to wider cultural currents represented by organisations such as the Nation of Islam. This film is both more complex in its treatment of its subject than *Spinal Tap*, and interesting as a parodic study in American racial discourse.

Mock–soap–documentary

Waiting for Guffman (1996)

This final degree 1 mock-documentary presents the preparations, rehearsals for and performance of a play celebrating the 150th anniversary of the founding of a small town in Missouri called Blaine. It is an interesting example of a mock-documentary which, in a similar way to mock-rockumentaries, draws upon and plays with a specific form within the documentary genre, in this case docu-soap.

The film is constructed as if a documentary film crew was dropped into Blaine to gain a slice-of-life look or exposé of small-town America. All of the people involved appear in the same terms as the minor 'stars' that are constructed within docu-soaps. They are seemingly unaware of how they appear, and that their shortcomings are being exploited for the purposes of entertainment. The documentary crew themselves remain anonymous. There are no shots of the 'crew', but they obviously have terrific access (and this is perhaps the only compromise made with the discourse of realism, otherwise the film is consistent with how it would look if a documentary crew actually operated in such a small town). All of the participants are happy to open themselves to the scrutiny of a camera crew; they demonstrate a kind of naiveté of the media, and are more than happy to present themselves to the audience.[33]

As is characteristic of docu-soaps (see Chapter 2), the characters tend to represent people at the lower ends of the socio-economic hierarchy. They are largely reduced to subjects of voyeuristic spectacle (a reflection of the class agenda of this form of documentary, and its subtle denigration of American 'failure'). It becomes obvious that these characters have been chosen as subjects not for their talent but because of their lack of musical or dramatic skills; the mediocrity of these people is the theme and subject of the film. Much of the film's humour stems from the fact that the characters obviously feel that their efforts are worthy (and in part this is reinforced by the fact that they are being 'filmed' by a 'documentary' crew). The dramatic high points all appear to grow from the nature of the characters themselves: their excitement at being involved in the production of the play, the frustrated ambitions of peripheral characters and the cast's petty egos and jealousies.

Ultimately, this film works especially as a satire of small-town American values. It never occurs to the townspeople that the 150th celebration of the founding of Blaine is nothing momentous to celebrate. The cast all represent stereotypes of small-town America; an unacknowledged gay thespian,[34] a humourless Jewish dentist who wants to be a comedian,[35] a frustrated high school music teacher, a repressed gay town councillor, an empty-headed cheerleader-type working at the Dairy Queen, and a frustrated middle-class couple displacing their energies into small-town dramatic ambitions – there is even a local man who claims to have been abducted (and probed!) by aliens.

The film targets above all the mediocrity of the people of Blaine. Even the town's founder (the apparently near-mythical Blaine Fabin) was a mediocre pioneer, someone who was unable to lead his group of settlers to California and simply stopped their pioneering trek in Missouri.[36] All of the cast (of the play titled *Red, White and Blaine*) are slight talents, but fail to realise their shortcomings, and even by the end of the film demonstrate an almost touching lack of self-awareness. The local audience for *Red, White and Blaine* are carried away by the show, and there is a kind of pathos to the fact that such a terrible show can elicit feelings of excitement and recognition for the people of Blaine. The best/worst song is 'Nothing Ever Happens on Mars', which features Allan Pearl the dentist (Eugene Levy) in a paper-maché head with multiple eyes explaining that he came to Earth because it was so boring on Mars (the song is rewritten as 'Nothing Ever Happens in Blaine' for the final credits), with the cast repeating 'boring' eight times to end the song. There is also an obligatory flag-waving finale, 'Blaine Panthers Fight Song', which brings a standing ovation from their local audience.

The film is based around reconstructions of observational footage, interspersed with largely individual interviews with the main cast members and crew of the play, either at their homes, or later at their first performance. These interviews are confessional, in the sense that the characters either express their immediate feelings, or unintentionally reveal themselves with what they do not say – in any case, we are in no doubt about their motivations (as with *Spinal Tap*, the quality of the film's parody stems from the fact that the characterisations contain enough detail to suggest a real history and depth; their hopes and dreams are both endearing and also slightly pathetic).

The film also includes a number of details which add credibility to the existence and natural drama of Blaine, Missouri (such as the *Blaine Bugle* local newspaper). These work to incorporate elements of documentary codes and conventions into a conventional fictional narrative. There are various sections of the film (with titles announcing 'The Auditions', 'The First Rehearsal' and 'The Day of the Show') which construct a conventional three-part dramatic structure. The pacing of the film also increases as the cast of the show prepare for their premiere and perform the play in all of its mediocrity (during the play itself, there are frequent inserts of reaction shots of peripheral characters in the audience). There is also an epilogue to the film which has the conventional '3 Months Later' interviews, revealing the expected mediocre achievements of all of the cast members (the best of these is Corky with his memorabilia store, proudly displaying his 'Dinner with Andre action figures', and 'Remains of the Day' lunch boxes which he insists will be popular with kids).

Notes

1 See Chapter 5 for a brief discussion of the role of this series in the development of the mock-documentary form.

2 Significantly, the sharpest comments in the film are directed at individuals who are seen to have interrupted the growth of the Rutles (Beatles) legend. The reporter abuses a record executive who turned down the first approaches of the band to record, while Yoko Ono is transformed into a character suggested to be Hitler's daughter (a reflection of both her position within Beatles mythology and perhaps also the unconscious misogyny of the *MPFC* series).

3 This is reinforced by an extensive use of music from the 1920s (such as 'I've Got a Feeling I'm Falling', 'Ain't We Got Fun', 'Sunny Side Up', 'Charleston'), as well as the songs which are supposedly composed in Zelig's honour after he becomes a media phenomenon (including 'Leonard the Lizard', 'Doin' the

Chameleon', 'Chameleon Days', 'You May Be Six People But I Love You', 'Reptile Eyes' and 'The Changing Man Concerto').

4   As discussed in Chapter 5, *Forrest Gump* (1994) exhibits a similarly complex treatment of archival material.

5   These are variously labelled as Pathé News, Metrotone News, Universal Newspaper Newsreel, Hearst Metrotone News and Hearst Movietone News. Blake notes that these 'newsreels' are interesting because they seem to be based more on the form of newsreel seen at the beginning of Orson Welles's *Citizen Kane* (1941) than actual documents from the period (Blake, 1995: 99).

6   These are virtually the only *private* moments within the film, and it is significant that they appear as grainy, hand-held footage which is constructed as more 'authentic' evidence of the relationship between Zelig and Fletcher than the manufactured or mediated images supposedly obtained from public archival material. This conforms to the ways in which home movies are often more typically used in fictional movies (see Chapter 5 for a discussion of the role of such sequences in the development of the mock-documentary form).

7   Including Leonard Zelig pens and lucky charms, clocks and toys, watches and books, a 'famous Leonard Zelig doll', aprons, chameleon-shaped earmuffs and a game called 'The Little Chameleon Boy'.

8   These sequences are intended specifically to parody the interviews in Warren Beatty's *Reds* (1981), which in that film provide corroborating evidence for the exploits of the main character – but in that film, the 'experts' and eyewitnesses are fictional, while the main character is based on an actual historical figure (Pym, 1983: 283).

9   Zelig is strongly reminiscent of Alfred E. Neuman, from *MAD* magazine – a character who can be placed into any context (in particular, cultural and political), retaining his distinctiveness but also adopting the dress or look or behaviour of the people he is with. Neuman is a more complex satirical figure than Zelig, and has a richer history and is designed towards different ends. Neuman exists to parody personalities and the context in which they appear – he is an element of absurdity and chaos who is inserted into a situation in order to highlight how precarious its sobriety and rationality truly are. Zelig does not have the subversive aspect of Neuman, and *Zelig* is too steeped in nostalgia really to take its parody of 1920s figures to any similar lengths (Reidelbach, 1991: 136–52).

10   It is interesting that Allen never allows Zelig to transform himself into a *woman* – with the exception that he becomes a psychiatrist and an aviator in mimicry of Dr Fletcher.

11   Tuttle really is a retired dairy farmer, Blachly a former state representative, and there are local media personnel and (even Fred's pet animals) in minor roles.

12   Fred's campaign slogans include 'Fred for Congress, Why Not?', 'a Man with a Plan', 'better Fred than dead', and his F.R.E.D. acronym – Friendly, Renewable, Extra-Terrestrial and Dinky.

13 Tuttle has gained a small number of votes for President (in Tunbridge), US Representative, governor, lieutenant governor, state treasurer, secretary of state, attorney general, state senator, state representative and high bailiff. *The New York Times*, 8 November 1996.

14 The arguments both in this discussion, and on *Forgotten Silver* in the following chapters have appeared in Roscoe and Hight (1996 and 1997).

15 This contrasts with the failure of science to deal with Zelig's condition.

16 Or even the computer 'enhancement' of the newspaper date in the Pearse footage, which supposedly records a pre-Wright-brothers controlled flight.

17 Gallipoli was the site of a minor battle on the Turkish coast during the First World War in which New Zealand (and other Allied) forces suffered heavy casualties. Within New Zealand (and Australia) it has achieved a mythical status as one of the places where the nation was forged.

18 Campbell (1991) offers a breakdown of the various narrative formulas commonly offered by (American) magazine-style news programs. These feature reporters in roles as detective, analyst and tourist.

19 In a completely unconscious way, the New Zealand television coverage of the 1995 America's Cup competition appealed to this same mythology. Here it was the supposed small-town technology which defeated that of the American superpower, and in a fashion acclaimed as being true to some of the basic values of the country itself (hard work, persistence and a sense of fair play).

20 *Spinal Tap* was apparently intended not only as a commentary on the heavy metal musical idiom but also partly as a specific parody of Martin Scorsese's *The Last Waltz* (1978) – a film more complex than most rockumentaries in that it looks to address directly the nostalgia which is inherent to these types of documentaries (Hall, 1998: 30) and to attempt to position the subject of the film (the music and seventeen-year career of The Band) as an art form. From the perspective of *Spinal Tap*, however, *The Last Waltz* is simply a more pretentious example of a suspect form of documentary.

21 Plantinga also makes a detailed analysis of the film and draws a useful distinction between its successful attempt to parody the rockumentary form and its ultimately limited satire of heavy metal mythology. (Plantinga, 1998)

22 The character's name is a sly reference on 'Martin Scorsese', and is played by *Spinal Tap*'s actual director, Rob Reiner.

23 Interestingly, these are virtually the only time when the band's fans are seen. This might be a pointer to explaining the film's cult status; hard-core heavy metal fans can enjoy the parody because it does not seek to target themselves directly. Perhaps they recognise traits of the band in the multitude of terrible bands who are not worthy of the name, but see great heavy metal groups as being able to transcend all of the clichés which Spinal Tap represents.

24 The film itself involved a significant degree of improvisation on the part of the main actors – which is partly revealed by out-take scenes played behind the film's closing credits.

25 This is just one part of the film's parody of the typical history of an ageing rock group. A running joke throughout the film is the series of unbelievable fatal accidents that befall a succession of drummers, and at one point David states that there have been thirty-seven members in the band (like other long-serving rock groups, Spinal Tap is virtually a brandname centred on a couple of strong personalities).

26 The film also includes a number of pointed digs at the inability of ageing bands to admit that their time has passed. In an act of desperation, after Nigel leaves, the remaining members even re-enact the late-1960s, early-1970s shift to progressive-jazz rock, as heavy metal descended into pompous stadium rock.

27 This is one of a number of sequences which directly parodies similar scenes from Pennebaker's *Don't Look Back*.

28 This list does not include another pair of mock-documentaries which feature a television documentary crew attempting to profile a heavy metal band: *Bad News Tour* (1983) and its sequel *More Bad News* (1987). Both are covered in the following chapter.

29 This presents an alleged biography of the 'first' supermodel, and features interviews with actual cult figures such as Debbie Harry. This text is interesting because it is a mock-documentary episode from an otherwise conventional biographical series.

30 'Chef' is one of the core characters of the series, with voice provided by Isaac Hayes, and this episode is based around a series of testimonials from rock figures, who all reveal the decisive influence which he supposedly has had on their careers. This is a notable mock-documentary text only in that it mixes interviews with *cartoon* sequences.

31 The relatively recent rise in the importance of promotional videos means that *Fear of a Black Hat* is able to use these as a rich source of parody in ways which *Spinal Tap* could not.

32 The film directly targets a number of well-known figures within rap, or modern black pop, such as Public Enemy, NWA, LL Cool J, PM Dawn, C + C Music Factory, as well as the emergence of black directors such as Spike Lee and John Singleton. For a detailed listing of these references see George (1994).

33 The film was apparently constructed without a detailed script – instead the actors developed their characters from key plot points conceived by scriptwriters Christopher Guest and Eugene Levy.

34 Corky St Clair (Christopher Guest), who is the main creative force behind the show. One of the film's best jokes is that his homosexuality is never acknowledged, or even noticed, by the rest of the townspeople.

35 The only way his character could be any more perfect would be if he was an undertaker.

36 Fabin's story is hilarious, as if all the truly great pioneer stock arrived in California, while the more hopeless participants of America's Manifest Destiny are those who reside in the Mid-Western states.

7

Degree 2: critique and hoax

Like degree 1 mock-documentaries, examples of the form which we categorise as degree 2 explicitly highlight their own fictionality, but generally do so in order to ask their audience to reflect upon the validity of the cultural or political position of their subjects. These texts tend to be characterised by an 'ambivalent' appropriation of documentary codes and conventions: appropriating documentary codes and conventions, but also incorporating more explicit commentaries on media practices themselves as part of their subjects. These texts, then, represent a greater exploration of the complexity of parody than degree 1 mock-documentaries.

Within this degree, we further distinguish texts which develop a reflexivity toward factual discourse in three different ways. Some degree 2 mock-documentaries feature muted critiques of media practices, others offer a sustained political critique of aspects of culture using the mock-documentary form and a third category comprises texts which generate reflexive interpretations because of their (intentional or not) success as hoaxes.

Muted critique of media practices

These mock-documentaries collectively offer an interesting textual complexity. They appropriate documentary aesthetics, but also include differing degrees of criticism towards media practices. In this sense, they are good examples of the reflexive potential which is inherent to mock-documentary's reconstruction of documentary codes and conventions; to varying degrees, their commentary on media practices contradicts their underlying acceptance of factual discourse.[1]

33

Bad News Tour (1983)

This is an offering from the British television Channel 4's *Comic Strip* series, and is a text which falls within the same mock-rockumentary 'tradition' as *This Is Spinal Tap*. It features a 'documentary crew' covering a brief tour by a completely unknown and conspicuously talentless heavy metal band. In contrast to *Spinal Tap*, however, *Bad News Tour* offers a more complex commentary on the nature of popular music and the role played by the media in the creation of rock mythology.

The most distinctive aspect of this mock-rockumentary is a noticeable tension between the crew (especially the director) and the band (Bad News). There seems to be a definite class basis to this tension (unlike *Spinal Tap*, where the band's lower-class origins are part of their appeal for Di Bergi). Here the director seems to be a BBC-trained or styled documentary-maker who is intent on creating a stereotypical portrayal of the band as part of a deliberate (and cynical) myth-making exercise. He has an explicit agenda – to portray the band as an emerging young talent representative of their generation – but his efforts to fulfil this agenda are constantly frustrated by the open hostility and ineptitude of the band and the indifference of his crew.

The documentary crew neither develop a sense of empathy with their subject nor make any effort to represent the tour from their viewpoint. The crew suggest the everyday struggling documentary-maker in the same way that the band represents the talentless hacks who make up the vast majority of local bands – the meeting between the two is hilarious because neither is inspired by the other. There is the sense that it is not that the crew are necessarily inept, but that the band are so stupid that they derail the normal filming procedures of the crew. The director becomes more and more frustrated at the band's inability to 'play along', the way documentary subjects normally do.

The more humorous sequences in *Bad News Tour* feature the disintegration of the collective, pathetic efforts of crew and band to create a rock myth. There is an interesting ambivalence here between the revealing of the deliberately constructed nature of 'art' documentaries, and the fact that the footage itself is capable of revealing the 'truth' of what happened during the encounter between band and crew. The band consistently fail to perform 'on cue', with the director trying to keep things 'natural' by telling them to keep going. One member, Den, keeps asking if they can 'cut that bit out', such as when he mistaken calls lead singer 'Vim' by his real name (Alan). The band are supremely conscious of being filmed; one of the guitarists (Colin) and a 'groupie' they pick up are absolutely thrilled to be filmed and constantly pose for the camera. An early scene in the programme has the drummer (Spider) paying a girl to give him a tearful on-camera goodbye.

At the same time, the band genuinely do not seem to realise how poorly they are coming across on film. In this sense, the footage reveals the 'truth' of the band; the frustrated ambition of lead singer Vim, the heavy metal posing of Colin the guitarist, the cynicism of Spider and the lack of intelligence of Den.[2] There are also a series of practical disasters which keep inhibiting filming, both wearing down the crew but also suggesting the effort that goes into making a documentary look effortless. The best of these scenes is where the band's van breaks down, and they and the director have a roadside debate over whether or not the crew should tow them. The van has obviously been directed to drive on a particular part of the motorway so that the crew can get a good shot, and the director initially thinks they are playing games with him when the van stops. He complains that to tow the van would constitute 'interference'; a blatantly hypocritical stance which effectively sums up all of the compromises which a documentary crew typically adopts towards its subject, while maintaining the pretence that what is being filmed is 'natural'. The sequence works as a sharply accurate (and hilarious) critique of the claim (as outlined in Chapter 2) that the observational mode of documentary is capable of merely 'recording reality'.

The final scenes in the programme show the collapse of any possibility of collaboration between band and crew. The director has told a theatre owner not to pay the band, in order to generate some dramatic tension, and in retaliation two members of the band (Vim and Den) beat up the crew and steal their equipment. This sequence marks the real difference between this film and *Spinal Tap*. Instead of a band that somehow succeeds despite itself, that manages to find a base of fans, Bad News are perhaps more typical of a hopelessly and helplessly self-destructive segment of rock culture. They are merely one of the thousands of British bands struggling to be recognised, and failing to escape from their class position. In the final scene, characteristically, their ineptitude extends to their efforts to complete the documentary using their own ideas. The band reveal that they have neither the talent nor the unity to have any hope of using the stolen equipment.

The sequel to *Bad News Tour*, *More Bad News* (1987), follows more closely in the tradition of *Spinal Tap*, and revisits the band in an openly nostalgic exercise. In order to construct a compelling narrative the 'documentary crew' engineer the reformation of the group, gain them a recording contract (which allows them to make a typically misogynist and apocalyptically styled heavy metal video) and appear at an actual established heavy metal festival (Castle Donington). Unlike the first *Bad News* mock-documentary, however, here the director and his crew are virtually anonymous, and there are few instances where documentary conventions are openly parodied.

The final scenes of the programme, where Bad News make a disastrous appearance on-stage at Castle Donington (after Vim declares he is the reincarnation of Jimi Hendrix, the heavy metal audience beat up the band), offer the best and most interesting examples of reflexivity toward the rockumentary form. When the band arrive at the festival they are initially told that they are not booked, and a Donington promoter explains that he was told they were part of a 'joke documentary'. The band momentarily look confused, then turn accusingly toward the crew, and there is a beautifully ambiguous moment where the mock-documentary crew are pretending to be making a mock-documentary in order to get a 'real' response from a fictional band. The band's festival appearance itself offers further interesting suggestions of a confusion of the band's ontological status. In a more deliberately satiric manner than *The Return of Spinal Tap*, here it is not clear whether or not the (real) heavy metal bands that were interviewed on Bad News's musical abilities were aware of the fictional nature of the band – and there is the suggestion that at least some of the audience at Donington were left wondering why such a terrible band was included on the bill.

ER (episode entitled 'Ambush', 1997)

This is one of the more openly reflexive examples of a degree 2 mock-documentary, with the ambivalence towards factual discourse which characterises this Degree represented at a variety of levels. This mock-documentary episode of a dramatic television series is consequently able to develop an unusual complexity in its relationship with documentary aesthetics.

The title of the series refers to a fictional Emergency Room of a Chicago hospital, and this was the premiere episode for the 1997 season. (It was unusual not only in its use of the mock-documentary format but because it was performed live on national American television.[3]) The episode was filmed to resemble a conventional observational form of documentary, the product of a Reality-TV crew visiting the ER in order to gain an exposé on the activities of the hospital and its personnel. It was constructed using two hand-held cameras and a 'surveillance' camera set up in the fictional doctor's lounge. There is a series of continuous one-shot takes, with the majority of the footage coming from the hand-held cameras. The programme cuts between these, with increasing speed towards the end of the programme, but always consistently with the notion that there are three cameras which are realistically able to capture all of the action which is presented. Overall, the programme itself is structured to give the appearance of a 'slice-of-life' text, with the length of the programme supposedly close to that of the action it portrays.

The *ER* series itself is a good example of the *vérité* style adopted by many mainstream American television drama series.[4] This particular episode is notable in that it features much slower pacing than that characteristically employed by the series, which has an established editing style combining hand-held footage with rapid cuts to give a heightened, but seamless, appearance of reality. Ironically, the editing style used for this particular episode partially acts against the efforts to present the events it depicts as a convincing reality. Regular viewers of the series become accustomed to the rapid editing technique as a central part of a supposedly 'realistic' representational style, and the attempts to operate within the observational mode have the converse effect of highlighting the constructed nature of this episode's narrative.[5] The dramatic success of this particular episode stems more from the continuity of plot-lines from the previous series, and the stability of the characters and basic situation themselves. Even if the characters are presented in a (for the series) unconventional manner, these are still the same 'people' whom the audience is familiar with.

The initial broadcast of the episode also operated with a certain amount of tension between the effort to highlight the technical achievement of the cast and crew in staging this 'live-to-air' event, and the failure to continue the 'realistic' editing style favoured and popularised by the series. Both the 'live performance' aspect and the mock-Reality-TV aspect are emphasised through the episode repeatedly highlighting the presence of the cameras and crew. The first camera operator we see explains how things are going to look; where the cameras are and what the style of presentation is going to be. Characters continually look at the camera, accidentally bump into it, wave 'Hi mom', ask the cameraman if a line should be repeated, tell the cameraman to move – and at one stage the camera is physically 'assaulted' by Dr Greene (Anthony Edwards) and an irate gang leader in the waiting room.

There are frequent addresses by characters 'to camera' (which records their efforts to explain medical procedures, and the 'climactic' final scene where Greene confesses the trauma of being the victim of an assault in the previous series). The cast fiddle with their microphones, and Dr Carter (Noah Wyle) is reminded to speak in a normal tone of voice. In a nicely reflexive commentary, there are also repeated references to the notion that these fictional characters are role-playing for the fictional documentary crew. In keeping with both a subtle highlighting of the constructed nature of the episode and a degree of humour within the series overall, there are a number of knowing jokes made by the ER staff. A male nurse is disappointed that the footage is intended for PBS rather than the network television, Dr Ross (George Clooney) tells Greene 'you look like a star out there', and there are references to *Dr Welby* (a predecessor to their own dramatic television series) and *I Love Lucy*.

A muted commentary on the documentary genre is generated from the many moments of tension between the ER personnel and the documentary crew. In an argument over a consent form, we see characters discuss the rights and responsibilities of the filmmakers, and the control which the filmmakers have over what is seen and not seen. (There is the brief suggestion that a non-consenting doctor could easily be cut from the film. She reluctantly signs the form, saying 'just keep my piece off *Hard Copy*, okay?') There are numerous aspects of the episode which specifically and deliberately critique the intentions and style of Reality-TV programmes – but, significantly, these are not extended to a more extensive critique of the whole documentary genre itself.

The argument over a consent form is quickly rendered irrelevant by the activities of this Reality-TV crew, which repeatedly violates characters' privacy with intrusive camerawork. The episode itself is entitled 'Ambush', and some characters explicitly suggest that the crew might be there for an exposé of the emergency room. The female director and cameraman repeat the usual proclamations of Reality-TV filmmakers – that they are committed professionals, who would just like to give the doctors an opportunity to share their stories or give their point of view – but they also emphasise that they will do the story anyway. The crew are ready to jump on the suggestion that some patients are receiving preferential treatment; they are continually looking for some scandal rather than recognising the inherent drama of everyday activities at the ER, and there is also the pointed suggestion that the presence of the film crew helps to escalate a confrontation between gang members and the ER's security guards. The footage gained by the crew is often shallow and deliberately titillating or exploitative, such as a cameraman panning down the crippled leg of a senior doctor, their close-ups of pain or death and their refusal to respect the idea that an administrator's heart attack is off-limits for filming.

Ultimately, then, the relationship which this episode constructs towards the documentary genre, despite the open critique of Reality-TV programmes, is complex. As mentioned above, the series itself is distinctive in its consistent use of *cinéma vérité* conventions of representations (although typically these are dramatically heightened through the use of editing and musical accompaniment[6]). The subtext to the dramatic quality of such representations is the 'grounding' of the series in some notion of 'reality'. In one sense, then, this mock-documentary episode serves to reinforce this dramatic device, by having a television current affairs crew 'cover' the emergency room as if it were part of the social-historical world. (And, conversely, the mock-documentary format also reveals itself as the perfect promotional device for such a dramatic series.)

This particular episode makes pointed reference almost exclusively to the recent Reality-TV hybrid forms of the genre.[7] Such programmes, at least as they are represented within this episode, effectively downplay the social responsibilities inherent to the origins of the documentary project, in favour of collating audio-visual material which is exclusively spectacular, dramatic and emotional; they operate purely as entertainment programmes. The media 'professionals' responsible for these programmes are represented here as pursuing a narrow, exploitative agenda. They establish a conventional 'contractual' relationship with their subjects (the doctors and staff), but then repeatedly violate the privacy of these people in order to gain as much visually and emotionally dramatic footage as possible. They interrupt the 'normal, everyday' activities of their subjects, and the filming becomes as much about the problematic aspects of their relationships with their subjects as it is about the ER staff. The director, her cameraman husband and the rest of the crew become characters in their own right – an intrusion both in the medical procedures they are covering and on the personal lives of the ER personnel.

There is the sense here that these types of Reality-TV programmes need to be reintegrated back into the documentary fold, to have more awareness of their ethical responsibilities. And, in fact, a strong underlying theme of the episode is that the filmmakers' encounter with these 'real' doctors and health professionals in some sense serves to 'educate' the filmmakers on how exploitative their actions are (or at least to make this obvious to the audience). At the end of the episode, a doctor 'educates' a cameraman when he accosts her in a lift, accusing her of preferential treatment towards a patient. He is lectured on his responsibilities and forced to acknowledge that he needs to respect his subjects more (at which point the camera literally droops in shame).

Because of our familiarity with the show's characters, we (the audience) are able to recognise where the filmmakers fail to represent accurately the complexities of the demands placed on the ER medical staff. Our status as 'insiders' to this fictional world allows us to be confident that we will be allowed access to the psychological motivations of all of the characters, that we are not reduced to the level of mere voyeurs, as the film crew are seen to be. In this sense, the episode, somewhat indirectly, highlights the partial nature of any documentary approach to its subject, and critiques the validity of the documentary project itself. However, these ideas serve very much as a subtext of the text, and are not the most prominent aspects of its critique of Reality-TV shows.

The Games (1998)

The final example in this first section of degree 2 texts is *The Games*, one of a small number of mock-documentary television series (another is *Tanner '88*[8]) of which we are aware. It was broadcast by the Australian Broadcasting Corporation (ABC) and looks to use the mock-documentary form to provide a social and political commentary on a public event – in this case the Sydney 2000 Olympic Games. This series is largely intended as a satire of the political and economic machinations behind the construction of such a high profile sporting event. The 'documentary crew' are present to record the administrative and political achievement in the construction of a modern Olympics, but they also have an implicit agenda to gain a behind-the-scenes exposé of the administrative office.

The series is deceptively simple in its construction. Although the majority of the action occurs within one setting (a number of offices of the Administration and Logistics section of the Sydney Olympics organising body), it manages to touch upon a complex variety of issues. Budget problems, construction delays, political agendas, the corruption of the International Olympic Committee and issues such as the level of drug-taking within elite sporting circles are all satirised. The series is brilliantly effective in revealing the conflicts of interest and blatant politicking which lies behind the internationalist/sporting rhetoric associated with the modern Olympics; in particular how the events themselves are never able to become the arena for pure sporting endeavours which they are promoted to be.

The focus of the series is really on the discourse of administration, within an Australian context. The main writer and actor is John Clarke, a New-Zealand-born comedian with a style of delivery which seems particularly suited to mock-documentary. Clarke's comic material usually focuses on the semantics of language, and he typically 'deadpans' his punchlines. Most scenes in *The Games* revolve around characters arguing over the semantics of administration, and especially attempting to make a problem disappear by relabelling it. (All of the cast use their real names, a transparency of characterisation which is also typical of Clarke.) The style of the series is related to that of the *Monty Python* tradition – the treating of an absurd notion in a logical way – although this series is considerably more subtle. Each episode begins with an improbable premise (for example, the administrators discover that the 100 metre track built for the Olympic Stadium is inexplicably only 94 metres long) and details the slow panic of the bureaucratic mind attempting to rationalise it, or seek someone else to blame.

The series operates with reconstructions of the observational mode of documentary, with frequent use of captions to introduce days and times, locate settings and identify characters. Episodes have the appearance of having captured the actions using two cameras, with series director Bruce Permezel operating one of the cameras. The presence of the crew is frequently acknowledged by their fictional subjects. They are greeted by characters and quickly become participants in the office activities (the most humorous is where they are encouraged to simulate an aerial shot surveying the model of a local proposal for the construction of the five Olympic rings for the opening ceremony – the camera shakes a little to simulate the action of a helicopter while the cameraman makes 'chopper' noises).

Within an overall construction which suggests that we are viewing an accurate and insightful look 'behind the scenes', the series incorporates some subtle commentary on the tensions inherent to any collaboration between documentary filmmaker and his/her subject. Throughout the series there are continual references to the contest between the need for good public relations (on the part of the administration team) versus the crew's need to get good footage. At one point, for example, John tells the cameraman to shut his camera off, 'because this is important' (as he makes a phone call) – with the inference that everyone knows that the crew will only be allowed to film within specific parameters.

Some of the best scenes where this tension is explored occurs in an episode revolving around an attempt at a cover-up by John and his colleagues. An IOC delegate has died in potentially scandalous circumstances, and the Secretary to the Minister of the Games has placed the body in the offices of Administration and Logistics until a publicly acceptable death scene can be arranged. Despite John's efforts to keep this from the film crew (by herding them into an office) they discover the plot by secretly filming through a window. When John spots them, he admits that it might be helpful to have a record of the cover-up (to cover his own involvement), but then says 'I want your word as an Australian journalist that *that* won't appear on television' (pointing at the camera).The crew solemnly agree (then obviously break their promise).[9] When the Secretary to Minister and John try to hustle the body of the IOC delegate out of the offices, in order to escape a news journalist arriving to interview the delegate, another member of the office team (Gina) literally tap-dances to distract the camera. As the Secretary struggles to hold up the body of the IOC delegate, he complains that the documentary crew should have more respect for the dead than to film them. The episode features one of the series' many scenes in which it targets the ethics of documentary practitioners, but also openly parodies the variety of ways in which a filmmaker and his/her subjects continually negotiate their conflicting agendas.

Political critique

This next group of texts consists of those degree 2 mock-documentaries which are characterised by a greater engagement with political commentary, an aspect of parody which would seem a natural subject for the mock-documentary form, but one which is rarely explored with any depth. As with the other examples discussed in this chapter, these texts demonstrate an ambivalence towards factual discourse, but they also arguably develop reflexivity through their engagement with issues related to the legitimacy of wider political processes, as much as from the complexity of their use of the mock-documentary form. The best example of this tendency is *Bob Roberts*.

Bob Roberts (1992)

Bob Roberts is something of a landmark text in the development of mock-documentary. It is a comparatively rare text which fully exploits the satiric potential of the form – in this case, in order to examine media practices and their role with the American political system. *Bob Roberts* covers the final stages of the Pennsylvania campaign of a folk-singing Republican senatorial candidate, played by Tim Robbins. Robbins first designed the Roberts character for a *Saturday Night Live* sketch, and has cited both *This Is Spinal Tap* and *Tanner '88* as significant influences (Francke, 1996; Kempley, 1992).[10]

The film is a sophisticated blend of the full range of documentary codes and conventions. Structurally the film is located around the conventional expositional narration provided by the character of a British journalist named Terry Manchester. He acts as an archetypal figure of a documentary-maker, allowing the film to perform a *Citizen-Kane*-like investigation into a political figure. The fact that he is a *British* journalist is key to his construction as an investigative reporter. He serves as a cultural outsider to the corrupted, sanitised, trivialised, sensationalist coverage provided by the American news media culture, with the implication that the BBC acts as a repository of those public service ideals which have been lost by these news programmes. Manchester represents the ideal political watchdog (distanced, objective, even turning to Thomas Jefferson for solace in the final scene) who attempts to gain insight into a complex political phenomenon; Roberts's campaign strategy (and, by extension, modern American political culture).

The film combines Manchester's coverage of Roberts with other artefacts, including 'documents' such as photos of his childhood and early life, and most notably Roberts's music albums and videos. Just as an expositional documentary would, the film makes use of a number of specific reference points from recent political history (the Boland Amendment, Iran-Contra, the Savings and Loans scandal, Panama's Noriega and the 1991 Gulf War against Iraq). There are also fictional news reports of the electoral contest between Roberts and incumbent Senator Brickley Paiste (Gore Vidal) and, as suggested above, these are an important part of the film's political critique. The superficial nature of these reports suggests that the mainstream American media are incapable of countering the degree of sophistication and subtlety exhibited by modern political candidates, and are reduced to accepting at face value any political spin offered by the candidates.

Most of the insights into Roberts come from Manchester's interviews with people on the campaign team, and especially those on the periphery; Roberts's ardent supporters and those who are bitterly opposed to him (Paiste, a leftist reporter named Bugs Raplin (played by Giancarlo Esposito) and television reporter Kelly Noble[11]). Roberts himself is rarely within the reach of Manchester;[12] instead it is his campaign manager MacGregor and the shadowy figure of Lucas Hart III who represent the cynicism of the modern political machine. MacGregor is the slick, perhaps apolitical, public relations expert, while Hart is from the conservative lunatic fringe, a more credible and subdued version of Oliver North.[13] The other members of the campaign team are all yuppies who, to varying degrees, recognise the basic immorality and cynicism that lies behind Roberts's façade.[14]

Manchester is in some sense an 'innocent' who tags along with Roberts's campaign, observing the militarist and monetarist nature of his campaign strategy, encountering the figures who are variously attracted or repelled by Roberts, and eventually becoming himself yet another pawn in the Roberts campaign strategy (being choreographed so that he will film the faked 'assassination' attempt on Roberts that is used to frame Raplin). The documentary crew, however, also witness and record the variety of types of carefully crafted performances which are associated with Roberts – including his concerts, press conferences, television interviews, political debates and ultimately his wheel-chair presence after the 'assassination' attempt. Their footage effectively captures the 'truth' of Roberts's Machiavellian political campaign.

The film works as a savage critique of a number of aspects of American culture, particularly the brand of modern conservatism of the Reagan and Bush eras. Roberts is a slightly exaggerated version of the modern American conservative. He has a sophisticated understanding of the media, and is comfortable with his political stance and wealth. His political discourse perfectly reflects the achievement of American conservatism of the 1980s; the ability to regain the moral high ground. Where Democratic politics in the 1960s and 1970s was able to define itself as being outside the establishment and representing the basic values of the American system, Republicans during the 1980s were able to appropriate this rhetorical position, to naturalise their own discourse of individualism, monetarism and 'family values'.[15]

Robbins's satiric representation of modern American conservatism is most perfectly realised through his character's folk-singing. As a singer, Bob Roberts directly inverts the stance and music of Bob Dylan, in sequences which epitomise this transformation in American political discourse. Bob Dylan's album *The Times They Are A-Changin'* becomes here an attack on the 1960s called *The Times Are Changing Back*. Every slogan used to mobilise anti-establishment movements from that decade is reinvented by Roberts as a call for a revitalised conservative politics. Woody Guthrie's 'This Land is Your Land' (an early labour solidarity anthem which had already been sanitised of any subversive content) is turned into an anthem for a conservative vision of individualism. In an MTV video called 'Wall Street Rap',[16] Roberts even uses Malcolm X's phrase 'by any means necessary' to refer to generating wealth, rather than the struggle for self-determination for African-Americans.[17]

The film's representation of the American media is complex. At one level there is a savage parody of the shallowness of political coverage within daily network television. All of the television news presenters (played by liberal actors such as Susan Sarandon, James Spader, Fred Ward and Helen Hunt) lack credibility and do not engage in any critical examinations of the political spins that they are fed. The continual repeating of manufactured allegations of sleaze made against Paiste are a good example of these networks' lack of depth and repetitiveness in their political coverage. The dominance of conservative discourse is also suggested as a reason for this stance. Roberts, in an exchange with Raplin, argues that any critique of his policies constitutes an abandonment of a journalist's objectivity, while after Raplin's arrest his lawyer is asked if it is true that his client is a 'card-carrying member' of the ACLU (American Civil Liberties Union), a perfect example of the naturalisation of conservative discourse.

There are also characters, such as Manchester, Raplin and Noble, who represent the more credible sectors of the media, who are able to draw upon and generate alternative political discourses in order to examine Roberts's politics. These characters explicitly draw upon and epitomise the journalistic rhetoric which is such an important part of the documentary discourse.[18] There is, however, the sense that these types of journalists have been negated or marginalised; Noble is merely left embittered and aware of her powerlessness, while Raplin sacrifices far more for attaining knowledge of the true nature of the political process (he is eventually assassinated by a fanatical Roberts supporter). Manchester represents the potential of investigative documentary to uncover the 'truth', to peel back the layers of political intrigue and make the political system more responsible to the public. He is able to gain enough evidence to suggest the corruption of Roberts; however there is no real suggestion that his film will make a difference to the American political process. In some sense, he is merely able to record the deception, rather than to attempt to act as a people's champion in the manner of Raplin. Manchester's final retreat to the Jefferson memorial is both an effort to find refuge and an acknowledgement of how far the American state has fallen from its original ideals. These final images can also easily be read as reflective of a profound sense of unease with the inability of a hopelessly tabloid fourth estate to counter this fall.

Hoaxes

The texts in this last category of degree 2 are among the more interesting of all mock-documentaries; texts where reflexivity has been generated as much through the specific context of *reception* as through the form or content of the text itself. As we argue throughout this book, audience are fully capable of engaging with mock-documentaries at a variety of levels, from an appreciation of the more superficial levels of parody, to an open acknowledgement of the form's inherent reflexivity. We include within this section, then, instances of almost accidental reflexivity – encounters between degree 2 texts and audiences unable to recognise them as fiction. The examples discussed below are media 'hoaxes' which to some extent forced their audiences to acknowledge the subversive nature of the mock-documentary form. Interestingly, they represent contrasting intentions on the part of their directors and producers.

Forgotten Silver (1995) has been discussed in the previous chapter as a degree 1 text, but it is placed here because of its status as an unintentional hoax. The filmmakers have stated publicly that they did not intend viewers to believe in its subject (a supposed long-forgotten pioneering filmmaker called Colin McKenzie), and have insisted that there are many cues in the text itself to highlight its fictionality. However a significant section of the programme's initial New Zealand audience were left either confused or taken in by the sophistication of the programme's simulation of the documentary form. In contrast, *Alien Abduction* (1998) appears to be a deliberate hoax, one created within a particular programming agenda, which similarly angered a sizeable portion of its audience. Both mock-documentaries are also interesting examples of the importance of the role played by the television broadcaster in framing the expectations and assumptions of viewers – in encouraging a documentary mode of reading and hence becoming accomplices in the generation of a hoax.

Forgotten Silver (1995)

A discussion of *Forgotten Silver*'s use of documentary aesthetics in the creation of a convincing biography of McKenzie is included in the previous chapter. What follows is an outline of the *contextual* factors which aided the programme's success as a mock-documentary, and the reaction of its New Zealand audience. The first screening of the programme on New Zealand television was accompanied by a variety of factors which effectively served to reinforce the text's documentary credentials with its audience.

Firstly, the programme was screened (by Television New Zealand on 8 Sunday November 1995) in the 'quality drama' *Montana Sunday Theatre* slot. In previous weeks, this slot had screened a series of original New Zealand dramas and the finishing of that series with a documentary about an apparently forgotten New Zealand filmmaker seemed appropriate, if somewhat unusual. A wider cultural context also served to further legitimate, justify and authenticate the programme and its subject matter. New Zealand was celebrating the centenary of cinema as an entertainment medium, with the New Zealand Film Commission spending much time, effort and resources in promoting an awareness and celebration of this milestone both nationally and locally.

One such activity organised through the national Film Archive has particular relevance here. Over the previous couple of years the Archive had been conducting a nationwide film search, encouraging the public to hand over old films which had largely been left to disintegrate in garages and attics. Peter Jackson makes specific reference to this search at the start of *Forgotten Silver* when explaining how he first encountered the work of Colin McKenzie. Although most of the materials collected by the archive have been home movies and similar short excerpts of film, it was certainly the hope (if not the reality) that the search would uncover material of historical importance. *Forgotten Silver* claimed to be presenting a film 'find' that matched and even exceeded the dreams of the Archive and of the many people who had contributed to the search. Given this context, it seemed reasonable to accord the announcement of the discovery and a presentation of McKenzie's work a place in a slot known for its promotion of high quality and original material. The fact that the Film Commission and New Zealand On Air[19] had supported the project financially only served to reinforce the legitimacy and significance of the programme. It was, then, with some excitement and curiosity that an estimated audience of four hundred thousand viewers tuned into TV1[20] that Sunday night to learn more about a pioneering New Zealand filmmaker.

This first screening was preceded by a significant amount of publicity focusing on the importance of the find. *Forgotten Silver* was first brought to the attention of the New Zealand audience in an article in the New Zealand *Listener* which 'broke' the story, claiming to herald a 'sensational find' with the discovery of a hoard of long-lost films by a previously unknown New Zealand filmmaker, Colin McKenzie (Welch). The article placed directors Peter Jackson and Costa Botes in the role of discoverers and celebrants of McKenzie's assumed legacy. In hindsight, the article contains a number of cues as to the real nature of *Forgotten Silver*,[21] and in fact is written in the same tones as the discourse of *Forgotten Silver* itself; excitement at the importance and relevance of the work of McKenzie, and of the implications which this discovery seemed to hold for both New Zealand and world cinematic history.

The first public screening of *Forgotten Silver* was not unprecedented in New Zealand television broadcasting. The programme could in fact be seen as part of a well-established 'tradition' of mock New Zealand television reports. Perhaps the best-known examples (for local audiences) have been the numerous mock reports of agricultural developments or inventions featured on *Country Calendar*.[22] The two main nightly news programmes also produce mock news items immediately before the conclusion of their 1 April broadcasts. What was perhaps unique was the level of secrecy which went into maintaining the pretence that the programme was a legitimate documentary, and the publicity surrounding this first screening. Here *Forgotten Silver* went beyond this tradition of spoof news items to enlist the complicity of a national print publication (the *Listener*) which generally enjoys a reputation for responsible journalism.

From a cursory survey of responses reported in the media, the New Zealand audience apparently reacted to *Forgotten Silver* in a number of varying and interesting ways. The written responses to the *Listener* itself (which featured the original article publicising *Forgotten Silver*) demonstrates a range of these audience reactions to the programme. The magazine states that of 'the writers of the 24 letters the *Listener* has received on the *Forgotten Silver* hoax, 16 express disapproval, five approve, and three still believe'.[23] This public response could be divided roughly into the three categories listed below. These are by no means exhaustive, nor mutually exclusive, but they do serve as a useful starting point for any discussion over the willingness of the New Zealand audience to allow, in particular, for the subversion of many of the basic assumptions exploited by documentaries, and news services in general.

Uncertain

Some responses reflected confusion over whether or not Colin McKenzie could be considered a New Zealand historical figure; whether *Forgotten Silver* was in fact a documentary. One viewer was inspired to conduct background research into 'Maybelle', the heroine of the film, and examined adoption records for Dunedin – coming to the conclusion that she had located a young woman who was almost certainly the daughter of either Brooke or Colin McKenzie.[24] Even local journalists were apparently fooled, with some not realising it was a spoof until they phoned TVNZ in order to contact the filmmakers for follow-up stories.[25] These kinds of audience response to *Forgotten Silver* testified to the effectiveness of Jackson and Botes in perpetrating their hoax, and to the quality of the craft which went into the programme itself.

The confusion of some viewers was perhaps also due to an expectation that there is a clearly demarcated line between reality-based television and fictional programmes; that there should be something either preceding or during the programme which makes this division obvious to the viewers. *Forgotten Silver* does have a degree of reflexivity – it does feature a number of clues as to the nature of its subject[26] – but these were very subtle and perhaps overwhelmed by the effectiveness of the programme's other devices. These viewers were apparently unaccustomed to being asked to judge the validity of an entire programme itself. This first category of responses could perhaps be summed up by the following quotation in a fax sent to the producers of the programme, Wingnut Films (with unconscious irony): 'It was such an amazing story that I half expected to find out at the end of the programme that it was fictional!'

Positive

A portion of *Forgotten Silver*'s audience, apparently initially a minority, expressed some appreciation of the degree of directorial ability which went into the making of the programme, and to some extent supported the idea that there were some national myths which New Zealanders should be able to laugh at:

The producers have done us all a service by showing how easy it is to hoodwink a viewing public that has been conditioned to believe that anything labelled 'documentary' is necessarily the truth.

Viewers should bear this experience in mind, and keep a pinch of salt handy, when watching supposedly more serious documentaries or 'infodocs' on current issues, especially controversial ones.[27]

In a follow-up article in the *Listener*, Botes offered the following response as his favourite: 'One Network News admitted that last night's *Montana Sunday Theatre* was a hoax. Well, all credibility has gone down the tubes – I won't be believing in TVNZ's news anymore.'[28] These viewers could perhaps be termed 'televisually sophisticated', in that they did not automatically assume that information structured within a documentary discourse was accurate, or even non-fictional.

Negative/hostile

The most interesting responses to the programme were those which
expressed anger at having been taken in by the hoax, and especially at the
willingness of the filmmakers to play with some of the more central
aspects of the rhetoric of objectivity which is central to factual discourse.
The implicit acceptance of viewers to this same ideology apparently led
many to express a feeling of betrayal at having their expectations and
assumptions in some sense 'violated' by *Forgotten Silver* not having been
labelled as fictional. In this case the violation is of an apparent trust which
these audience members feel exists between themselves and Television
New Zealand as an institution, a trust which is itself a legacy of TVNZ's
history as a BBC-styled public broadcasting service.[29]

Because of the damage to true documentary and the misuse of that honoured
term, I for one, after a lifetime of interest in film, have resigned my membership
of the Film Society.[30]

I am very irate that I was misled in thinking that this documentary was true.
TVNZ should be ashamed that they can show this sort of rubbish on TV. I don't
pay my licence fee for nothing you know.[31]

If this sort of thing is allowed to develop where will it end? From now on anything
that the media produce, whether it be by word or film, will be regarded with
disbelief. This is a sad state of affairs when we can't believe what we read, see
and hear.[32]

A third aspect of the negative reaction to the programme was also a
degree of anti-intellectualism – the idea that this was a hoax which was
just too clever, that it could not have been unravelled except by the most
visually sophisticated viewers. Here the anger seems to be directed at filmmakers who would supposedly play with some of the more treasured popular New Zealand legends (such as the alleged pre-Wright-brothers flight
of Richard Pearse) largely for their own amusement.

I can't express my disappointment at having lost a genius and gained another
'clever' film-maker. A wise film-maker of yesteryear (when standards were more
stodgy) warned against tricking or insulting your audience. Whatever its motive,
this film could not be said to be in sympathy with its audience. I doubt if I'll ever
look at the work of Peter Jackson (or the *Listener*) in quite the same light again.[33]

As one of the 'gullible' who viewed *Forgotten Silver*, I felt I was not deceived or
cheated at having been a victim of such an elaborate ruse. But I am saddened that
Colin McKenzie is not part of my heritage as a New Zealander, and that the dis-
play of determination and spirit was not more than a figment of imagination in
the guise of a documentary.

The role of the documentary, in my mind, is to reveal and educate, and the programme does not qualify. It does reveal that intellectual arrogance is to be found
among those whose vacation it is to entertain or inform.

I trust that the groups which funded *Forgotten Silver*, New Zealand on Air and
the New Zealand Film Commission, are delighted at having perpetrated a great
New Zealand myth that artisans are forever biting the hand that feeds, and that
their intellectual vanity is matched only by their egos.[34]

Finally, there is the issue of whether the local audience reactions to *Forgotten Silver* are complicated by a degree of uncertainty and 'immaturity'
over the basic character of national identity – within a national culture
which is still comparatively young. These viewers are perhaps representative of social groups which are unable to cope with challenges to its more
'sacred' national myths and symbols of national identity. At this stage
in New Zealand history such myths and symbols are perhaps still too
vulnerable to be able to face such an exercise in deconstruction. It is the
programme's insistence on violating not only these integral aspects of
New Zealand heritage, but also the 'sacredness' of fundamental aspects of
the documentary genre itself which made *Forgotten Silver* more than an
exercise in entertainment.

National insecurities

Jackson and Botes apparently intended that their audience would realise
the joke while viewing the programme.[35] Both expressed surprise that there
was a group of viewers who seemed unable, or unwilling, to move from
a documentary mode of viewing to an appreciation of the filmmakers'
original intention.

We never seriously thought that people would believe it because we kept putting
in more and more outrageous gags – custard pies in the Prime Minister's face,
making film out of eggs, and the Tahitian colour film. We wanted the audience to
start out believing it and although by the time it was finished they no longer
believed it they would still have had a good time.[36]

This was fiction, but it was a full-blown celebration of Kiwi ingenuity, asking
people to wake up and see what's in their backyard. Picasso said, 'We all know that
art is not truth. Art is a lie that makes us realise truth.' [37]

If *Forgotten Silver* causes people never to take anything from the media at face
value, so much the better. Our film was better researched and, on the whole, more
'true' than most products of the 'infotainment' industry.[38]

As Jackson claimed in his own defence – in a television news story on
Forgotten Silver the day after its first screening – he is 'in the business of

creating illusions', a *raison d'être* which could be extended to the very form which his film effectively attempted to demythologise. This is perhaps a fear of some of the audience members who reacted so negatively to the first screening of *Forgotten Silver*. One of the more interesting public responses to the programme was the following: 'The connection with Richard Pearse was tasteless and left many in South Canterbury disappointed and angry. It also may have the effect of discounting any claim that he might have of being the first to fly, for many may now dismiss his life as part of the hoax that the film has perpetuated.'[39] *Forgotten Silver* shows, above all, the polysemic nature of mock-documentaries – in other words, the varying degrees of reflexivity with which audiences can engage with these texts. Viewers of this programme were divided on the degree to which they were prepared to accept the 'inappropriate' use of documentary codes and conventions, and the degree of their appreciation of the text's implicit subversion of factual discourse.

Despite the sophistication of *Forgotten Silver*'s simulation of documentary aesthetics, the programme none the less makes a concerted effort to highlight its fictionality. In this sense, for the audience to be taken in by the text (for them to accept it as 'real'), they have effectively to read against its intended (preferred) meaning (which is why we have placed it initially in degree 1). The more negative responses to the initial screening were from people who had their faith in factual discourse reinforced by the very fact that documentary codes and conventions appeared to have been used. The more complex responses (that is, those were initially taken in by *Forgotten Silver*, but who developed varying degrees of appreciation of its parody of New Zealand culture, and degrees of reflexivity toward the constructed nature of factual texts) suggests the engagement of a number of different levels of reading.

Forgotten Silver, then, demonstrates the ability of the audience to engage with a mock-documentary text in a variety of ways. Obviously, context is important. The success of the hoax had to do with a number of factors, both deliberate and fortuitous for the filmmakers, associated with the immediate context of the initial screening of the text. Once the programme was known as a hoax, audiences would presumably approach it with interpretations more in line with the preferred meaning intended by directors Jackson and Botes.

Alien Abduction – Incident in Lake County (1998)

It is interesting to compare the reception of *Forgotten Silver* to that of this second example, a mock-documentary text which appears to have been deliberately constructed as a hoax. *Alien Abduction – Incident in Lake County* aired in the United States, on UPN, on 20 January 1998. UPN released the following advance promotion:

UPN will present a one-hour special centered on an alleged videotaped account of a family's purported encounter with what may be extraterrestrial life forms when 'Alien Abduction: Incident at Lake Country' airs Tuesday, Jan. 20.

The recently acquired videotape is the sole testament to the fate of the McPherson family, missing since last Thanksgiving Day.

Apparently recorded and, at various times, narrated by the family's 16-year-old son, Thomas McPherson, the startling footage shows the family gathering with friends to celebrate Thanksgiving on Thursday, Nov. 27, 1997. A series of strange occurrences, caught by the camera, culminate in what appears to be a frightening encounter with strange creatures.

During the special, several people who claim to have had similar experiences relate their ordeals, and experts on aliens discuss the authenticity of the videotape.

Like *Forgotten Silver, Alien Abduction* uses a combination of expositional, observational and interactive techniques to 'document' the experiences of the missing McPhersons.[40] The central piece of 'evidence' of their supposed experiences is the surviving videotape, and this forms the basis of a debate constructed between various interviewees. There is a conventional authoritative, male voice-over narrator, who offers a structure and frame for the text. At various points he notes some aspect of the tape (for example, he emphasises the fact that the McPhersons appear to forget a shooting incident as soon as it happens).

Some of the interviewees offer personal experience of alien abduction, but mostly they appear as 'experts', offering a number of competing hypotheses to explain the nature of the McPhersons' experience and disappearance.[41] The programme even groups these competing theories under explicit titles ('cover-up theory', 'hoax theory', 'reality theory'). The videotape itself is effectively treated by most of the experts as capturing a 'slice-of-reality', with debate centring on the precise meaning of the experiences it portrays. In other words, the tape is used as the basis for competing narratives of the events it purports to present, with each of the experts looking to frame the events in terms of a (for them) plausible scenario. The images themselves are examined and used in a variety of contexts. They are slowed down for particular emphasis, there are frequent freeze-frames when there needs to be commentary on the meaning of a particular scene, and there are some blown-up sections of still-frames (such as the climactic scene where Tommy supposedly encounters an alien). Collectively the experts construct the conventional range of debate; assessing the truth and validity of the alien abduction footage by drawing upon a range of scientific discourses. A final debate at the end of the programme implicitly accepts the validity of the tape as a given, as speculation turns to possible reasons for the 'visitation'.[42]

The videotape sequences themselves are interesting in that they are capable of standing alone as narrative constructions. There is generally no ambiguous information in the tape, at least in terms of the McPhersons and their experiences. The characters all explain clearly what they are thinking and feeling; they openly debate possible courses of action and even give 'direction' to each other. As in any conventional piece of fictional narrative, their motivations are clear. All of the key points of 'evidence' eventually debated by the 'experts' are carefully highlighted, either by explicit dialogue, direct camera shots or the use of music at dramatic climaxes.[43] Structurally, the tape offers a series of clearly defined episodes, all escalating from previous action, which eventually lead to the 'climax' of the final encounter between Tommy and an 'alien'.

The portrayal of the McPherson family itself is also extremely conventional. They are a traditional middle-class, white,[44] patriarchal family (the men have use of the guns, while the women merely become hysterical). Tommy (the apparent cameraman) acts as the point of identification for the audience; both because the camera records events by acting as his 'eyes' and because he constantly reacts to, comments on and asks 'common-sense' questions about the action.

Like *Forgotten Silver*, the reception of this mock-documentary generated confusion over its accuracy, in part because of the context in which it was screened. The initial broadcast of *Alien Abduction* was immediately preceded by a programme called *Real Vampires: Exposed!*, which offered a tabloid-like investigation of 'vampires' and in some sense can be said to have created expectations concerning the 'alien' documentary which followed. Although the producers of the vampire programme obviously adopted a tabloid approach to a trivial subject (*Alien Abduction* appears conventional in comparison) there is nothing in the programme to suggest that they have manufactured sequences.

Alien Abduction also needs to be seen in the context of an increasing trend within mainstream American television of both series and one-off specials which purport to operate with both documentary and explicitly fictional agendas. The programme was created by Dick Clark Productions, which is responsible also for a television series screened on Fox TV network called *Beyond Belief: Fact or Fiction*, hosted by Jonathan Frakes (an actor from *Star Trek: The Next Generation*). This series offers allegedly true stories mixed with acknowledged fake stories and challenges its audience to identify their fictional or factual status.

It also need to be acknowledged that the whole subject of alien mythology and investigation has been a productive area for some documentary filmmakers. There are a wealth of both mainstream and low-budget texts which, with varying degrees of sobriety, purport to examine the subject and to herald the discovery of an apparently convincing piece of evidence. There are obvious science fiction connotations to the possibility of alien contact with Earth, as Orson Welles himself claimed in his defence of involvement in the infamous 1938 *War of the Worlds* radio broadcast.[45] Consequently, there is a fine line between 'conventional' documentary treatments of the subject, and a mock-documentary such as *Alien Abduction*.

An interesting comparison to the text can also be made with a 1995 documentary called *Alien Autopsy: Fact or Fiction?* Also hosted by Frakes, it focuses on footage of an alleged alien autopsy from the famous Roswell 'alien crash landing' in July 1947. The documentary examines the seventeen-minute (black and white, hand-held) footage, interviewing eyewitnesses and various experts on claims that it is a historical document (including a pathologist, Hollywood special effects technicians, photographic technicians, a documentary filmmaker and the same physicist who appears in *Alien Abduction*: Stanton Friedman). This programme similarly draws upon scientific rhetoric (including photographic and medical sciences), but includes explicit disclaimers at the beginning and end. Frakes states that the programme makers have their own doubts, but encourages the audience to decide for themselves the validity of the autopsy tape.

The controversy surrounding *Alien Abduction* centred on the absence of any similar disclaimers for the McPherson tape, the supposed lack of obvious cues that the footage was faked, and the questionable manner in which some of the experts were included in the programme. There were three authentic UFO researchers (Stanton Friedman, Yvonne Smith and Derrel Sims) included in the programme, none of whom were shown the videotape prior to being interviewed, nor given a clear idea on the nature of the show.[46] The main public debate over the programme's status as hoax apparently occurred on internet chat rooms and bulletin boards. There it was quickly discovered that 'Tommy McPherson' was in fact an

actor (Kristian Ayre) who had his own website. According to responses
posted on the internet, even after the screening Dick Clark Productions
apparently told some viewers that the programme was true.

From the internet debate, the responses to the broadcast generally followed the same pattern as that for *Forgotten Silver*, with some viewers
confused, some appreciative and others openly angry at the deception.

Anyone who watched the so-called abduction video on UPN tues. (1/20/98) was
subjected to the most worthless and incompetent hoax this investigator has ever
seen. I wish aliens would abduct those people and all of UPN's people responsible
for putting it on TV. And don't bring them back. Ufology has been insulted if not
kicked in the testicles. I don't blame people for laughing at the subject now. Please
send angry letters and insults to UPN. Make them pay for this travesty.[47]

Some viewers were prepared to accept that parts of the programme
were faked but that the McPhersons' experiences were real. The most
interesting responses were those of an apparent minority of viewers, especially UFO researchers and those believers in alien abduction, who argued
that the mock-documentary was evidence of some wider conspiracy.[48] As
with some responses to *Forgotten Silver*, there was some concern within
this minority of UFO believers over the potential harm done to the legitimacy of extraterrestrial sciences.

I consider the reactions to your show as evidence that a major affront has occurred
to the advancement of scientific knowledge and understanding of these phenomena. If any individual employed by your company are of the opinion that this is all
nonsense and should be ridiculed, I would like the opportunity to educate them.
What we don't need are producers and editors who think that TV ratings are
so much more important than presenting the truth (presented in an objective
and neutral environment) that they will intentionally frighten for entertainment
TV audiences.[49]

The broadcast of *Alien Abduction* in New Zealand (in February 1998)
offers some interesting parallels to that of *Forgotten Silver*. The mock-
documentary was screened on TVNZ (although on TV2, its more openly
commercial channel, rather than TV1 which still retains remnants of a
public service ethos). In perhaps an attempt to achieve the same notori-
ety which *Forgotten Silver* had obtained, the channel sought deliberately
to confuse the question of the programme's factual status. Immediately
before the broadcast, a disclaimer was printed on screen (and read by an
announcer): 'Alien Abduction – Incident in Lake County was obtained
exclusively from America's U.P.N. Television Network and is presented as
received. Its authority is still under much debate in the United States. We

invite you to decide for yourself.' Despite the claim that the programme is 'presented as received', the channel opted to cut the final credits for *Alien Abduction*. This prevented New Zealand audiences from noting that the McPhersons were played by actors, an action which prompted complaints by the New Zealand Skeptics Society, both to TVNZ and eventually to the Broadcasting Standards Authority. TVNZ justified cutting the credits on the grounds that it was similar to the promotional campaigns for the science-fiction series *Millennium* and *X-Files*, and that it was done to 'aid in a seamless transition to another science fiction fantasy' which followed (Hyde, 1998). In a justification which echoed that of Jackson and Botes for *Forgotten Silver*, they also argued that the programme was clearly a 'spoof' that viewers would not take seriously. Both television mock-documentaries, then, were 'hoaxes' in large part because of contextual factors, not least of which was the attitude of network broadcasters who appeared willing to participate in promotions which encouraged a confusion of these programmes' ontological status.

Notes

1 See Chapter 2 for a discussion on the differences between mock-documentary and reflexive documentary.
2 There is a strong element of docu-soap in these character constructions (see Chapter 2). Vim seems to be the only one in the band who understands how terrible they truly are – he does not want to be in 'just a heavy metal band', he is constantly frustrated that the others don't respect his 'vision', but he is still under the illusion that he himself is 'multi-talented'.
3 There was a huge promotional campaign focusing on the 'live' aspect of the premiere, including a build-up to the broadcast in which fans could participate on websites. The episode was actually performed live twice, once for each coast of the United States, and was apparently ranked among the four most popular teledramas of all time (with two episodes of *Dallas*, and the series finale of *Magnum PI*) (Paskin, 1998).
4 For a discussion of the origins of this style see Chapter 5.
5 In this sense, the episode is a classic example of the difference between a classic realist narrative (which employs codes and conventions already accepted by the audience, and hence naturalised by them) and a style which attempts to record an event accurately and faithfully.
6 In this episode, the usual dramatic music during the action sequence is replaced with a patient who drums an accompaniment to the action, to the annoyance of Greene. This is an openly reflexive moment which echoes the sudden appearance of a full orchestra, from the soundtrack into the diegesis of

the narrative itself, in Mel Brooks's *Blazing Saddles* (1974) and *High Anxiety* (1977).

7 Again, see Chapter 2 for a brief discussion of the position of Reality TV within the documentary genre.

8 We have been unable to track down copies of any of the episodes of this series, but from its reputation it appears to conform to the characteristics of a degree 2 mock-documentary (Francke, 1996: 342–3). Directed by Robert Altman (who co-wrote with *Doonesbury* cartoonist Garry Trudeau), *Tanner '88* (1988) features the political campaign of fictional Democratic congressman Jack Tanner (Michael Murphy). The television series was broadcast on the American cable channel HBO during the lead-up to the 1988 presidential eection, contested between Republican George Bush and Democratic candidate Michael Dukakis, and has Tanner interacting with actual candidates Gary Hart, Bob Dole and Pat Robertson.

9 Throughout the series, a recurring joke is the suggestion that Australian journalists' adherence to any ethical standards is easily expressed but effectively non-existent.

10 This mock-documentary's origins in the *Saturday Night Live* comedy series mirrors that of *The Rutles*, which developed from the *Monty Python* tradition, and both texts demonstrate the importance of these television series as precursors of the mock-documentary form. (See Chapter 5.)

11 Both Raplin and Noble are African-American, and are painfully aware of the racial overtones of Roberts's populist appeal. Raplin represents the complete antithesis to Roberts; he has an Arab middle name, is crippled, obsessed and paranoid, and pure of conviction in total contrast to Roberts's corruption. While Senator Paiste acknowledges that he himself has been corrupted by the Washington environment, Raplin symbolises all that is left of the promise and political ideals of the New Left from the 1960s. Similarly, Noble is a figure who has benefited from the advances of the 1960s, such as the civil and women's rights movements, and has the intelligence to recognise how radically the political situation has back-tracked since those days. Like Raplin, she has a voice within the media, but a marginalised one that is not able to make up for the overall mediocrity of television news.

12 This eerily foregrounds real political documentary such as *The War Room* (1993), where Bill Clinton is almost seen as an unnecessary addition to his campaign team.

13 He is shown at the Iran-Contra hearings justifying illegal activities in Central America through assertions of his patriotism.

14 An African-American member denies any racism within Roberts's politics, a female campaigner named Delores is the political innocent who realises too late how she has been duped, while Polly is the anonymous political wife – polished and totally irrelevant, even to Roberts.

15 The campaign style of Ronald Reagan is parodied brilliantly through

Roberts's re-creation of Reagan's presidential re-election commercials, which used the image of a 'new morning' in American to suggest a rebirth of American power and wealth.

16 As Hall notes, this is a direct take on Dylan's 'Subterranean Homesick Blues' from D. A. Pennebaker's documentary account of Dylan's 1965 England tour, *Don't Look Back*. *Bob Roberts* also directly quotes from other scenes from this early observational documentary, including the film's opening shot of Roberts coming into the lights of the stage, and the meeting of a local official and her three teenage sons. See Chapter 6 for a brief discussion of *Don't Look Back* in relation to rockumentary.

17 Robbins apparently refused to issue a soundtrack for the film, out of fear that right-wing politicians would use the songs for their own anthems – just as Reagan appropriated Bruce Springsteen's *Born in the USA* as a campaign song, despite the song's cynicism towards American patriotism and its negative commentary of 1970s America. Robbins's decision is partly a recognition of the slippery nature of political discourse, but it also reflects a sense of uncertainty over the ability of the American *audience* to be able to deconstruct such messages.

18 See Chapter 1.

19 New Zealand On Air (NZOA) is a public body which has a brief to 'foster New Zealand culture and identity' through funding local broadcasting. NZOA represents the last institutional remnant of New Zealand's public service broadcasting system – it was previously funded through a (now scrapped) universal licence fee, and its funding choices typically attract political debate.

20 TV1 is one of two channels provided by the publicly owned (former public service) television broadcaster Television New Zealand (TVNZ), and four hundred thousand represents a sizeable audience for a nation of just over three million.

21 In the article Jackson is quoted as stating that there 'was some pressure on us at first to possibly dramatise some aspects of Colin's life, but frankly, even though it's a documentary, the events of his life were so dramatic that the word drama is not inappropriate', and Botes offers the claim that 'It's as gripping as any fictional story'. Among other clues, the article also specifically highlights the fact that *Forgotten Silver* was to be featured within a programme slot reserved for dramatic productions.

22 *Country Calendar* is a long-running agricultural information programme screened by TVNZ. Mock items have surfaced occasionally during the long run of the series, and have included 'reports' on a remote-controlled sheep-dog, day and night sheep grazing, alternative sheep shearing with blow waves and soft music, a farmer using his fence as a musical instrument, and an episode featuring the lifestyle of 'farmer' Fred Dagg (comedian John Clarke – who has more recently been responsible for the Australian mock-documentary series *The Games*).

23 Letters to the editor, *Listener*, 25 November 1995: 12. TVNZ itself received hundreds of telephone calls about the programme, which broadly fell into the same categories.

24 Letter to *New Zealand Listener*, 18 November 1995, from Ann Else, Northland, Wellington.

25 *Hollywood Reporter*, 31 October 1995.

26 The clues include the tenuous nature of the 'scientific' basis to the egg and plant chemistry experiments from which McKenzie supposedly developed film stock, an interview with an *Alexandra* Nevsky at the Russian embassy, the numerous references to Taurus (bull) symbols, and so on. The final image of the programme itself has McKenzie grinning while filming himself in a mirror, with credits for the writing and direction of Jackson and Botes superimposed.

27 K. C. Durrant (Upper Hutt), letter to the editor, *Listener*, 25 November 1995: 12.

28 G. Chapple, 'Gone, Not Forgotten', *Listener*, 25 November 1995: 26.

29 It is interesting to speculate whether TV3, the much younger and more openly commercial rival to TVNZ, would have received the same degree of vilification from members of its audience if it had broadcast *Forgotten Silver*.

30 W. J. Gaudin (Christchurch), letter to the editor, *Listener*, 25 November 1995: 12.

31 Anonymous call to TVNZ.

32 Olwyn Rathgen (Waimate), letter to the editor, *Timaru Herald*, 6 November 1995.

33 G. A. De Forest (Te Atatu Peninsula), letter to the editor, *Listener*, 25 November 1995: 12.

34 Michael Rudd (Taupo), letter to the editor, *New Zealand Herald*, 9 November 1995.

35 The programme starts with Jackson iterally leading viewers down a garden path, and McKenzie's supposed films are found under a status of a bull. Botes has stated that he had wanted to make such a film since he saw the early hoax BBC mock-documentary *Alternative Three* (1977).

36 Interview with Peter Jackson (1996) *Midwest Art Magazine*, Issue 10: 23.

37 Costa Botes, quoted in *New Zealand Listener*, 25 November 1995.

38 Botes, letter to the editor (written in response to negative letters), *Evening Post*, 16 November 1995.

39 W. J. Gaudin (Christchurch), letter to the editor, *Listener*, 25 November 1995: 12.

40 In fact, outside of their content, each falls into the classic model of documentary, drawing from all of the basic codes and conventions of the documentary genre (see Chapter 1).

41 The interviewees include a local sheriff, a female reporter, a former government employee, authors, an abduction researcher, a special effects technician, a nuclear physicist, a UFO investigator, abductees and a child psychiatrist.

Interestingly, in an apparent effort to cue the appropriate audience response, they are filmed using different techniques, with eyewitnesses interviewed in domestic surroundings (with a hand-held camera), and experts shown in more formal settings (and the ex-government-agent in a darkened warehouse with his face disguised).

42 The explanations offered are all still presented using scientific rhetoric – including the suggestion that the aliens are on earth to study an inferior species.

43 The points include a transformer exploding, the loss of electricity, the sighting of an alien craft, the youngest girl's unnatural behaviour, the appearance of triangular scars on the McPhersons' necks, the entry of an alien 'probe' into the house, the loss of time on the tape (stated by the narrator, then reinforced through an exchange between two of the women) and so on.

44 The only African-American man is left in the house with the women and children, while the men explore outside. He is not allowed a gun and is effectively given no voice at all.

45 See Chapter 5 for a discussion of Welles's radio text as a precursor to mock-documentary.

46 They were apparently asked general questions on alien abductions and their answers edited into the programme at appropriate points to suggest that they were responding to the opinions of the fictional experts. CNI News, 27 January 1998.

47 Joel Henry, Minnesota MUFON Webmaster and Field Investigator.

48 One hilarious, and widely repeated, claim was that the government was behind the programme in order to distract the country from the Clinton–Lewinsky scandal.

49 Public email from Bruce Cornet to Joe Passarella, programming UPN, 26 January 1998.

8

Degree 3: deconstruction

The mock-documentary texts which we place within degree 3 are those which may or may not expect their audience to easily identify their fictionality, but which incorporate a more explicit degree of reflexivity towards the documentary genre. These mock-documentaries represent the 'hostile' appropriation of documentary codes and conventions, and can be said to bring to fruition the 'latent reflexivity' which we argue is inherent to mock-documentary's parody of the documentary project. Despite their apparent subject matter, these are texts where the documentary form itself is the actual subject. Here the filmmakers are attempting to engage directly with factual discourse, and effectively to encourage viewers to develop a critical awareness of the partial, constructed nature of documentary.

Mock-documentaries such as *Forgotten Silver* (1995) could be placed within this degree, because of their status as documentary hoaxes; texts which have generated a reflexivity towards documentary outside of the intentions of the filmmakers. It is important to reiterate that our schema of degrees is largely based on an assessment of the preferred readings constructed by these texts. As discussed in the previous chapter, *Forgotten Silver* clearly illustrates the importance of the role played by audiences (and their wider viewing context) in constructing reflexive interpretations of mock-documentaries. As noted in previous chapters, this was a television programme intended, by its makers, as a parody of aspects of New Zealand culture. It has been read by sections of its audience variously as a *critique* of New Zealand media culture and as an exercise in *deconstructing* the expectations or assumptions of factual discourse.

We have found that mock-documentaries which are designed to operate within degree 3 are, to date, comparatively uncommon. The mock-documentary form seems to be more typically used by filmmakers to parody aspects of popular culture, particularly media culture, than to encourage viewers to question their adherence to the assumptions and expectations associated with documentary. The examples of degree 3 texts discussed in this chapter, then, suggest both the *potential* of the mock-documentary form to serve as a site for the active subversion of factual discourse and the degree to which this potential has remained relatively underdeveloped.

David Holzman's Diary (1967)

This is a comparatively early example of a mock-documentary, but it still remains one of the few to deal openly with a range of issues inherent to the documentary project – such as the implicit collaboration between filmmaker and subject, and the nature of the relationship between filmed images and reality. This film also offers a more personalised narrative than later examples of degree 3 texts. Presented as a *cinéma vérité* document, and filmed in black and white, it presents the story of an attempt of a young filmmaker, David Holzman (L. M. Kit Carson), to put his life in order by making a diary using a camera and a tape recorder.

The film is set over the course of eight days in July 1967,[1] and is ostensibly prompted by recent unemployment and the arrival of a draft notice. In order to uncover the 'truth' about himself and his relationships, David explicitly calls upon the statement by Jean-Luc Godard that film is 'truth 24 times a second', a given which he adheres to despite the frustrations of its explicit failure, and an apparent understanding of the complexity of photographic 'reality'. Throughout the film he acts especially on Godard's statement that the camera is capable of recording the true nature of people and events,[2] and implicitly appears to believe that his life has no meaning outside of these recordings.

The film consists mainly of extended monologues to camera by David, and long tracking shots around the neighbourhood where the film is set. These exterior scenes are filmed, at times in slow-motion, either from a car or from David walking along the sidewalk. These provide some information about his neighbourhood, and the surrounding streets, as he points out buildings. The exterior shots which are without commentary are the most effective – they are the most like 'pure documentary' because they escape the subjectivity which David cannot help imposing on images of his relationships with other people (Hogue, 1993: 3).

The other interesting sequences in the film feature a number of simple special effects, which David uses to capture 'reality'. There is the montage

where he attempts to represent all of the images which 'passed through
and into' his head in an evening; a rapid series of shots of the programmes
he watched on television, with a shot for each time the image on the
screen changed.[3] The resulting montage is extremely dense, and, although
some of the images can be identified only if the sequence is slowed down,
most are familiar enough to be instantly identifiable. There are shots from
a number of commercials featuring well-known products, glimpses of
what appear to be news reports of civil rights protests and the Vietnam
War, and snapshots of many of the popular television programmes of the
period (including *Batman, Star Trek,* the *Merv Griffin Show,* a Liberace
performance on the *Dean Martin Show,* the *Joey Bishop Show* and a
Shirley Temple movie). This sequence obviously highlights the fact that
David belongs to the first American generation to grow up with television, but it also indirectly suggests the importance which images increasingly have in constructing that generation's perspective on the world. In
other words, the montage records the importance of mediated images,
and the assumptions and expectations which they bring, for David (and
by extension, the audience).

A second special effect is used in scenes later in the film where David
walks down the street, and gets his final phone message from his now
ex-girlfriend Penny, while filming with a fish-eye lens. These scenes
mark the point where he attempts finally to retreat into the (now explicitly distorted) representation of his world which he is constructing on
celluloid. The distortion of the lens also represents something of the
warping of control which David starts to feel over his own life. In both
senses, these are *expressionist* sequences which none the less still adhere
to the illusion that what is being filmed is 'reality'.[4] David enjoys the
effect of the lens, playing with it like a child with a new toy, and this perhaps also suggests the limitations of what he has been able to achieve as
a filmmaker. His obsession with the camera destroys his relationship
with Penny, and he is unable to use the recording instrument to suggest
a way to 'fix' his life – he can only 'play' with the camera as he would
with a friend.

David from the beginning of the film develops just this kind of relationship with his film equipment. An early sequence 'introduces' the
equipment he uses to construct most of his diary.

> [a white screen, followed by a variety of specifications shots from a camera
> manual, including directions for how to hold for hand-held shooting, with the
> following voice-over:]

'I would like you to meet my friend, my eyes, my camera. Eclair NPR, Noiseless

Portable Reflex camera. She weighs about eighteen pounds. I carry her on my shoulder or under my arm, wherever I go.
This is the Angenieux 9.5 to 95 lens, through which Eclair takes a pictures of everything 24 times every second.
This is a Niagara tape recorder, and this is the lavelier mike, which I use for recording inside.'
[blank screen]
'When I go out on my adventures, I tie all of my friends onto me, and this is how we look.'
   [amateur black and white still of David and equipment, in front of building, with two people watching from the balcony behind him]
'As we walkabout, seeing and hearing, getting it all down.'

This 'relationship' with his recording friends becomes a frustrating one for David. As Hogue notes, David has an 'obsessive, complex and contradictory attitude toward photography'. He is fascinated with the possibility that the instruments can provide him with an accurate record of his life, one which he can use to determine its 'truth'. However, he also seems to acknowledge that images are capable of lying, of distorting rather than merely reflecting reality (Hogue, 1993: 3). This is a tension which is also central to the documentary project (as discussed in Chapter 1). Eventually the tension between what he wishes from his 'friends' and their inherent limitations becomes too much for him, and he angrily rebukes the camera for not providing him with the truths that he feels it should. The film ends with David's equipment having been stolen, and with him reduced to representing himself using a series of photography booth snapshots and a scratchy homemade record. His obsession with his camera has led him to disappear into its frame, and without it David ceases to exist.[5]

David's obsession with the seductive possibilities of his camera literally frames his relationships with other people, especially with women. As Hogue notes, the film suggest that David 'prefers reel women to real women' (Hogue: 1993, 3). He introduces his girlfriend, Penny, to the camera firstly through a series of her fashion photographs; she is a model. Penny is clearly uncomfortable with David's insistence on filming aspects of their life together, something which he cannot comprehend. In some sense, her character represents the dichotomy between public and private worlds, between 'reel' and 'real' women.

Penny's first 'live' scene has her attempting to escape from David's lens, and literally squirming in a chair as he circles her and positions her within the frame in artful compositions (including one with a poster for Alfred Hitchcock's *Suspicion* (1941) on the wall in the background). She is

clearly disturbed by David's attempts to transform their personal relationship into a movie (however 'real' David assumes his recording to be).
David says he cannot understand how she can happily model for hours,
but refuses to let *him* film her, when all he wants is herself. He says he
cannot 'get her sense of privacy', and tries to win her collaboration by
intoning to her the documentarist slogan 'the camera is your friend' and
suggesting that she should just ignore it.

Despite Penny's explicit objections, David repeatedly violates her
wishes and attempts to 'capture' her on film. In the scene where she finally
leaves him, she wakes to find that he has filmed her asleep in the nude (as
he attempts to fix her on celluloid, like one of the pristine rooms behind
glass at the Smithsonian). Eventually David is reduced to being a peeping
tom outside her apartment window, where he is caught by a police officer. This is an implicit reference to the film which apparently served as a
direct inspiration for director McBride: Michael Powell's *Peeping Tom*
(1960) (Thompson and Christie, 1990: 18).

Peeping Tom has as its main character a serial killer (named Mark Lewis)
who derives sexual gratification from filmed documents of himself killing
his victims (with a blade hidden within one of the legs of his camera
stand). He is himself the victim of a father's obsession with attempting to
construct a complete filmed record of Mark's childhood, an obsession
which has literally driven his son insane. Effectively this 1960 film suggests
the intellectualism, coldness and ultimately violence inherent to the documentary project.[6] In *David Holzman's Diary*, David's obsession with
recording the truth of a moment contains implicit elements of sadism, as
he drives his girlfriend crazy with his lack of respect for her privacy.

David's preference for 'reel' woman is clearly behind his voyeuristic
fascination with a girl who lives in an apartment building opposite his. He
films her through her window at night, speculating on her television
tastes and habits, and names her 'Sandra' (having taken the initial of her
Christian name from her letterbox). 'Sandra' mostly exists in the frame of
her window.[7] She is a 'reel woman', one who is distant enough for David
to have a degree of narrative control over, although David also eventually
follows her down the street. Significantly, his filming of Sandra mostly
occurs when he has had an argument or is frustrated in his attempts
to communicate with Penny. In a sense, he retreats to the 'reel' woman
who offers an uncomplicated (one-way and effectively non-existent)
alternative relationship.[8]

David's filming of Sandra leads to a creepy scene where he follows
either her or another woman off the subway, and up the street. The

woman becomes increasingly uncomfortable at his presence and eventually turns around and tells him to 'beat it'. As she confronts him, the
camera suddenly goes out-of-focus, a perfect visualisation of David's
uncertainty when confronted by the irritated response of a real woman.[9]
The dichotomy between 'reel' and 'real' woman is reinforced by David's
encounter with a woman from the neighbourhood who attempts to chat
up David from her car. She is framed by the window of her car, he refers
to her as a 'street goddess', and unlike Penny she is completely at ease with
his camera. He firstly explains (in voice-over) that he has arranged to
'interview' her when his 'camera is loaded'.[10] In a conversation rich with
Freudian irony, she asks about the size of his equipment, and eventually
the scene ends when his camera equipment fails (and their intimate
filmed encounter draws a crowd).

Perhaps the most interesting encounter in the film is the interview
which David conducts with a friend, who challenges the assumptions
which frame David's filmed diary. In a direct contrast to David's beliefs in
the purity and 'truth' of capturing people and events on film, his friend
offers a different (vaguely postmodernist) notion of filmed images: 'You
don't understand the basic principle. As soon as you start filming something, whatever happens in front of the camera is not reality any more. It
becomes something else. It becomes a movie.' Like a critic, his friend
complains that neither David's nor Penny's life is a good movie ('I'm sure
you can write a better script than that. Your life is not a very good script').
He specifically deconstructs the notion that events and people can be
filmed naturally once the presence of a camera is known, suggesting
instead that when you are aware that you are being filmed 'your decisions
stop being moral decisions and become aesthetical decisions'. This is a
statement which echoes the complaints which have been made against
observational documentaries since their rise in popularity in the 1960s.
David, he argues, cannot gain the truth through film (in direct opposition
to David's faith in Godard's insistence that film is 'truth 24 times a
second'). Interestingly, he also proposes that David could get closer to the
truth only if he stood completely naked in front of his camera for hours,
in order to totally break down any pretences. (This is effectively what
David then tries with a sleeping Penny, without her consent – an act that
ends their relationship.) Otherwise, he insists, David will get only half-
truths, which are worse than lies.

This assault on David's motivation for filming is left unchallenged,
even by David, as his friend refuses to let him control the encounter (at
the end of his monologue he directs David to 'cut', a complete inversion

of the power relationship which David constructs with Penny). The encounter offers the most explicit articulation of the basic tension within *David Holzman's Diary* between Godard's axiom, and the notion that filmed images can offer only a partial and subjective representation of reality. This is a tension which drives the film's narrative, as David moves from a naive belief in the first perspective to a grudging and frustrated acceptance of the second. As Hogue argues, David's 'strength is not the image of reality, but the reality of the image' (Hogue: 1993, 3), and ultimately *David Holzman's Diary* offers a deconstruction of a (documentary) filmmaker's faith in the purity of any relationship which photographic images may claim with 'reality'.

The Falls (1980)

The Falls is a mock-documentary by British filmmaker Peter Greenaway. The work of an auteur whose films have traditionally been challenging for the mainstream audience, it requires an active and critical engagement on the part of its viewers. It explicitly develops a reflexivity towards the classic expositional form of documentary, asking its audience to question their adherence to assumptions and expectations of factual discourse. Constructed over a five-year period, and combining both original and found film material, this three-hour film develops the mock-documentary tendencies of Greenaway's earlier short films *Vertical Features Remake* (1976) and *A Walk Through H* (1978).[11]

The Falls is an example of the wider tradition of experimental filmmaking that looks to investigate matters of form and content. The film was partly intended to parody the work of colleagues at the Britain's Central Office of Information (where Greenaway had worked):

Here were people collating absurd statistics about the number of sheepdogs in South Wales or Japanese restaurants in Ipswich, so I thought I could put the classic BBC techniques, the paraphernalia of apparently 'real' information, to entirely fictional ends. [*The Falls* is] a total travesty of the documentary tradition. (quoted by Johnston 1994)

Greenaway had studied that documentary tradition with the British Film Institute, an experience which apparently led him to grow disillusioned with any notion of documentary 'truth'. 'It seemed to me more ethically acceptable to say "This is a lie, this is a fiction, but let's try to tell the truth within fiction" (always acknowledged as fiction). None of this pretense of the English system' (Lawrence, 1997: 11). *The Falls*, then, was designed as a deliberate subversion of the codes and conventions of British documentary. It adopts the specific form of government-produced documentaries and effectively undermines that form by exhaustively applying it to a fictional subject.

The film opens with blue-tinged footage as a low-level camera races over a rocky field. Superimposed over this footage is scrolling blue text, consisting of a listing of names which all have the letters 'Fall' in their surname. The main title to the film is followed by white text, which is read by an authoritative male voice-over.

The ninety-two people represented in this film all have names that begin with the letters 'FALL'.

The names are taken from the latest edition of the Standard Directory published every three years by the committee investigating the Violent Unknown Event – the VUE for short.

The names are presented in the alphabetical order in which they stand in the Directory and represent a reasonable cross-section of the nineteen million other names that are contained there.

This is followed by a further screen of text: 'The FALLS is presented in ninety-two different languages of which this is the most recent English version.'

The remainder of the film consists of ninety-two segments, each offering a thumbnail biography of a name from the alphabetical list. Each segment begins with a black screen, with a large number in orange in the left of the screen, and a name in smaller type underneath. These segment titles are often accompanied by a voice-over presenting a summation of the person and their relationship with the VUE. Each of the persons is particularly identified according to 'gender' (which soon fails to conform to the binary of male–female), age, and any unusual physical attributes caused by the VUE. An intriguing feature of these people's characteristics is the language which they have acquired (or rather, created) as a result of their exposure to the VUE.

These segments include a variety of forms of representation, and a listing of these suggests the lengths to which Greenaway has gone to provide a convincing detail to his fiction. There are exterior shots of landscapes and cityscapes where these VUE victims lived or where they were first afflicted by the VUE; black and white photographs; visual presentation of artefacts such as records; close-ups of diagrams (including a recurring body diagrammatic, with coloured marks showing the position of unusual features caused by the VUE), drawings, illustrations, maps and colour slides made by subjects; and a recurring close-up of a typewriter as it types out the victim's name. Other footage has the appearance of being 'extracted' from black and white newsreels, or home movies (both usually placed within a frame on a black screen), or extracts of films made by people from the directory.[12] In addition to these visuals are occasional shots of interviewees, either in the street or in their own dwellings, reading the testimony they gave to the committee investigating the VUE.

Along with this complex presentation of visual material, these segments collectively use a variety of voice-overs. Voice-over narration is used to present an exhaustive wealth of information. The main voice used is that of a conventional authoritative male, but at times VUE victims themselves are heard, either in the form of recordings or in person as they read their testimony in their VUE language. There are also other voices reading stories and letters and especially a variety of voices of 'translators' (both male and female) who summarise or read verbatim extracts from victims' testimony.

Increasingly throughout the film, there are shots of the various narrators themselves. The later part of the final segment features frequent visits to shots in a projection booth, as narrators speak into a microphone (as if offering real-time commentary for the images), with a projectior running next to them. And there are more informal settings shown for narrators, often seated at a desk in a darkened room, with a desk lamp for illumination as they read aloud. While the studio shots suggest the constructed nature of documentary, these 'home' settings offer more explicit hints of the narrative style of a storyteller.

The voice-over narrations themselves are clear and concise, but each segment may have multiple voices, often overlapping as they summarise other voices, or present updated information. The language is always presented soberly, drawing especially upon scientific rhetoric, but at the same time the connections which are made between characters and the nature of their VUE suffering is very much within the *Monty Python* tradition. There is here the same delight in the rhythms of nonsense language presented as coherent rationality (using the BBC model of factual presentation). The difference is that, unlike *Monty Python, The Falls* does not work to highlight its fictionality using form, relying instead on the audience's ability to discern the absurdity of the *content* of the narration.

The biographies contained within these segments focus on a number of ornithological themes, with most of the information relating to the avian preoccupations of the people themselves (their efforts at mechanical or natural flight[13]), or the abilities or languages they gained from the VUE (many victims, like the committee, exhaustively categorise birds or the bird-like characteristics of VUE sufferers). Increasing reference is made to the films of Alfred Hitchcock, such as *Psycho* (1960), *Marnie* (1964) and especially *The Birds* (1963). Tippi Hedren from *The Birds* is a recurring icon (described as 'another bird victim'), and one victim suggests that the VUE was a 'hoax perpetrated by A. J. Hitchcock to give some credibility to the unsettling and unsatisfying ending of his film *The Birds*'. Among the hypotheses (invariably with apocalyptic ornithological themes) offered by narrators for the origins of the VUE is one called the Theory of the Responsibility of Birds. Gradually developed is the suggestion that the VUE has succeeded in partly transforming its victims into birds.

The absurdity of this proposition stands in direct contrast to the expositional mode of presentation. What becomes apparent is the fragility of this documentary mode, and in particular the tenuous manner in which it seeks to represent its relationship to reality (Lawrence, 1997: 2). All of the biographical segments seek to represent their subjects (the VUE victims) through forms of evidence signified as remnants of their presence. The overall subjects of the film, the VUE itself and the nature of its effects on people are constructed indirectly. It is as if a filmmaker had gone to Hiroshima decades after the 1945 dropping of an American nuclear bomb, and attempted to reconstruct the event purely through the testimony of its surviving victims. The victims offer testimony, evidence is collated and various experts are consulted – all to test the relative validity of a number of hypotheses concerning the origins of the VUE.

In effect, then, the film is a case study in the creativity and partiality of the expositional form of historical inquiry. It becomes obvious that everything depends on the frame of reference, the organising structure, the investigative perspective which is adopted by the documentary makers. The 'lesson' of this case study is that any effort to reconstruct a narrative of the social-historical world can be achieved only through methods which are governed by the concerns of the filmmakers themselves. Greenaway has the segments become progressively more explicit in detailing the absurdity of pretending that there is a clear line between fictional and factual narratives.

As Lawrence argues, the ultimate theme of *The Falls* is a theory of reading (Lawrence, 1997: 43). Documentaries (and any other form of audiovisual narrative) inevitably construct information into easily understood relationships between characters, events and a social-historical milieu. Both filmmakers and audiences rely on an assumption and expectation

that documentary forms of representation entail a more privileged relationship with reality than fictional forms. Over the course of *The Falls*,
however, Greenaway undermines this special status. An increasing
amount of contradictions between the testimony of VUE victims, the
repeated undermining of the validity of experts and scientific knowledge
and of the integrity of audio-visual forms of evidence itself, eventually
forces the viewer to conclude that nothing can be authoritatively understood about the film's subject. In other words, the more we learn about
the VUE, the more we realise that it cannot have happened.

As Lawrence phrases it;

> *The Falls* is the exhaustive, thorough documenting of an event that did not
> happen, which affected people who did not exist, verified by experts who also do
> not exist, and ultimately invented by an array of possible authors, none of whom
> exist either. As the film ends we see that the figure of the author is simultaneously
> everywhere and nowhere, a fiction that can seem particularly sturdy or can dis-
> solve before you. (Lawrence, 1997: 48)

The ultimate effect of the film is a reflexivity towards factual discourse, one
which is carefully and convincingly developed over the course of the film.
By the final segments (especially numbers 88 to 92), the viewer is encouraged to recognise that factual forms of presentation rely on 'a plain,
rhythmic language suitable for the telling of a steady, uncluttered narrative' (number 92) – a language which is no more reliable for presenting
truthful, objective and balanced perspectives on the social-historical world
than that provided by any fictional narrative form.

Man Bites Dog (1992)

The remainder of this chapter discusses the last of the mock-documentaries
covered within this book, one which especially exemplifies the reflexive
potential of the form. *Man Bites Dog* is a multi-layered mock-documentary
produced in 1992 by three Belgian film students: Remy Belvaux, Andre
Bonzel and Benoit Poelvoorde. It is a feature-length film about a serial killer
and the documentary crew who are engaged in filming his everyday life and
killings. The crew start off by simply filming him, but end up becoming
fully implicated in his horrendous deeds. *Man Bites Dog* uses the mock-
documentary form to engage deliberately in a debate about documentary
and, in particular, the authority of the documentary look. The polemic also
highlights the obsession of 'actuality' programmes with the extraordinary

or bizarre. The title itself, *Man Bites Dog*, underlines this focus by referring to the journalistic desire for entertaining and newsworthy stories.[14]

Man Bites Dog plays ruthlessly with the codes and conventions of the documentary screen, in particular that of the observational form. It is perhaps the observational documentary which best illustrates the documentary ideology in terms of what it claims to promise and what we, as viewers, expect from it. As outlined in Chapter 2, observational documentaries expect viewers to take part in the pretence that the camera is not there and to accept the filmmaker's presence as absence. Further, we are asked to participate in the belief that the events presented to us would have unfolded in exactly the same way if the camera had not been present (Nichols, 1994: 95).

It is this 'documentary look', the look that bears knowledge, fact and truth, that is deconstructed and destabilised within *Man Bites Dog*. Through the utilisation of conventions such as the objective 'third person point of view', a documentary gaze or look is set up. As the film opens we watch Ben, the killer and subject of the film, strangle a woman on a train. Framed within such a gaze, it has the appearance of reality, a far cry from the choreographed violence (complete with special effects) of Hollywood blockbusters. With no evidence of the presence of the film crew we are allowed direct access to that which is usually hidden. We become voyeurs, but at a safe distance. Documentary relies on there being a distance for its claims to objectivity. This distance, no matter how small, reinforces the notion that what is being seen is evidential and that we are 'onlookers' rather than participants in the sphere of action.

The 'realism' of the film is heightened in several ways which work to certify this objective documentary look. As well as being filmed in black and white, which serves (in this case) to give an air of authenticity to the film, it also has a 'camcorder' feel to it. Camcorder footage[15] is very popular within current documentary and 'actuality' programming and works to promote the idea of immediacy and the experience of being a 'fly on the wall'. The camcorder is a central component of 'Reality TV', which Dovey describes as factual programmes which use camcorder footage together with reconstructions to construct 'a raw high energy and sensationalist "tabloid TV."' (Dovey, 1995).[16] *Man Bites Dog* both embraces this and comments on it. The film takes as its subject matter a serial killer and joins Reality TV's fascination with the perverse, yet at the same time refuses to sensationalise its subject. *Man Bites Dog* invites viewers to take up this opportunity to engage with this screen form at a different ideological level, rather than remain passive consumers of such texts.

Continuity editing, longshots and mid-range shots are used most effectively in the scenes where Ben is shown at home, with his family at their
shop and during the disposal of the dead bodies. The use of long seamless
shots allows the 'look' to be suitably distanced. The repetition of these
scenes and situations works to reinforce their 'reality' by locating them
within a historical time and place (Nichols, 1991: 41). A capturing of 'naturalistic' sound and lighting, and the use of real people, rather than (paid)
actors further works to promote a sense of realism and factuality. This
final point is underlined by the knowledge that the three students who
made the film also star in it and use their real names: Benoit Poelvoorde
plays Ben the serial killer and so on.

Throughout *Man Bites Dog* the 'direct address' is used effectively as a
means through which Ben can impart his philosophical wisdom (especially within the context of his local pub). This direct address has the
effect of calling into existence an audience for Ben and his life. In an early
scene Ben addresses the camera and crew directly when discussing his
methods for the removal of dead bodies. Looking them straight in the eye
(lens) he explains the importance of assessing the weight, size and bone
density of victims to ensure the correct ratio between the bodies and
materials used to weigh them down. His information conveys the idea
that this procedure ensures that bodies will remain safely at the bottom of
lakes and rivers.

Documentary participants usually address viewers directly in the
knowledge that they are being invited to act upon information being
shared with them. While giving the impression of a documentary mode
of direct address, in another sense Ben seems to be ignoring the audience,
giving little consideration as to how we may react to what he says or what
he does.[17] The film's deconstruction of the documentary look is successful, in part, because of this refusal to acknowledge the implications of a
direct mode of address. This has three possible implications. Firstly, it
positions the crew as part of the action and narrative, rather than being
detached and outside of it. Secondly, it allows the viewer to recognise both
Ben *and the crew* as the object of the documentary gaze/look. Thirdly,
there is an ambiguity over exactly what knowledge viewers are being
invited to act upon.

Although the film attempts the establishment of a documentary mode
of presentation, early on that very form is de-stabilised. This is attempted
through parody and burlesque, and through a subversion of the traditional conventions. Often these moments are humorous, but they
also have a more serious implication in terms of the way in which they

can draw attention to the constructed nature of documentary's truth claims and myths.

The early observational style scenes which allow lingering, but static, shots of Ben and his family soon give way to moments in which this 'documentariness' is disrupted. For example, while filming Ben dumping a body over a bridge the camera (and our look) wobbles, thus alerting us of the actual presence of the camera. In a following scene, Ben attacks a postman in a darkened shop doorway. In the outer edges of the shot, the crew's reporter Remy can be seen and heard shouting 'Lights!'. Thus we are made aware not only of the camera and the crew but also of the artificial nature of such observational documentary moments.

As outlined in Chapter 2, documentary's claim of objectivity is perhaps one of its most treasured and protected myths and one that *Man Bites Dog* moves to dismantle. The film charts the movement of the crew from 'objective recorders' to active participants in Ben's activities. At first it is just a fleeting acknowledgement that they exist. For example, Ben makes a visit to Jenny, who is a prostitute. As Ben rings the bell he turns to the crew and asks if they 'got home okay' after their evening in the pub. He comments that they 'must be bushed'. In Jenny's flat the crew's presence is once again acknowledged, when she turns to them and asks what they would like to drink. These early signs of inclusion soon give way to scenes in which the crew begin to participate more fully. After Ben has killed an African-American man on a building site, he recruits Remy to help him to move the body. Remy starts to appear more consistently within shots and the crew seem to be moving from 'outsiders' looking in on the events to 'insiders' who are part of the action. The distance between the camera (viewer) and object begins to diminish both metaphorically and literally, and the documentary look starts to be de-objectified.

The crew's participation in the events allows for some humorous moments. Ben has chosen as his next victim an old lady living in a block of flats, and recruits the crew in his bid to gain entry to the old woman's flat. As the woman opens the door, he introduces himself as part of a television crew who are making a documentary on 'loneliness in high rise apartments'. As he sits down next to the old woman he requests the crew to start filming the 'interview'. This is funny not only because they themselves are in fact a documentary crew, but also because of the way it draws attention to the reputation that some documentarists have for using deception to gain access which would otherwise be denied.

The crew are not merely recording an act of murder but are themselves part of this act. After Ben has killed the woman, he and Remy are shown searching the flat for cash. Ben remarks, to Remy's obvious delight, that there will 'be plenty for everyone!' It is as if these events seal the developing collaboration between Ben and the crew. Outside, in the street, the status of this new relationship is explored. Ben declares that killing the old woman has 'whet his appetite' and offers to take the crew for a celebratory meal. Remy seems interested, yet the crew hesitate, apparently pondering the implications of Ben's friendship. Just as it looks as though they are about to reclaim their status as (objective) outsiders, there is a cut to the next shot which reveals the crew and Ben in the restaurant.

Documentaries are often criticised for exploiting 'real' people for their own ends. The participants typically do not get paid, they have little editorial control and are often in a powerless position. In *Man Bites Dog* this convention is consciously subverted. During the restaurant scene, Remy tells Ben that they are running out of money and may not be able to carry on with the film. To this Ben replies that he will fund the film, thus ensuring himself a screen presence. His position changes from that of a powerless 'object' of study through to one of power and control; he becomes the film's producer. This has the effect of, once again, subtly shifting the object of study from himself to himself and the crew.

During a shoot-out in a disused factory, the sound man, Patrick, is shot. Patrick's body is disposed of without ceremony and, as usual, the day's events are subject to a post-mortem in the local pub. Again, it is both Ben and the crew who are the object of scrutiny. Ben and Remy share the screen space while the presence of the cameraman, Andre, is indicated through a glass of beer sitting on the counter.

The death of Patrick allows for a moment of parody. On returning from the pub, Remy sets up the camera and delivers a memorial monologue. With a bottle at his side and tears in his eyes Remy proceeds to explain that the job was always tinged with danger; death is an occupational hazard that could strike any of them. However, they would continue the film for Patrick, his girlfriend Marie-Paul and for their unborn child (a eulogy which is hilariously revealed to be meangingless when Remy gives the almost word-for-word same speech after a further crew member is killed). This moment specifically parodies the authors of war documentaries and reporters who seem so willing to put themselves in obvious danger in order to bring the 'truth' back home to the public. Here, there is little talk of courage or sacrifice and the death is almost trivialised. Patrick did not die for the 'truth', and his lack of a proper burial not only makes fun of such documentary claims but also effectively reveals their insincerity.

Until now the crew have been only indirectly participating in the killings, as accomplices in the disposal of bodies. As yet they have not actually killed anyone themselves. As they become more actively involved with Ben so they become more and more detached from their original roles as observers. While they cruise a suburban street Ben challenges the crew to choose a house and the next victim. It is a choice that has consequences, and the crew are expected to play a part. This is an interesting moment as their victims, the members of a white, middle-class nuclear family, are the typical (ideal) viewers of television documentary. As the crew become active collaborators with Ben, their complicity forces a collapse of the audience's distance from the subject. Once inside the house, Vincent (the new sound man) heightens Ben's enjoyment of killing by capturing the sound of Ben breaking the husband's neck, and Andre uses his camera and lights to help track down the young son of the family, who has run off into the night. These events could be read as the symbolic death of the ideal television documentary viewer and of the safe distance which they are usually guaranteed through a participation in the discourses of objectivity. Here, this objective distance implodes back on to the audience. As we get closer to the subject, we become more aware of the constructed nature of the documentary look, and we can no longer take for granted its promise to allow access to the real without the consequences of having been there.

The final loss of Ben's and the crew's original roles and positions is symbolically played out in a scene in Ben's hideout, an old derelict warehouse. As they arrive in the building they hear movements in the floor above and Ben tells Remy that 'The Nightingale' (presumably an enemy of his) is present. Gunshots ring out and a second crew member is shot down (Franco). A chase across rooftops presents a spectacle that would not look out of place in any 'Reality-TV' programme. On return to the house, Ben and the crew encounter another documentary crew, there to film 'The Nightingale'. They are clearly 'rivals' of the crew (working on video rather than film), and possibly from a rival network 'Reality-TV' programme. They 'disarm' the video crew of the tools of their trade, effectively rendering them impotent. Without their cameras, they have no protective lens from behind which they can safely but vicariously take part in the action. The video crew are now merely another group of potential victims, and are quickly killed with all of 'our' crew participating.

There has been an almost total inversion of the conventional collaborative situation which was established at the beginning of the film. The dead film crew effectively represent the objective, distanced ethical role prescribed for documentarians. The implicit metaphor at the heart of the film, that documentary filmmaking ('shooting a doco') is equivalent to killing, is now explicitly realised (McNeil, 1993: 30). Having taken their acceptance of Ben's moral worldview to its logical conclusion, they join him on what can only be described as a rampage.

Remy and the new sound man, Vincent, are fully implicated now and the gang are firstly shown in the pub playing a game called 'dead baby boy'. This game involves an olive and a sugar cube tied together with a piece of string, which is then dropped in a gin and tonic. The aim of the game is to have your 'baby' rise to the surface last. It symbolises the 'ballasting of corpses' and during the game Ben refers to his earlier lecture on this subject, testing Remy and Vincent. Once again Andre's presence is indicated only through his glass. After several rounds, they leave the pub in search of action. They stop at an apartment block, and as Ben dances in a drunken stupor, we see for the first time the silhouette of Andre and his camera. They climb the stairs and burst into the kitchen of a young couple, caught naked. What follows is the brutal gang rape of the woman, with her partner forced to watch. Everyone takes a turn, including Andre (whose face we never see).[18]

After Remy has raped the woman, the camera frames him for a brief moment. There is a look of total disgust on his face. It is as if he has suddenly realised what he has done and what he has become. But it is also a look that realises there is no turning back. The whole scene seems gratuitous and unnecessary and as they wake up in the morning surrounded by death, there is little room for humour. As Remy comes to realise what he has done, so too, we as viewers begin to realise what we have been watching. 'The camera gaze that actively sides with agency of death legitimates itself through the same codes as the taking of life in the first place' (Nichols, 1991: 85). The documentary gaze, and by implication our voyeurism, are implicated in the deaths.[19] Documentary asks us not only to engage with its representations but also to act upon those knowledges. Perhaps *Man Bites Dog* is unsettling because it is presenting to us truths or knowledges which we would rather not engage with or act upon.

Man Bites Dog, as with the most effective mock-documentaries, invites us to participate in a documentary mode of engagement, *as though it were a documentary*. In doing so, it creates a space within which viewers can negotiate a reading which deconstructs the documentary look. This is not a one-sided critique of the documentary form, but rather a deconstruction which questions not only the authority of documentary, but also the position of documentary makers and viewers. Old dichotomies such as the

objective/subjective and insider/outsider that have shaped both the production and reception of the documentary are challenged within *Man Bites
Dog*, specifically through the complicity of the film crew in the killings.
As the distance between the subject (Ben) and the observers (the crew)
disappear, the documentary look finds a new subject. The whole process of
documentary production comes under scrutiny and open to question.

In joining Ben in his 'work', the crew lose the safety of their outsider
status, and so too we as viewers are left without the protection of the documentary look – a look that is supposed to be objective and distanced,
allowing voyeurism without the risks of being located within the action.
The loss of a 'neutral, 'objective' perspective in *Man Bites Dog* works to
de-stabilise the authority of the documentary gaze.

Documentaries do not merely present the social world but comment
upon it. Since the early days of the Grierson movement, documentarists
have not only 'recorded' but have interpreted, analysed and commented
upon the social world (Winston, 1995: 11). Even the purest observational
documentary has at its core an argument which may give indications of
the ideological or ethical perspective of the documentarist but also produces certain ideological or moral subject positions. That this moral positioning may be overlooked is in itself an indication of how successful
documentary has been in passing its versions of reality as naturally occurring within that reality rather than a construction derived from it.

One of the unsettling aspects of *Man Bites Dog* is its refusal to take up
fully a position in which Ben and the killings are explicitly condemned. It
is not that the film takes an *amoral* stance on the murders, but rather it is
ambiguous about its position. In effect, it refuses to speak with the
authoritative moral voice traditionally associated with documentary.
Instead it leaves us with a series of ambiguous moments from which we as
viewers have to construct our own moral response.

It is possible to trace the textual tendencies in *Man Bites Dog* within a
number of examples of the 'subgenre' of serial killer films. Among the
most significant reference points for serial killer cinema are *Psycho* (1960)
and *Peeping Tom*. Both implicate the voyeuristic tendencies of their audience within their representations of serial murder. Taubin notes that the
recent generation of serial killer movies are generally not able to live up to
the complexity of the model presented in *Psycho* (Taubin, 1991: 16),
which is effectively a black comedy perpetrated on viewers. The audience
is unwittingly drawn into the world of a serial killer, then left with the
implications of their identification with him, when he is revealed as the
killer at the end of the film. *Peeping Tom*, meanwhile, makes explicit the

links between voyeurism and sadism. As mentioned earlier in this chapter, it features a filmmaker who derives sexual pleasure from viewing films he has made of the moments when he kills young women. The implicit message is that viewers of the film perform a similar ritual, and must share some of the same perversions.

Both fictional and fact-based narratives about serial killers have become an increasing part of popular culture, particularly in the United States. What are central to many of these portrayals are killers represented as pathologised individuals often from broken homes or as victims of child sexual abuse. These representations typically reinforce the stereotype of the serial killer as an abnormality outside of mainstream society. In doing so, they take a particular type of moral position which has certain political and social implications. In *Man Bites Dog* a very different representation is made available. Ben is presented as a cultured and educated middle-class male. Far from being a product of a deviant upbringing, his family embody 'normality'. Further, Ben himself is in a long-term stable relationship and seems to have no other anti-social traits. This 'normalisation' of the serial killer is reinforced by the repeated shots of Ben with his family, with his partner and in the pub, all 'normal' everyday ways of being. This naturalisation of Ben attempts a subversion of the usual moral positioning that is produced by the documentary gaze. It works against what we expect a documentary to do: that is, to comment upon (and condemn) what society has deemed evil.

Ultimately, *Man Bites Dog* seems to suggest that there is a kind of obscenity, or at least questionable moral attitude, underlying the ideological pretensions associated with factual discourse. The distanced, objective view which the documentary genre claims to hold is revealed as a thin veneer covering a far more mundane and easily corrupted moral agenda. As McNeil (with self-conscious irony) suggests, *Man Bites Dog* should be censored, 'not because unbalanced individuals may become sociopathic after seeing it, but because they might want to become documentarists'.

Notes

1   The film only suggests the summer of 1967 through David's stating of the date of each 'diary entry', and partly through faintly overheard news reports of the Vietnam War and ghetto riots.

2   This is also an axiom which effectively summarises the rationale behind the

development of the observational mode of documentary. (See Chapter 1 for our summary of Nichols's modes of documentary representation.)

3   The montage has David's voice-over introduction for the first few seconds, then is entirely silent.

4   This is an aspect of the film which perhaps also mirrors the group of documentary sequences which Nichols groups under the label of 'performative mode'. (See Chapter 2.)

5   At least, David ceases to exist for the audience. There is an interesting ambiguity to the ending of the film. David's existence is no longer recorded, and recognised, by the all-important media eye that the camera represents; but there is also the possibility that he was been forcibly 'weaned' from this dependence on 'friends' who can only ever reflect his own subjectivity as a filmmaker.

6   Mark himself seeks to make a documentary of his killings and the police investigations. There is a link here to *Man Bites Dog* (1992), discussed later in this chapter, and its link between cinematic representation and a voyeuristic fascination with killing.

7   In another implicit reference, this closely resembles the sequences from Hitchcock's *Rear Window* (1954), where James Stewart and Grace Kelly speculate on the lives of the people they see through the windows visible through Stewart's own 'frame'.

8   Because Sandra is a fetishized object, David is able to elevate her above the ordinary and refers to her in abstract artistic terms. He compares her to a model in Italian paintings, and makes reference to François Truffaut's comments about Debbie Reynolds in *Singin' in the Rain* (1952).

9   David eventually loses his fascination with 'Sandra' in a similar way. After his final failure at reconciliation with Penny he attempts to telephone Sandra (as he films her answering the phone through her window). She does not recognise the name David has given her, tells him he has a wrong number and hangs up on him.

10   She has been present as a blurred figure in the background of the still photo of David in the sequence where he introduces his camera 'friends'.

11   These have been described by Johnston as attempting their own classification procedures on a fictionalised universe 'with a mad logic reminiscent of Swift and Lewis Carroll'. Lawrence argues that Greenaway's early films such as *H is for Horse* (1974), *Windows* (1974) and *Dear Phone* (1976) can also be seen as virtual parodies of English documentary of the time (Lawrence, 1997: 11).

12   These film extracts include samples from Greenaway's own short films.

13   Victims share a fascination with aircraft, kites, hang-gliders and experiments with natural abilities for flight that many gain from the VUE – including trials with other creatures (such as dogs and cats).

14   'Dog bites man' is nothing exceptional and hence does not constitute news, but 'Man bites dog' is and does. Journalists are keenly aware that they are required to hunt out 'Man bites dog' stories (Winston, 1995: 214).

15 The 'camcorder look' can be characterised as one which is grainy and has a cluttered screen, jump cuts, discontinuous or incomplete narratives, and so on.

16 See Chapter 2 for a fuller discussion of Reality TV and its position within the documentary genre.

17 In part, this is because Ben seems to take for granted the idea that the presence of the documentary crew itself confers a degree of legitimacy on his 'profession'.

18 It is perhaps through the character of the cameraman, Andre, that the audience is implicitly implicated in the action throughout the film.

19 However, it is also the case that this same gaze could be seen as commenting on such discourses. See for example David Monaghan's discussion of his documentary *Executions*, which has caused much controversy for breaking the screen taboo against showing real deaths. 'My bloody documentary is the antidote to the Hollywood hype dumbing and dripping blood from the shelves of our video stores' (Monaghan, 1995: 31).

Conclusion

Documentary is undergoing various transformations in response to a variety of external and internal challenges. This process, although to some extent inherent to the form since its origins, has more recently resulted in a number of new hybrid documentary formats that effectively problematise traditional notions of fact and fiction as distinct entities. They can be characterised as border genres which inhabit the space between the still potent public perception of a fact/fiction dichotomy. Mock-documentary is one of the more interesting and significant of these screen forms, in large part because it plays in the space 'in-between' and works to subvert the fundamental discourses that underpin the documentary genre.

Documentary's privileged status derives from a sense that documentary is distinct from fictional screen forms. Its truth claims are based on the notion of referentiality: that there is a direct relationship between the image and the referent, and further that it is only documentary that can construct such a direct relationship with the real. As we have argued, these claims are based on documentary's close association with the discourses of factuality and sobriety. Ultimately, documentary also relies on the wider discourses of photography and the assumed power and ability of the camera to access and portray reality.

Both reflexive and performative documentary problematise documentary's reliance on the power of its referentiality. These modes offer the notion that documentary has an inherently partial and constructed nature that depends heavily on the interpretative framework adopted by the filmmaker. Like the drama-documentary, such texts can easily be seen to expand the possibilities for representation within documentary. Drama-documentary allows for greater fictional representation, while still being closely aligned to the assumptions and expectations of factual discourse. In effect, the reflexive mode and drama-documentary texts challenge the notion of fact and fiction as distinct entities, and blur concepts of 'truth' and 'fact'.

The performative mode takes this even further through its conscious turn away from the referential role of documentary. Its playfulness undermines the objective stance taken by documentary, and challenges the audience to move beyond narrow conceptions of truth. However, reflexive and performative modes are still seen as 'acceptable' because they openly acknowledge what has always been implicit within documentary: that there are contradictions between its claims to truth and the fact that the filmmaker inevitably and necessarily needs to impose a structuring argument on a documentary text's portrayal of reality.

While these modes problematise documentary representations of the socio-historical world, they do not challenge what is the essential basis of documentary: that is, its claim to offer a direct referent to the real world. Perhaps the reflexive and performative modes are, in fact, not that radical after all, and do not have mock-documentary's potential to go to the core of the documentary genre. While reflexive and performative documentaries show how elastic the truth is, and work to destabilise any adherence to the notion that there is one Truth, they do not question the assumption that there is a truth to be gained.

Mock-documentary arguably provides the greatest challenge in terms of what documentary claims to be. It provides a direct contest to the truth claims made by documentary on the basis of the power of the image, and its referentiality. It takes up the ground of the reflexive and performative documentary, furthering the challenge to any assumed fact/fiction dichotomy, and extending the range of representational strategies available to filmmakers. It deliberately raises issues about the nature of representations and the claims which documentaries present.

One of the aims of this book has been to develop a theoretical framework through which mock-documentary can be analysed, and in particular through which it can be distinguished from other fact-fiction screen forms such as drama-documentary, Reality TV and docu-soap. Our objective has been to describe and identify the range of mock-documentary texts and in the process to illuminate the differing relationships such texts build between texts, audiences and the discourse of factuality. It has not been our intention to provide a fixed or static taxonomy of different (idealised) mock-documentary types, but rather to explore and analyse the complexity that distinguishes this broad corpus of texts.

In claiming that the mock-documentary is now a recognised screen form with a coherent corpus of texts, it would be tempting to proclaim for it the status of a new 'genre'. Certainly our approach to the study of the mock-documentary, involving a focus on integrating the intentions of the mock-documentary filmmaker, the representations which they offer as a corpus of texts and the conventional roles which are constructed for their viewers is consistent with much genre criticism. 'Genre may be defined as patterns/forms/styles/structures which transcend individual films and which supervise both their construction by the filmmaker and their reading by an audience' (Tom Ryall, quoted in Neale, 1980: 7).

To some extent, we have been able to identify particular patterns in form, various stylistic traits, and distinctive roles constructed for the viewer. We suggest it is possible to argue that in most examples of mock-documentary (with the obvious exceptions of hoaxes) there is an understanding, or implicit contract, between the filmmaker and the viewer, another key characteristic of a genre.

However, it needs to be acknowledged that the attempt to discuss mock-documentary in purely generic terms would neglect key characteristics of these texts – in particular, the very fluid nature of the form. We would argue that it is more productive to think of mock-documentary as a *discourse*: informed and shaped through the particular relationships it constructs with documentary proper, with the discourses of factuality, and especially through the complexity of its engagement with viewers. To conceive of mock-documentary as a genre would ultimately lead us to obscure the diversity of textual strategies which fall under this umbrella, and to diminish the shifting nature of the form. In (tentatively) conceptualising the form as a discourse we are suggesting that the various relationships which mock-documentary constructs with documentary rhetorics, and the inherent implications of these relationships, cannot be wholly contained within the theoretical and analytical frameworks currently on offer within genre theory.

We have provided an initial schema through which to begin the process of identifying and analysing the ways in which mock-documentary relates to, and critically comments upon, the documentary form. This initial categorisation of mock-documentary texts into three 'degrees' is intended to demonstrate the complexity and diversity of this growing screen form. No doubt our schema will rapidly prove inadequate to properly detail what is still an emerging form. As we have argued, mock-documentary has been able to respond rapidly, and inventively, to the changes taking place within the documentary genre – for example, with its witty commentary on the comparatively recent emergence of docu-soap (*Waiting for Guffman, The Games*).

While our approach seeks to collectively examine the intentions of the filmmaker(s), the specific textual strategies which they adopt and the roles constructed for the audience in order to understand fully the distinctiveness of the mock-documentary form, we give particular emphasis to the last of these three aspects. We argue that all mock-documentary texts contain the potential for critical reflexivity, as an inherent part of their appropriation of documentary aesthetics, and that it is this role constructed for the viewer that consistently marks the mock-documentary out from other recent fact-fiction screen forms.

Central to our understanding of the mock-documentary form is an appreciation of the multi-layered possibilities offered by parody. The general intention of the form is to 'mock', and the role constructed for the audience allows the viewer to interpret and engage with each text in a number of ways. Through a foregrounding of humour, parody allows viewers to enjoy the pleasures of being 'in on the joke'; to appreciate and engage with the 'mocking of the subject of the parody. Mock-documentary assumes a sophisticated viewer able to recognise and participate in the form's largely parodic agenda; in other words, a viewer both familiar with the codes and conventions of documentary and ready to accept their comedic treatment.

Yet parody is double-edged, its playful nature often working in tandem with a more openly critical agenda. While parody can be read as a homage or appreciation of its mimic, it also harbours an invitation for audiences to reflect critically upon the object of the mimic. Every mock-documentary similarly contains an invitation to the viewer to take up this critical stance towards the object of the parody: the documentary.

In degree 1 mock-documentary texts we can see the playful appreciation of documentary, and of certain cultural icons, prioritised over any critical agenda. These texts still contain an invitation to reflect, but it is less explicit than in other degrees. The reflexivity inherent in the appropriation of documentary aesthetics is present, but typically left unexplored by the text itself. The popularity enjoyed by fictional bands such as Spinal Tap or The Rutles, or political figures such as Fred Tuttle (*Man with a Plan*) and Jack Tanner (from *Tanner '88*) suggests that audiences enjoy the opportunity to engage with filmmakers in the parody of authoritative forms of representation. We assume that some of these audiences will also discern these texts' subtextual subversion of documentary. As we have outlined previously, our approach towards mock-documentary derives from a complex understanding of the potential of viewers to engage in the active reading of texts, shaped by the variety of contextual factors which distinguish any instance of viewing. Our discussion of these texts is necessarily limited to their 'preferred' reading; however, the complexity of mock-documentary's parodic intent in itself should suggest a variety of viewer interpretations.

The double life of parody constructs an ambivalence which is more fully expressed in the degree 2 mock-documentary texts which we have discussed, such as *Bad News Tour*, the 1997 premiere of *ER* and *Bob Roberts*. Their playful re-constructions of documentary codes and conventions operates in tandem with a muted form of critique of documentary aesthetics and ethics. These texts support comic and critical agendas more or less equally, resulting in a number of often-contradictory positions and interpretations to be constructed for viewers.

The mock-documentaries we term 'deconstruction' texts (degree 3 mock-documentaries) assume that audiences are capable of resolving the tension between these levels of reading and actively engaging in a critique of documentary. In the current context, where 'fakes' are becoming more commonplace, these texts are playing to an increasingly wider audience, as audiences are less able to retain a naive faith in factual practitioners and their programmes and are perhaps more willing to engage in critical commentary on these forms. It is none the less interesting to note that few filmmakers have chosen to explore the potential offered by this degree. The notable exceptions such as *Man Bites Dog*, *The Falls* and *David Holzman's Diary* collectively offer a challenge to future mock-documentary filmmakers to explore this potential.

It needs to acknowledged that the majority of mock-documentary texts we have studied foreground their fictionality and tend to provide only a muted critique of documentary. Hoaxes (whether intentional or unintentional) tend to deny the audience the opportunity to participate actively in their parodic exercise. Perhaps this is why some (New Zealand) audiences felt provoked to anger by such texts as *Forgotten Silver*, which a significant section of viewers read as playing a joke on *themselves*, rather than as playing with the status of documentary.

What appears to be the most important issue in relation to mock-documentary is the extent to which it, unlike the reflexive or performative modes of documentary, both exploits and helps to construct a new set of relationships between the audience and factual discourse. It offers the audience an opportunity to reflect on the wider cultural acceptance of factual and sober discourses and potentially to move towards a position of critical awareness, distrust or even incredulity of such discourses. More specifically, mock-documentary offers a critique from outside of documentary and puts the audience at the centre of that critique.

Clearly our work here would be significantly expanded by the addition of an audience research component. Future studies on mock-documentary would be incomplete without research that seeks to explore how specific, culturally-located audiences engage with these texts, and in particular the extent to which viewers take up the critically reflexive role towards documentary which we argue is inherent to these texts.

The development of the mock-documentary form has a number of implications for documentary proper. It is of key importance that mock-documentary offers an *external* challenge to documentary. As we have argued, the reflexive and performative modes of documentary have failed to undermine the foundations of documentary because of their inability to abandon their connection to the 'real'. When these modes move beyond a pretence at representing reality, they transgress the boundaries of the genre itself and cease to be accepted by audiences as 'documentary'.

However, it is also worth noting that the potential challenge that mock-documentary presents to the documentary project is here displaced on to a form which can still be dismissed as 'fictional'. Instead of a *documentary* mode exploring the contradictions inherent to factual discourse, we have a group of *fictional* texts posing the troubling questions or representation. Mock-documentary's subversion of documentary can be nullified by viewers turning away with the cry of 'it's only fiction'. This response would leave documentary untroubled by the mock-documentary critique, essentially leaving the privileged status which documentary still enjoys unchallenged. In this regard, it is interesting to reiterate that so few mock-documentaries look to engage aggressively with the assumptions and expectations of factual discourse in the manner of degree 3 mock-documentaries such as *Man Bites Dog*.

The future of mock-documentary is difficult to predict at this point. As we have argued throughout our discussion on mock-documentary, the real key to the development of the form lies with its audience. The central issue here is perhaps the extent to which viewers are willing to become complicit in the subversion of factual discourse. It may be that audiences will be quite willing to allow the form to grow and develop in much the same way that we already accept (and perhaps even demand?) the pleasure of April Fools' Day news reports. Viewers can enjoy the muted critique of the status of factual discourse, but with stories which are none the less invariably flagged for their fictional status. In the same way, mock-documentary could allow audiences to approach documentary codes and conventions in an increasingly complex but essentially unproblematic way: retaining a basic belief in factual discourse, but appreciating the sophistication of a filmmaker's parody.

Degree 2 mock-documentaries which offer a muted critique of documentary are the perfect example of such tendencies, and in this sense they perhaps best illustrate the ambivalence of viewers toward factual genres such as documentary. While the genre is increasingly fragmented and challenged from within, it is perhaps too integral to patterns of representation within visual culture to be easily dismissed. It may be that audiences are not ready to abandon the pretence of a fact/fiction dichotomy in favour of the seamless representational soup offered by post-modernism. We argue that, however the genre itself evolves, the mock-documentary will always pose a challenge to documentary proper because it does contain the potential to offer a sustained reflexive perspective on the genre.

The mock-documentary does appear to be becoming an accepted form within both mainstream cinema and television, most recently achieving popular exposure through films such as *The Blair Witch Project* (1999). This feature-length horror film has prompted much discussion over the possibility of mock-documentary becoming merely the latest trend or style to be adopted by low-budget filmmakers. Such discussions conveniently side-step any debate about the potential critique offered by the form, instead merely viewing the use of documentary aesthetics as a way of heightening the potential horror of the film. *The Blair Witch Project* is an important mock-documentary because of the success it has enjoyed in the mainstream, which has, despite the film's focus on horror, allowed audiences greater access to those key debates and issues surrounding documentary proper (Roscoe, 2000).

Mock-documentary has already enjoyed a degree of acceptance; for example, with the mainstream television series *The Games* in Australia, and *Tanner '88* in the US, *People Like Us* in the UK, and the continuing cult status of key texts such as *This Is Spinal Tap*. It is also the case that there are mock-documentary episodes of popular television dramatic series such as *ER* and *The Practice*, as well as in animation series such as *The Simpsons* and *South Park*. These are examples which perhaps support the argument that mock-documentary has become another identifiable style with a developing set of conventions which can be easily adopted, but also point to a greater acceptance by the audience of an increasingly sophisticated form.

Despite these popular appropriations of the mock-documentary form, we argue that it still contains potentially damning critiques of documentary.

As well as generating specific parodic commentaries of the various subcate-
gories within documentary (Reality TV, docu-soap and so on), the form
also raises more fundamental questions concerning the nature of the documentary project itself. We would argue that there is a difference between
what documentary *is* and what documentary *does*. Mock-documentary's
critique addresses both of these strategic concerns.

Mock-documentary provides a direct challenge to what documentary
is, by presenting faked images that give the appearance of being 'true to
life', of bearing witness, and of representing a true and direct relationship
between an image and its referent. The mock-documentary uses technology to undermine the status of the camera, and the photograph, both of
which are shown to be suspect. The relationship between the image and
the referent is not only broken, it is in fact completely destroyed when the
images can be shown to have no referent in the real world.

But to what extent does mock-documentary provide a challenge to the
notion of what documentary does? As Plantinga (1997) suggests, documentary takes an assertive stance toward the social world, a call to action
and so on. Given that the discourse of factuality is intimately linked with
the presentation of visual and verbal testimony in documentary, a challenge to these fundamental axioms is a direct challenge to the discourse of
factuality, to the underlying discourse of documentary. A key issue for
documentary is whether it can realise its claims to truth and complete
knowledge in the face of the mock-documentary challenge.

We are not making a call to bolster the referentiality of documentary,
although this is one route that is likely to be taken by both academics and
practitioners. A move towards a firmer evidentiality, and a strengthen-
ing of its referential claims could allow documentary to close off recently
opened transgressive spaces, leaving little room for forms such as the
mock-documentary. As documentary's ability to capture reality has
been undermined, it is paradoxically bolstered by technological
advances that allow the documentary to penetrate the social world in
newer and deeper ways. In some sense, the development of Reality-TV
(including an infatuation with surveillance footage) and docu-soap represent a search for a more 'authentic' form of documentary representation. Despite its enduring popularity through these forms, the genre's
privileged cultural status is arguably more tenuous now than at any time
in the past.

The challenge for documentary is how to take up the critiques offered
by forms such as (and most particularly) mock-documentary, yet
still retain some notion of documentary's difference to other screen

forms. That is, what makes the documentary different from the mock-documentary when they can both look, and act, the same?

The mock-documentary form has attracted a wide audience, outside of the academic and visually sophisticated elite which have been the main viewers for the form's factual cousin, the reflexive documentary. It is this popularity of (admittedly largely degree 1) mock-documentary which we argue contains the potential for this form to succeed where reflexive documentary has, to date, failed. As we suggest above, however, the reflexive potential of the mock-documentary form is by no means assured.

In the next few years, we suggest that there is likely to be continued exploration of mock-documentary. One possibility is that this form will eventually become exhausted, with audiences tiring of its irreverent stance towards factual aesthetics, and filmmakers moving to explore other modes of expression. Mock-documentary might be considered as a transitional discourse, a form that takes full advantage of technological developments and our insecurities concerning factual discourse. Having pushed those issues to their logical endpoint, the form itself could easily give way to new configurations within the fact–fiction continuum. Alternatively, the continued emergence of mock-documentary could lead to a more fundamental reappraisal of the essentials of documentary proper. In the near future, might we conceivably think of mock-documentary as the offspring of documentary, a member of the 'next generation' that emerges and is inspired by the exhaustion of the documentary genre itself?

Filmography

Mock-documentaries

The following list contains film and television texts which the writers have been able to identify as mock-documentaries. Those which have summaries, and are categorised according to degree, are texts which we have been able to actually locate and analyse.

Alien Abduction: Incident in Lake County (1998, aired 20 January), 50 min.
Director: Dean Alioto
Country of origin: United States
Mock-doc degree: 2
A television mock-documentary which presents excerpts and analysis from what
   is claimed to be the discovery of documentary evidence proving the existence
   of extra-terrestrial visits to Earth (videotape of the alien abduction of a family
   in Lake County, Minnesota). This text is notable not only as an initially suc-
   cessful hoax but for its inclusion of unrelated interview material with actual
   UFO experts (an aspect which had many UFO cultists speculating that the ultimate objective of the programme was in fact to discredit any popular belief in
   UFO visitations).

Alternative 3 (1977, aired 20 June), 52 min.
Director: Christopher Miles
Country of origin: Britain

An Alan Smithee Film – Burn Hollywood Burn (1998), 86 min.
Director: Alan Smithee
Country of origin: United States
Mock-doc degree: 2
'Alan Smithee' is the Director's Guild of America's official pseudonym credited to
   a film when a director believes that it is too incompetent or compromised to
   put on his/her resume. The premise of this mock-documentary is that a direc-
   tor whose 'real' name is Alan Smithee would be left with no option but to

destroy the master negative of the film itself. The text largely comprised a series of interviews, and attempts to construct a (heavy-handed) satire of Hollywood. (N.B. Ironically, the film is credited to Alan Smithee because the actual director, Arthur Hiller, has disavowed it.)

The Appleby Sensation (1997)
Director: Aaron Orullian
Country of origin: United States

A Self-Made Hero (1996), 105 min.
Director: Jacques Audiard
Country of origin: France

Bad News Tour (1983), 30 min.
Director: Sandy Johnson
Country of origin: Britain
Mock-doc degree: 2
A British television mock-documentary following the pattern of *This Is Spinal Tap*, with a documentary crew following an inept and talentless heavy metal band as it struggles to start a regional tour. Unlike *Spinal Tap*, however, the best scenes in this offering from Channel 4's *Comic Strip* are those which reveal an escalating tension between the crew and the band. The 'director' and his crew can barely disguise their lack of respect for their subject and are constantly frustrated by the band's complete inability to aid in the construction of their own myth. (See also the sequel, *More Bad News*.)

Bigger Than Tina (1999), 90 min.
Director: Neil Foley
Country of origin: Australia

The Blair Witch Project (1999), 89 min.
Director: Daniel Myrick and Eduardo Sánchez
Country of origin: United States
Mock-doc degree: 2
A highly successful mock-documentary feature film which purports to present the discovered footage of three student filmmakers who disappeared while attempting to investigate the legend of the Blair Witch of Maryland. After a brief opening caption, the film is presented entirely as observational footage, and focuses on the gradual descent of the amateur filmmakers into fear and confusion, apparently at the hands of supernatural forces. This text is notable both as a rare example of a horror mock-documentary, and for the variety of promotional material designed for its release which sought deliberately to confuse the film's fictional status. (See also *Curse of the Blair Witch*.)

Bob Roberts (1992), 101 min.
Director: Tim Robbins
Country of origin: United States
Mock-doc degree: 2
A political mock-documentary which follows the final stages of the Pennsylvania
senatorial campaign of Bob Roberts (Tim Robbins), during the lead-up to the
Gulf War. This film is presented by 'Terry Manchester', a British journalist who
rides along with Roberts and his campaign team of young professionals, and
encounters both supporters and opponents of Roberts's archetypal brand of
conservatism. The film works effectively as both a critique of modern American conservatism during the Reagan and Bush eras, and a wider attack on the
nature of the modern American political process (including the news media)
which allows candidates like Roberts to be successful.

Cannibal Holocaust (1979), 95 min.
Director: Ruggero Deodato
Country of origin: Italy

Children of the Revolution (1996), 102 min.
Director: Peter Duncan
Country of origin: Australia
Mock-doc degree: 1
An Australian feature film which operates at the fringes of the mock-documentary
form. This film purports to reveal a previously hidden story from recent
Australian political history: how, in May 1990, the Australian-born son of
Joseph Stalin nearly took over the Australian government. Presented largely in
interactive documentary mode, this film features 'interviews' with the son,
Joseph Welch, members of his family and political commentators with 'recon-
structions' of incidents which they describe. Set over the three decades of
Welch's life, the film is presented against the backdrop of Australian anti-
communist politicians of the era and the fall of socialist Eastern Europe.

Curse of the Blair Witch (1999), 50 min.
Director: Daniel Myrick and Eduardo Sánchez
Country of origin: United States
Mock-doc degree: 1
This television mock-documentary screened on a cable science-fiction channel as
part of the promotional campaign surrounding the release of the feature mock-
documentary *The Blair Witch Project*. A more complex (but less effective)
appropriation of documentary aesthetics than the film itself, this programme
uses a combination of expositional, interactive and observational documentary techniques to develop the Blair Witch mythology. It presents historical
background to the Blair Witch legend (including debates between 'experts'

over its validity), the biographies of the three student filmmakers and additional details (including television news reports) of their mysterious disappearance while in pursuit of documentary footage of the phenomenon.

Dadetown, (1996), 93 min.
Director: Russ Hexter
Country of origin: United States

David Holzman's Diary (1967), 73 min.
Director: Jim McBride
Country of origin: United States
Mock-doc degree: 3
An early black and white example of a mock-documentary, this features a young
   filmmaker (Holzman) who attempts to discover the 'truth' about his life by
   recording it on film, drawing on Jean-Luc Godard's observation that 'film is
   truth 24 times a second'. The film covers eight days in July 1967, as Holzman
   documents his neighbourhood, stalks female strangers, interviews a friend and
   a neighbour, drives his girlfriend away with his continuous filming, and eventually
   becomes frustrated himself with the lack of revelations provided by his
   camera. Although more introspective than any of the other texts listed here,
   this film is also more direct in its examination of the nature of film and its relationship
   to reality.

Dill Scallion (1999), 91 min.
Director: Jordan Brady
Country of origin: United States

The Disappearance of Kevin Johnson (1995), 102 min.
Director: Francis Megahy
Country of origin: United States
Mock-doc degree: 2
This mock-documentary has a British documentary crew attempting to locate
   and interview a British producer in Hollywood. Their attempts to investigate
   the producer's disappearance reveal that he was a con-man who was able to
   manipulate the ambition, greed and vulnerability of people looking to succeed
   in the American film industry. (The film constructs a critique of Hollywood
   which is similar to Robert Altman's *The Player.*)

Drop Dead Gorgeous (1999), 93 min.
Director: Michael Patrick Jann
Country of origin: United States

Elvis Meets Nixon (1997), 95 min.
Director: Allan Arkush
Country of origin: United States

ER ('Ambush') (1997), 50 min.
Director: Thomas Schlamme
Country of origin: United States
Mock-doc degree: 2
This was the fourth season premiere of the popular primetime television series
   ER, set in a Chicago hospital emergency room. The episode was performed live,
   and achieved substantial ratings in the United States. Constructed as a 'fly-on-
   the-wall' documentary, the regular characters of the series are here 'visited' by
   a documentary crew for a day. This text is most interesting for its construction
   of the documentary crew themselves, who emerge as tabloid, Reality-TV-style
   'journalists' attempting to gain a sensationalist exposé of hospital practices.

Faces of Death (1979), 85 min.
Director: Conan le Cilaire
Country of origin: United States

The Falls (1980), 185 min.
Director: Peter Greenaway
Country of origin: Britain
Mock-doc degree: 3
In ninety-two segments, Greenaway documents the impact of a Violent
   Unknown Event (VUE) on a representative sample of its victims. Each segment represents a case study in the representational methods typically
   employed by documentary filmmakers (especially BBC documentarists)
   working within the expositional mode; each constructs a biography of an
   absent victim through a complex blend of contemporary and archival material. The result is a film which exhaustively details an event which is increasingly
   acknowledged to be a fiction – in the process, deconstructing any suggestion
   that documentary codes and conventions can achieve a directly referential
   relationship with reality.

Fear of a Black Hat (1993), 82 min.
Director: Rusty Cundieff
Country of origin: United States
Mock-doc degree: 2
Virtually a re-make of *This Is Spinal Tap*, this mock-documentary follows a rap
   group, N.W.H. or Niggerz With Hats, through the same cycle of success, disin-
   tegration and rebirth (and comes close to surpassing the original film). This
   film parodies especially the political and artistic stances adopted by a number

of well-known figures within American rap culture, but also works to target business and cultural practices within the wider music industry.

Forgotten Silver (1995), 50 min.
Director: Costa Botes and Peter Jackson
Country of origin: New Zealand
Mock-doc degree: 1 or 2
A mock-documentary which heralds the discovery of a long-lost New Zealand world pioneer in film-making (Colin McKenzie). This uses a sophisticated blend of expositional, interactive and observational modes to present a biography of McKenzie's life (through interviews with local celebrities, McKenzie's 'widow', and film experts – including Leonard Maltin). This is intercut with footage of an expedition by Botes and Jackson as they travel into the depths of the New Zealand bush to rediscover the site of McKenzie's greatest silent epic, *Salome*.

The Games (1908), 25 min. episodes
Director: Bruce Permezel
Country of origin: Australia
Mock-doc degree: 2
An Australian mock-documentary television series which satirises the efforts of administrators preparing for the Sydney Olympics in 2000. The series purports to offer an inside view of economic and political forces behind the construction and organisation of the modern Olympics. Drawing on the comedic style of its main writer/actor (John Clarke, who specialises in dry observation), the focus is on the discourse of administrators and politicians, with most of the action taking place within one set.

Ghostwatch (1992), 90 min.
Director: Lesley Manning
Country of origin: Britain

Hard Core Logo (1997), 92 min.
Director: Bruce McDonald
Country of origin: Canada

The Hellstrom Chronicle (1971), 90 min.
Director: Walon Green and Ed Spiegel
Country of origin: United States

The History of White People in America (1985), 48 min.
Director: Harry Shearer
Country of origin: United States
Mock-doc degree: 1

Hosted by Martin Mull, this mock-documentary series surveys the culture of (American) white people, largely through the experiences of the Harrison family. Mull also interviews experts from the Institute of White Studies, who present the latest 'research' on white people. This mock-documentary essentially parodies a number of the ethnic stereotypes characteristic of American television and popular culture. (See also the sequel.)

The History of White People in America Volume II (1986), 100 min.
Director: Harry Shearer
Country of origin: United States
Mock-doc degree: 1
A sequel to *The History of White People in America*, which features four episodes from the series following the Harrison family through various crises.

Husbands and Wives (1992), 108 min.
Director: Woody Allen
Country of origin: United States
Mock-doc degree: 1
A mock-documentary which follows the friendships and romantic relationships surrounding two New York couples. This uses especially the interactive documentary mode, combined with *cinéma vérité* aesthetics. At regular points the characters are interviewed for their insights into both their own actions, and those of their friends and partners. A conventional comedy-drama, the mock-documentary form here becomes largely another way to allow audiences to gain an understanding of the psychological motivations of characters. (See also Allen's *Take the Money and Run* and *Zelig*.)

The Idiots (1998), 117 min.
Director: Lars von Trier
Country of origin: Denmark
A feature film which operates at the margins of mock-documentary. This is one of a series of films from Dogme 95, a group of Danish filmmakers committed to an anti-Hollywood aesthetic which prioritises techniques such as naturalistic lighting and hand-held camera work. Here a group of middle-class dropouts pretend to be mentally and/or physically handicapped (in public), in order to expose the hypocrisy of social attitudes toward the handicapped, and to get in touch with their 'inner idiots'. This film features 'interviews' in which characters explain their motivations, and much of the effectiveness of its narrative derives from its adherence to a *vérité* style of filmmaking.

King of Chaos (1998), 50 min.
Director: Bryn Higgins
Country of origin: Britain

Mock-doc degree: 2

A British television mock-documentary set in the near future which is part biography, and part murder investigation. The central characters are Liam Keller, a billionaire who has been branded the 'King of Chaos' after his 'revolutionary internet software changed the face of world television', and a female journalist who attempts to uncover the political and industrial conspiracy responsible for Keller's death.

L7: The Beauty Process (1998), 47 min.
Director: Krist Novoselic
Country of origin: United States

Larry David: Curb Your Enthusiasm (1999), 65 min.
Director: Robert Weide
Country of origin: United States

The Last Broadcast (1998), 86 min.
Director: Stefan Avalos and Lance Weiler
Country of origin: United States

The Legend of Boggy Creek (1972), 90 min.
Director: Charles B. Pierce
Country of origin: United States

The Making of ... And God Spoke (1993), 82 min.
Director: Arthur Borman
Country of origin: United States

Man Bites Dog (1992), 88 min.
Director: Remy Belvaux, Andre Bonzel and Benot Poelvoorde
Country of origin: Belgium
Mock-doc degree: 3

An extremely subversive Belgian mock-documentary which charts the collaboration between an independent film crew and small-time serial killer Benoit Patard (featuring the three directors themselves in the main roles). Filmed in black and white, this follows the format of a classic observational documentary as Ben and the crew develop a complex relationship which reveals all of the compromises necessarily adopted by documentary makers towards human subjects. On one level, the film is a disturbing black comedy which serves as a deconstruction especially of the moral and ethical pretensions adopted by all documentarists. The presence of the crew encourages Ben to greater excesses, and they in turn are gradually drawn into Ben's world, acting as his accomplices in robbery, murder, the disposal of bodies, gang rape and eventually Ben's

escape from prison. The film, however, can also be read variously as an indict-
ment of European tribal cultures (such as those underlying the disintegration
of Yugoslavia), an attack on the value system promoted by capitalist heroes, or
a wider critique of the dehumanising effects of modern society.

Man of the Year (1996), 88 min.
Director: Dirk Shafer
Country of origin: United States
Mock-doc degree: 2
A mock-documentary which incorporates elements of the real-life experiences of
the director, a gay man who was *Playgirl* magazine's Man of the Year. Structured almost entirely around a series of fictionalised interviews, but including
some actual footage of Shafer's appearances on American national talk shows,
the film presents an account of his career as a male centrefold. Its real intent,
however, is to offer a commentary on the difficulties of being homosexual
within an overwhelmingly heterosexual culture.

Man with a Plan (1996), 90 min.
Director: John O'Brien
Country of origin: United States
Mock-doc degree: 1
A mock-documentary which chronicles the Vermont congressional campaign of
Fred Tuttle, a 75-year old ex-dairy-farmer from Tunbridge, as he challenges
six-term incumbent House Representative William Blachly. Structured around
the bemused narration of a political journalist, this mock-documentary has a
low-key, amateur style, and works as a gentle parody of the American electoral
process. The film is essentially a nostalgic fantasy which calls for a return to a
more personal and participatory political system. Fred's campaign style consists of making things up as he goes along, relying on an insignificant advertising budget and an often incoherent political agenda (his answer to waste
disposal is to send it all up into space). Most of the characters in the film play
themselves, including Fred's pets.

More Bad News (1987), 50 min.
Director: Adrian Edmonson
Country of origin: Britain
Mock-doc degree: 2
A mock-documentary sequel to *Bad News Tour*, this features the heavy metal band
Bad News being reunited by a documentary crew as part of a 'where are they
now?'-type programme. This time the band secure a record contract, make a
video and appear at a major heavy metal rock festival. This sequel is much
closer, in content than the original *Bad News Tour* to *This Is Spinal Tap*. Instead
of open conflict between the band and the documentary crew, here the

(unseen) documentary filmmakers aid the career of the band in an unsuccessful attempt to construct a narrative of popular success.

Norbert Smith: A Life (1989), 50 min.
Director: Geoff Posner
Country of origin: Britain
Mock-doc degree: 2
A British television mock-documentary from comic Harry Enfield. This features *The South Bank Show* host Melvyn Bragg parodying his own arts-programme interviewing style, as he presents the life and career of Sir Norbert Smith. Smith is presented as a distinguished British actor from the same generation as other knighted luminaries such as John Gielgud and Ralph Richardson. The chronicle of Sir Norbert's life allows the film to parody both the archetypal narratives of this acting generation and a wide range of British (and American) cinematic styles.

People Like Us (1999), 25 min. episodes
Director: John Morton and Peter Schlesinger
Country of origin: Britain

The Practice (1997), 47 min.
Director: Michael Shultz
Country of origin: United States
Mock-doc degree: 2
A mock-documentary episode from an American dramatic television series. Like the *ER* episode listed above, this features a documentary crew recording a day in the life of the ensemble cast (in this case, a legal firm, as it attempts to prevent the execution of a man on death row). The episode is less complex than the *ER* example, offering more of a 'straight' observational documentary, with less commentary on the relationship between filmmaker and subject.

The Protagonists (1998), 92 min.
Director: Luca Guadagnino
Country of origin: Italy

The Return of Spinal Tap (A Spinal Tap Reunion: The 25th Anniversary London Sell-Out) (1993), 110 min.
Director: Jim Di Bergi
Country of origin: United States
Mock-doc degree: 1
A rare mock-documentary sequel, this revisits the band Spinal Tap for a reunion concert in Albert Hall, London, to promote the release of the (real) album *Break Like the Wind*. Unlike the 'on the road' narrative of *This Is Spinal Tap*, this film is centred on a single concert, with various interview inserts of the

original band members and director as they provide updates on their personal and professional lives. The most interesting feature of the concert itself is the status of the band. The ability to attract a capacity audience to the Albert Hall, and their obvious familiarity with the lyrics of most of the band's songs, complicates the issue of whether Spinal Tap can still be considered to have a purely *fictional* musical career.

The Rutles (1978), 71 min.
Director: Eric Idle and Gary Weis
Country of origin: Britain
Mock-doc degree: 1
An early mock-documentary which parodies the popular narrative of the hugely successful musical career of the Beatles. Presented by a hapless and inept interviewer, this documents the rise of 'The Rutles', through interviews with various real and fictional celebrities (including Mick Jagger) and close parodic re-constructions of Beatles archival material. An openly fictional mock-documentary, this features a cast which includes members from both *Monty Python's Flying Circus* and *Saturday Night Live* – television programmes which helped to develop the mock-documentary form.

The Simpsons – Behind the Laughter (2000), 24 min.
Director: Mark Kirkland
Country of origin: United States
Mock-doc degree: 1
An episode of the popular animated series which parodies the format of tabloid accounts of figures within popular culture by 'documenting' the rise, decline, break-up and eventual reunion of the Simpson family. A rare example of an animated mock-documentary, this is obviously a text which foregrounds its fictionality (hence our decision to position it as essentially a degree 1 mockdocumentary). As is typical of the series, this episode develops a complex self-reflexivity incorporating a commentary on both itself and 'factual' entertainment forms.

South Park – Chef: Behind the Menu (1998), 24 min.
Director: Jennifer Heftler and Lisa Page
Country of origin: United States
Mock-doc degree: 1
This is essentially a promotional piece for a compact disc released to capitalise on the cult success of the *South Park* television cartoon series. A 'biography' of Jerome 'Chef' McElroy, one of the staple characters of the series, this episode features interviews with the various rock artists who contributed to the album, all of whom identify Chef as the legendary (but unacknowledged) genius who most influenced their musical careers. This episode is interesting as an example

of an *animated* mock-documentary (although it is a less sophisticated mock-documentary than *The Simpsons: Behind the Laughter*).

Take the Money and Run (1969), 85 min.
Director: Woody Allen
Country of origin: United States
Mock-doc degree: 1
A biographical mock-documentary which follows the 'career' of Virgil Starkwell (Allen), an inept New Jersey criminal. The film relies on a conventional expositional narrator and interviews to parody many of the generic conventions of American gangster and prison films. This was an early effort by Allen in the mock-documentary form and does not appropriate documentary aesthetics as consistently as his later mock-documentary films (*Zelig* and *Husbands and Wives*).

Tanner '88 (1988), 30 min. (10 episodes)
Director: Robert Altman
Country of origin: United States

Ted (1998), 84 min.
Director: Gary Ellenberg
Country of origin: United States

That's Adequate (1989), 82 min.
Director: Harry Hurwitz
Country of origin: United States

This Is Spinal Tap (1984), 82 min.
Director: Rob Reiner
Country of origin: United States
Mock-doc degree: 1
A mock-documentary which follows the American tour of a mediocre British heavy metal band as their new album descends into oblivion and the members of the band into acrimony, before an eventual triumphal rebirth in Japan. The film is a brilliant parody of 'rockumentaries' (those films which purport to adopt a documentary stance towards their subject, but which often tend more toward sycophancy). This classic mock-documentary manages both to savage every cliché of the heavy metal genre and also to generate an affection for the fictional band itself (it has attracted a real base of fans). (See also the sequel, *The Return of Spinal Tap*.)

To Die For (1995), 101 min.
Director: Gus Van Sant

Country of origin: United States
Mock-doc degree: 2
A feature film which, like *Children of the Revolution*, operates at the margins of the
mock-documentary form. This film presents the story of Suzanne Maretto, a
weather girl for a small local television station who manipulates two local
teenagers into killing her husband when he looks to stifle her ambitions. The
film seems to be partly based on a number of actual, sensationalised murder
cases in the United States, but serves to present a wider critique of aspects of
American culture in the 1980s and 1990s (such as the public's fascination with
the infamous, the brutally ambitious culture of the television industry, and a
perceived corruption of the American Dream).

20 Dates (1998), 97 min.
Director: Myles Berkowitz
Country of origin: United States

Unauthorized Biography: Milo – Death of a Supermodel (1997), 24 min.
Director: Andrea Black and Russell Firestone
Country of origin: United States
Mock-doc degree: 1
A mock-documentary episode of a non-fiction television series, this chronicles
the controversial life and eventual death of the 'first supermodel'. It incorporates interviews with both American cult figures (such as Debbie Harry) and
fictional acquaintances of Milo, who is presented as epitomising the excesses of
the 1970s (disco and Studio 54) and 1980s (drug abuse and punk).

Unmade Beds (1997), 100 min.
Director: Nicholas Barker
Country of origin: United States

Waiting for Guffman (1996), 80 min.
Director: Christopher Guest
Country of origin: United States
Mock-doc degree: 1
A classic mock-documentary about the production of an original musical
designed to celebrate the sesquicentennial of the small American town of
Blaine, Missouri. This mimics the format of soap-documentaries, and follows
the production from the first auditions of local hopefuls through to its tri-
umphant, but bitter-sweet, premiere in front of an audience of assorted
Blaineans. Underlying its simple narrative is a sharp satire of American small-
town 'values', especially the frustrated artistic ambitions, unaware mediocrity
and repressed sexuality of the middle class.

The Watermelon Woman (1996), 90 min.
Director: Cheryl Dunye
Country of origin: United States

Where Are the Bredstix? (1990).
Director: Mathew Tobey
Country of origin: United States

Zelig (1983), 79 min.
Director: Woody Allen
Country of origin: United States
Year of production 1983
Length 79 min
Mock-doc degree: 1
Another Woody Allen mock-documentary (see *Take the Money and Run* and *Husbands and Wives*), this presents the biography of Leonard Zelig, a man who has the chameleon-like ability to physically transform himself to blend in with any social group (except women). Zelig becomes a celebrity in 1920s America, and Allen has his character mingle with major cultural and political figures of the period. Largely a nostalgia piece, the film also serves as an interesting commentary on aspects of American culture.

Other texts:

The Abyss (1989) James Cameron, United States, 110 min.
Alien Autopsy: Fact or Fiction? (1995) Tom McGough, United States, 1995, 45 min.
All Quiet on the Western Front (1930) Lewis Milestone, United States, 138 min.
Apocalypse Now (1979) Francis Coppola, United States, 153 min.
A Walk in the Sun (1945) Lewis Milestone, United States, 117 min.
A Walk Through H (1978) Peter Greenaway, Britain.
The Battle of Algiers (1965) Gillo Pontecorvo, Italy–Algeria, 123 min.
Beauty and the Beast (1991) Gary Trousdale and Kirk Wise, United States, 85 min.
The Big Parade (1925) King Vidor, United States, 126 min.
The Birds (1963) Alfred Hitchcock, United States, 119 min.
Blazing Saddles (1974) Mel Brooks, United States, 93 min.
Blue in the Face (1995) Wayne Wang and Paul Auster, United States, 85 min.
Born on the Fourth of July (1989) Oliver Stone, United States, 135 min.
Breaking the Waves (1996) Lars von Trier, Denmark–Sweden–France–Netherlands–Norway, 159 min.
Buffalo Bill and the Indians, or Sitting Bull's History Lesson (1976) Robert Altman, United States, 123 min.
Cane Toads (1988) Mark Lewis, Australia, 46 min.

The Celebration (Festen) Thomas Vinterburg, Denmark, 1998, 105 min.
Chinatown (1974) Roman Polanski, United States, 131 min.
Citizen Kane (1941) Orson Welles, United States, 119 min.
Crumb (1994) Terry Zwigoff, United States, 119 min.
Culloden (1964) Peter Watkins, Britain, 71 min.
The Deer Hunter (1978) Michael Cimino, United States, 182 min.
Dr Strangelove (Or How I Learned to Stop Worrying and Love the Bomb) (1963) Stanley Kubrick, Britain, 91 min.
Don't Look Back (1967) D. A. Pennebaker, United States, 96 min.
Dragonheart (1996) Rob Cohen, United States, 99 min.
The Falcon and the Snowman (1985) John Schlesinger, United States, 131 min.
F for Fake (Vérités et mensonges) (1974) Orson Welles, United States, 85 min.
Forrest Gump (1994) Robert Zemeckis, United States, 137 min.
Frankenstein (1931) James Whale, United States, 71 min.
Gimme Shelter (1970) David Maysles, Albert Maysles and Charlotte Zwerin, United States, 90 min.
Goodfellas (1990) Martin Scorsese, United States, 148 min.
Health (1979) Robert Altman, United States, 102 min.
High Anxiety (1977) Mel Brooks, United States, 94 min.
Hoop Dreams (1994) Steve James, United States, 170 min.
Hospital (1970) Frederick Wiseman, United States, 84 min.
Independence Day (1996) Roland Emmerich, United States, 139 min.
JFK (1991) Oliver Stone, United States, 190 min.
Jurassic Park (1993) Steven Spielberg, United States, 120 min.
The Kingdom (Riget) (1994) Lars von Trier, Denmark–France–Germany–Sweden, Part 1: 133 min., Part 2: 146 min.
The Last Waltz (1978) Martin Scorsese, United States, 117 min.
The Long Goodbye (1973) Robert Altman, United States, 112 min.
Marnie (1964) Alfred Hitchcock, United States, 130 min.
M.A.S.H. (1970) Robert Altman, United States, 116 min.
McCabe and Mrs Miller (1971) Robert Altman, United States, 121 min.
Mean Streets (1973) Martin Scorsese, United States, 110 min.
Mr Smith Goes to Washington (1939) Frank Capra, United States, 129 min.
Monterey Pop (1968) D. A. Pennebaker, United States, 88 min.
Nanook of the North (1922) Robert Flaherty, United States, 55 min.
Nashville (1975) Robert Altman, United States, 161 min.
Natural Born Killers (1994) Oliver Stone, United States, 120 min.
Night and Fog (Nuit et brouillard) (1955) Alain Resnais, France, 32 min.
Night of the Living Dead (1968) George A. Romero, United States, 96 min.
Nixon (1995) Oliver Stone, United States, 191 min.
Paris, Texas (1984) Wim Wenders, West Germany–France, 148 min.
Patton (1969) Franklin J. Schaffner, United States, 171 min.
Peeping Tom (1960) Michael Powell, Britain, 109 min.

Platoon (1986) Oliver Stone, United States, 120 min.
The Player (1992) Robert Altman, United States, 123 min.
Prêt-à-Porter (Ready to Wear) (1994) Robert Altman, United States, 132 min.
Psycho (1960) Alfred Hitchcock, United States, 109 min.
Punitive Damage (1998) Annie Goldson, New Zealand.
Purple Rose of Cairo (1985) Woody Allen, United States, 82 min.
Raging Bull (1980) Martin Scorsese, United States, 128 min.
Real Vampires: Exposed! (1998) United States, approx. 50 min.
Rear Window (1954) Alfred Hitchcock, United States, 112 min.
Reds (1981) Warren Beatty, United States, 196 min.
Robocop (1987) Paul Verhoeven, United States, 103 min.
Roger & Me (1989) Michael Moore, United States, 87 min.
Salvador (1986) Oliver Stone, United States, 122 min.
Saving Private Ryan (1998) Steven Spielberg, United States, 169 min.
Schindler's List (1993) Steven Spielberg, United States, 185 min.
Sherman's March (1985) Ross McElwee, United States, 157 min.
Shoah (1985) Claude Lanzmann, France, 566 min.
Shoot to Kill (1990) Peter Kosminsky, Britain.
Singin' in the Rain (1952) Gene Kelly and Stanley Donen, United States, 102 min.
Smoke (1995) Wayne Wang, United States, 112 min.
Star Wars (1977) George Lucas, United States, 121 min.
Star Wars: Episode I – The Phantom Menace (1999) George Lucas, United States, 133 min.
The Steel Helmet (1951) Samuel Fuller, United States, 84 min.
Suspicion (1941) Alfred Hitchcock, United States, 99 min.
Taxi Driver (1976) Martin Scorsese, United States, 114 min.
Terminator 2: Judgment Day (1991) James Cameron, United States, 135 min.
The Thin Blue Line (1987) Errol Morris, United States, 96 min.
Titanic (1997) James Cameron, United States, 194 min.
Vertical Features Remake (1976) Peter Greenaway, Britain.
Wall Street (1987) Oliver Stone, United States, 120 min.
The War Game (1965) Peter Watkins, Britain, 47 min.
The War Room (1993) Chris Hegedus and D. A. Pennebaker, United States, 96 min.
War Stories (Our Mother Never Told Us) (1995) Gaylene Preston, New Zealand, 95 min.
Who Bombed Birmingham? (1990) Mike Beckham, Britain, 105 min.
When Harry Met Sally (1989) Rob Reiner, United States, 110 min.
When We Were Kings (1996) Leon Gast, United States, 87 min.
Willow (1988) Ron Howard, United States, 120 min.
Woodstock (1970) Michael Wadleigh, United States, 184 min.
Young Sherlock Holmes (1985) Barry Levinson, United States, 115 min.

Bibliography

Ang, Ien (1989) 'Wanted: Audiences: On the Politics of Empirical Audience Studies', in E. Seiter, H. Borchers, G. Kreutzner and E. Warth (eds), *Remote Control: Television, Audiences, and Cultural Power*, Routledge, London.

Ang, Ien (1991) *Desperately Seeking the Audience*, Routledge, London.

Ang, Ien (1996) *Living Room Wars: Rethinking Media Audiences for a Postmodern World*, Routledge, London.

Ansen, David (1997) 'Gotta Sing! Gotta Dance!: A Small Town Gets Bitten by the Broadway Bug', *Newsweek*, 10 February.

Arthur, Paul (1998) 'Media Spectacle and the Tabloid Documentary', *Film Comment*, Volume 34, Number 1, 74–80.

Bakhtin, M. M. (1981) *The Dialogic Imagination: Four Essays*, edited by Michael Holquist, translated by Caryl Emerson and Michael Holquist, University of Texas Press, Austin.

Barker, Adam (1992) 'Cries and Whispers', *Sight and Sound*, Volume 1, Issue 10, February, 24–5.

Barthes, Roland (1981) *Camera Lucida: Reflections on Photography*, Hill and Wang, New York.

Baudrillard, Jean (1983) *Simulations*, Semiotext(e) Inc., New York City.

Baxter, John (1996) *Steven Spielberg: The Unauthorised Biography*, Harper Collins, London.

Bazin, André (1971) *What is Cinema?* Volume 2 (translated by H. Grey), University of California Press, Berkeley.

Beaver, Frank (1994) *Oliver Stone: Wakeup Cinema*, Twayne Publishers, New York.

Becker, Karen E. (1991) 'To Control Our Image: Photojournalists and New Technology', *Media, Culture and Society*, Volume 13, Number 3, 381–97.

Bernstein, Mathew (1994) '*Roger and Me*: Documentaphobia and Mixed Modes', *Journal of Film and Video*, Volume 46, Number 1, 3–20.

Best, Steven and Douglas Kellner (1991) *Postmodern Theory: Critical Interrogations*, The Guilford Press, New York.

Bethell, Andrew (1999) ' A Job, Some Stars, and a Big Row', *Media Watch 99*, Sight and Sound, London.

Bhaskar, Roy (1989) *Reclaiming Reality: A Critical Introduction to Contemporary Philosophy*, Verso, London.

Björkman, Stig (1994) *Woody Allen on Woody Allen*, Faber and Faber Limited, London.

Björkman, Stig (1996) 'Naked Miracles', *Sight and Sound*, Volume 6, Issue 10, 10–14.

Blake, Richard A. (1995) *Woody Allen: Profane and Sacred*, The Scarecrow Press, Inc., Lanham.

Brady, Frank (1990) *Citizen Welles: A Biography of Orson Welles*, Hodder and Stoughton, London.

Britton, Andrew (1992) 'Invisible Eye', *Sight and Sound*, Volume 1, Issue 10, 26–9.

Bullert, B. J. (1997) *Public Television: Politics and the Battle Over Documentary Film*, London, Rutger University Press.

Caldwell, John Thornton (1995) *Televisuality: Style, Crisis, and Authority in American Television*, Rutger University Press, New Brunswick.

Campbell, R. (1991) 'Securing the Middle Ground: Reporter Formulas in *60 Minutes*', in R. A. Avery and D. Eason (eds), *Critical Perspectives on Media and Society*, The Guilford Press, New York.

Camper, Fred (1984) 'Review of *Shoah*', in Christopher Lyon (ed.), *The International Dictionary of Films and Filmmakers*, Volume 1, 820–2.

Cantril, Hadley (1940) *The Invasion From Mars: A Study in the Psychology of Panic*, Princeton University Press, Princeton.

Caughie, John (1980) 'Progressive Television and Documentary Drama', in T. Bennett, S. Boyd-Bowman, C. Mercer and J. Woollacott (eds) *Popular Television and Film*, BFI, London.

Cawelti, J. G. (1979) '*Chinatown* and Generic Transformation in Recent American Films', in B. K. Grant (ed.), *Film Genre Reader*, University of Texas Press, Austin, 1986.

Chang, Chris (1997) 'Planet of the Apes', *Film Comment*, Volume 33, Number 5, 68–71.

Chumo, Peter N. (1995) '"You've Got to Put the Past Behind You Before You Can Move On": *Forrest Gump* and National Reconciliation', *Journal of Popular Film and Television*, Volume 23, Number 1, 2–7.

Cockburn, Alexander (1992) 'John and Oliver's Bogus Adventure', *Sight and Sound*, Volume 1, Issue 10, February, 22–4.

Colbert, Mary (1996) '*Children of the Revolution*: Writer-Director Peter Duncan Interviewed by Mary Colbert', *Cinema Papers*, Number 113, 22–6.

Combs, Richard (1987) 'Beating God to the Draw: *Salvador* and *Platoon*', *Sight and Sound*, Volume 56, Issue 2, 136–8.

Combs, Richard (1996) 'Orson Welles' *F for Fake*', in K. MacDonald and M. Cousins (eds), *Imaging Reality: The Faber Book of Documentary*, Faber and Faber, London.

Connor, Steven (1997) *Postmodernist Culture: An Introduction to Theories of the Contemporary*, Second Edition, Blackwell Publishers, Oxford.

Corliss, Richard (1986) 'A Document Written in Blood', *Time*, 15 December.

Corliss, Richard (1987) '*Platoon*: Viet Nam, the Way it Really Was, on Film', *Time*, 26 January, 40–7.

Corliss, Richard (1999) 'Blair Witch Craft', *Time*, 16 August, 52–8.

Corner, John (1995) *Television Form and Public Address*, Edward Arnold, London.

Corner, John (1996) *The Art of Record: A Critical Introduction to Documentary*, Manchester University Press, Manchester.

Corner, John (1999) *Critical Ideas in Television Studies*, Clarendon Press, Oxford.

Cowie, Elizabeth (1997) 'The Spectacle of Reality and Documentary Film', *The Documentary Box*, Volume 10, June.

Dahlgren, P. (1992) 'What's the Meaning of This? Viewers' Plural Sense-Making of TV News', in P. Scannell, P. Schlesinger and C. Sparks (eds), *Culture and Power: A 'Media, Culture and Society' Reader*, SAGE Publications, London.

Darke, Chris (1997) 'Monsieur Memory', *Sight and Sound*, Volume 7, Issue 4, 24–6.

Davis, Karen D. (1997) 'Digital Lab Rats', *DOX*, Number 11, 20–1.

Deleuze, Gilles (1989) *Cinema 2: The Time Image* (translated bt Hugh Tomlinson and Robert Galeta), University of Minnesota Press, Minneapolis.

Doherty, Thomas (1998) 'Review of *Saving Private Ryan*', *Cineaste*, Volume XXIV, Number 1, 68–71.

Dovey, Jon (1995) 'Camcorder Cults', *Metro*, Number 104, 26–30.

Dyer, Richard (1997) 'Kill and Kill Again', *Sight and Sound*, Volume 7, Issue 9, 14–17.

Erens, Patricia (1986) 'Home Movies in Commercial Narrative Film', *Journal of Film and Video*, Volume 38, summer/autumn.

Ericson, R. V., P. M. Baranek and J. B. L. Chan (1987) *Visualising Deviance: A Study of News Organisation*, Open University Press, Milton Keynes.

Ericson, R. V., P. M. Baranek and J. B. L. Chan (1991) *Representing Order: Crime, Law, and Justice in the News Media*, Open University Press, Milton Keynes.

Felski, Rita (1998) 'Images of the Intellectual: From Philosophy to Cultural Studies', *Continuum*, Volume 12, Number 2, 157–71.

Fiske, J. (1989) 'Moments of Television: Neither the Text nor the Audience', in E. Seiter, H. Borchers, G. Kreutzner and E. Warth (eds), *Remote Control: Television, Audiences, and Cultural Power*, Routledge, London.

Fiske, J. (1992) 'British Cultural Studies and Television', in R. C. Allen (ed.), *Channels of Discourse, Reassembled: Television and Contemporary Criticism*, Second Edition, The University of North Carolina Press, Chapel Hill.

FitzSimons, Trish, Pat Laughren and Dugald Williamson (2000) 'Towards a Contemporary History of Australian Documentary', *Metro*, Number 123, 62–72.

Francke, Lizzie (1996) 'When Documentary Is Not Documentary', in K. MacDonald and M. Cousins (eds) *Imagining Reality: the Faber Book of Documentary*, Faber and Faber, London.

Gelley, Ora (1997) 'Narration and the Embodiment of Power in *Schindler's List*', *Film Criticism*, Volume 22, Number 2, 2–26.

George, Edward (1994) 'Beneath the Hats', *Sight and Sound*, Volume 4, Issue 11, 26–7.

Goldstein, Alyosha (1996) 'Total Communication: Cross-Examining the 'Universality' of Documentary and Digital Media', *MIA*, Volume 82, 30–9.

Goodwin, Andrew (1992) *Dancing in the Distraction Factory: Music, Television and Popular Culture*, University of Minnesota Press, Minneapolis.

Goodwin, Andrew (1993) 'Fatal Distractions: MTV Meets Postmodern Theory', in S. Frith, A. Goodwin and L. Grossberg (eds), *Sound and Vision: The Music Video Reader*, Routledge, London.

Graham, Adam H. (1998) 'On *Fargo*, Working with SAG, and the Local Life: An Interview with Vermont Filmmaker John O'Brien', *New England Film*, online.

Grant, Barry Keith and Jeannette Sloniowski (eds) (1998) *Documenting the Documentary: Close Readings of Documentary Film and Video*, Wayne State University Press, Detroit.

Gross, Larry (1995) 'Exploding Hollywood', *Sight and Sound*, Volume 5, Issue 3, 8–9.

Hall, Jeanne (1998) 'Don't You Ever Just Watch?', in B. K. Grant and J. Sloniowski (eds), *Documenting the Documentary: Close Readings of Documentary Filmed Video*, Wayne State University Press, Detroit, 223–37.

Hampton, Howard (1994) 'American Maniacs', *Film Comment*, Volume 30, Number 6, 2–4.

Hansen, Miriam Bratu (1997) '*Schindler's List* is not *Shoah*: Second Commandment, Popular Modernism, and Public Memory', in Y. Loshitzky (ed.) *Spielberg's Holocaust: Critical Perspectives on* Schindler's List, Indiana University Press, Bloomington.

Harrington, Richard (1994) 'Review of *Fear of a Black Hat*, *Washington Post*, 17 June, online.

Hartley, John (1996) *Popular Reality: Journalism, Modernity, Popular Culture*, St Martin's Press, London.

Helms, Michael (1994) '*Natural Born Killers*', *Metro*, Number 100, 14–17.

Hill, John (1997) 'Interview with Ken Loach', in George McKnight (ed.) *Agent of Challenge and Defiance: The Film of Ken Loach*, Flicks Books, Trowbridge.

Hinson, Hal (1993) 'Review of *Man Bites Dog*', *Washington Post*, 5 June, online.

Hoberman, J. (1996) 'Shoah: Witness to Annihilation, in K. MacDonald and M. Cousins (eds) *Imagining Reality: The Faber Book of Documentary*, Faber and Faber, London.

Hogue, Peter (1993) 'Images (*David Holzman's Diary*)', *Film Comment*, Volume 29, Number 6, 2–4.

Hogue, Peter (1996) 'Documentaries as Movies', *Film Comment*, Volume 32, Number 4, 56–60.

Hoijer, B. (1990) 'Studying Viewer's Reception of Television Programmes:

Theoretical and Methodological Considerations', *European Journal of Communication*, Volume 5, Number 1.

Horn, John (1999) 'The Outer Limits', *Premiere*, Volume 12, Number 6, February, 82–8.

Horowitz, Sara R. (1997) 'But Is It Good for the Jews? Spielberg's Schindler and the Aesthetics of Atrocity', in Y. Loshitzky (ed.), *Spielberg's Holocaust: Critical Perspectives on* Schindler's List, Indiana University Press, Bloomington.

Howe, Desson (1992b) 'Review of *The Falls, Vertical Features Remake, A Walk Through H'*, *Washington Post*, 11 December, online.

Howe, Desson (1993) 'Review of *Man Bites Dog*', *Washington Post*, 4 June, online.

Hughes, Peter (1995) 'The Documentary Caught in a Web?' *Metro*, Number 104, 45–52.

Hughes, Peter (1996) 'Strangely Compelling: Documentary on Television.', *MIA*, Volume 82, 48–55.

Hutcheon, Linda (1985) *A Theory of Parody*, Methuen, New York.

Hyde, Vicki (1998) '"Real TV"? How TVNZ Turned a Hoax into a Documentary', *New Zealand Skeptic*, Number 48, 1–5.

Izod, John (1998) 'Documentary Soaps: The British as Victims and Witnesses?' Paper presented to Visible Evidence VI, San Francisco State University, 13–16 August.

Jameson, Fredric (1984) 'Postmodernism: The Cultural Logic of Late Capitalism', *New Left Review*, Number 146, 53–92.

Jameson, Richard T. (1998) 'History's Eyes: *Saving Private Ryan*', *Film Comment*, Volume 34, Number 5, 20–3.

Jancovich, M. (1992) 'David Morley, The *Nationwide* Studies', in M. Barker and A. Beezer (eds), *Reading into Cultural Studies*, Routledge, London.

Jensen, K. B. and K. E. Rosengren (1990) 'Five Traditions in Search of the Audience', *European Journal of Communication*, Volume 5, Number 2–3.

Johnston, Trevor (1994) Liner notes to the British Film Institute's video edition of *The Falls*.

Kaplan, E. Ann (1987) *Rocking Around the Clock: Music Television, Postmodernism, and Consumer Culture*, Routledge, New York.

Kempley, Rita (1992) 'Review of *Bob Roberts*', *Washington Post*, 4 September, online.

Keough, Peter (1992) 'Death and Hollywood', *Sight and Sound*, Volume 2, Issue 2, June, 12–13.

Kerr, Paul (1990) 'F For Fake? Friction over Faction', in Andrew Goodwin and Garry Whannel (eds), *Understanding Television*, Routledge, London.

Keyser, Les (1992) *Martin Scorsese*, Twayne Publishers, New York.

Kilborn, Richard (1994) 'Drama over Lockerbie: A New Look at Television Drama-Documentary', *The Historical Journal of Film, Radio and Television*, Volume 14, Number 1, 59–76.

Kilborn, Richard (1996) 'New Contexts for Documentary Production in the UK', *Media, Culture and Society*, Volume 18, Number 1, 141–50.

Kilborn, Richard (1999) 'Discovering the Power of Real-Life Soap', Paper presented to Visible Evidence VII, University of California at Los Angeles, 19–22 August.

Kilborn, Richard and Izod, John (1997) *An Introduction to Television Documentary*, Manchester University Press, Manchester.

Kolker, Robert Phillip (1988) *A Cinema of Loneliness: Penn, Kubrick, Scorsese, Spielberg, Altman*, Oxford University Press, New York.

Krieg, Peter (1997) 'Docs Go Digital: Documentary in the Age of the Internet', *DOX*, Number 11.

Langer, John (1998) *Tabloid Television: Popular Journalism and the "Other" News*, Routledge, London.

Lawrence, Amy (1997) *The Films of Peter Greenaway*, Cambridge University Press, Cambridge.

Leahy, Gillian (1996) 'Fidelity, Faith and Openness: Rescuing Observational Documentary', *MIA*, Volume 82, 40–7.

Leitch, Thomas M. (1997) 'Know-Nothing Entertainment: What To Say To Your Friends on the Right, and Why It Won't Do Any Good', *Literature/Film Quarterly*, Volume 25, Number 1, 7–17.

Lipkin, Steve (1999) 'Defining Docudrama: *In the Name of the Father, Schindler's List* and *JFK*', in A. Rosenthal (ed.), *Why Docudrama? Fact-Fiction on Film and TV*, Southern Illinois University Press, Carbondale, 370–84.

Lockerbie, Ian (1991) 'The Self-Conscious Documentary in Quebec: *L'Emotion dissonante* and *Passiflora*', in P. Easingwood (ed.), *Probing Canadian Culture*, AV-Verlag, Augsburg, 225–34.

Lorenz, Janet E. (1984) 'Review of *The Battle of Algiers*', in Christopher Lyon (ed.), *The International Dictionary of Films and Filmmakers*, Volume 1, 82–4.

Loshitzky, Yosefa (1997) 'Holocaust Others: Spielberg's *Schindler's List* versus Lanzmann's *Shoah*', in Yosefa Loshitzky (ed.), *Spielberg's Holocaust: Critical Perspectives on* Schindler's List, Indiana University Press, Bloomington.

Louvish, Simon (1994) 'Witness', *Sight and Sound*, Volume 4, Issue 3, 12–15.

Lucas, George (1999) 'Movies Are an Illusion', *Premiere*, Volume 12, Number 6, February, 58–60.

Lumby, Catharine (1999) *Gotcha: Life in a Tabloid World*, Allen Unwin, St Leonards.

Lyotard, Jean-François (1984) *The Postmodern Condition: A Report on Knowledge*, University of Minnesota Press, Minneapolis.

MacDonald, Kevin and Mark Cousins (eds) (1996) *Imagining Reality: The Faber Book of Documentary*, Faber and Faber, London.

MacLennan, Gary (1993) 'Truth Propaganda Ideology Power and the Media Teacher', *Metro*, Number 94, 22–8.

Malik, Kenan (1996) *The Meaning of Race*, Macmillan, London.

Mapplebeck, Victoria (1998) 'The Mad, The Bad and The Sad', *DOX*, Number 16, 8–9.

Marks, Laura U. (1999) 'Fetishes and Fossils; Notes on Documentary and

Materiality', in D. Waldman and J. Walker (eds), *Feminism and Documentary*, University of Minnesota Press, Minneapolis, 224–43.

McBride, Ian (1999) 'Where Are We Going and How and Why?', in A. Rosenthal (ed.), *Why Docudrama? Fact-Fiction on Film and TV*, Southern Illinois University Press, Carbondale, 111–18.

McKnight, George (1997) 'Introduction', in George McKnight (ed.), *Agent of Challenge and Defiance: The Films of Ken Loach*, Flicks Books, Trowbridge.

McNeil, Shane (1993) '"We'll Never Get Enough…": *Man Bites Dog*, Documentary Theory and Other Andalsian Ethics', *Cinema Papers*, Number 95, 28–31.

McQuire, Scott (1997) *Crossing the Dgital Threshold*, Australian Key Centre for Cultural and Media Policy, Brisbane.

Meadows, Michael (1999) 'Cultural Studies and Journalism', *MIA*, Volume 90, 43–52.

Monaghan, D. (1995) 'Executions', *Metro*, Number 104, 30–6.

Morley, D. (1992) *Television, Audiences, and Cultural Studies*, Routledge, London.

Mullin, Tom (1993) '"Livin' and Dyin' in Zapruderville" A Code of Representation Reality and its Exhaustion', *Cineaction*, Number 38, 12–15.

Neale, Stephen (1980) *Genre*, London, BFI.

Neale, Steve and Frank Krutnik (1990) *Popular Film and Television Comedy*, Routledge, London.

Newman, G. F. (1990) 'Truth Ache', *Time Out*, 30 May–6 June, 21.

Nichols, Bill (1991) *Representing Reality: Issues and Concepts in Documentary*, Indiana University Press, Bloomington.

Nichols, Bill (1993) '"Getting to Know You…" Knowledge, Power and the Body', in M. Renov (ed.), *Theorizing Documentary*, Routledge, New York and London.

Nichols, Bill (1994) *Blurred Boundaries: Questions of Meaning in Contemporary Culture*, Indiana University Press, Bloomington.

Nightingale, V. (1996) *Studying Audiences: The Shock of the Real*, Routledge, London.

O'Neill, Edward. R. (1995) 'The Seen of the Crime: Violence, Anxiety and the Domestic in Police Reality Programming', *CineAction*, Number 38, 56–63.

Ophuls, Marcel (1985) 'Closely Watched Trains', *American Film*, Volume 11, Number 2, 16–22.

Orvell, Miles (1995) 'Documentary Film and the Power of Interrogation: *American Dream* and *Roger and Me*', *Film Quarterly*, Volume 48, Number 2, 10–18.

Paget, Derek (1990) *True Stories?: Documentary Drama on Radio, Screen and Stage*, Manchester University Press, Manchester.

Paget, Derek (1998) *No Other Way to Tell It: Dramadoc/Docudrama on Television*, Manchester University Press, Manchester.

Paget, Derek (1999) 'Acting the Real: Dramatic Practices in Television Dramadoc/Docudrama', Seminar presentation, University of Waikato, 23 November.

Palmer, Jerry (1987) *The Logic of the Absurd: On Film and Television Comedy*, British Film Institute, London.

Palowski, Franciszek (1998) *Witness: The Making of Schindler's List*, Orion Books Limited, London.

Paskin, Barbara (1998) 'Live and Dangerous', *Listener* (New Zealand), 28 February, 68–9.

Peary, Danny (1981) *Cult Movies*, Vermilion, London.

Peirce, Charles (1965) *Collected Papers: Vol. II*, Cambridge, Mass.: The Belknap Press at the Harvard Press.

Perlmutter, Ruth (1991) 'Woody Allen's *Zelig*: An American Jewish Parody', in Andrew Horton (ed.). *Comedy/Cinema/Theory*, University of California Press, Berkeley.

Petley, Julian (1996) 'Fact plus Fiction Equals Friction', *Media, Culture and Society*, Volume 18, Number 1, 11–25.

Petley, Julian (1997) 'Factual Fictions and Fictional Fallacies: Ken Loach's Documentary Dramas', in George McKnight (ed.) *Agent of Challenge and Defiance: The Films of Ken Loach*, Flicks Books, Trowbridge.

Philo, Greg (1990) *Seeing and Believing: The Influence of Television*, Routledge, London.

Plantinga, Carl R. (1997) *Rhetoric and Representation in Nonfiction Film*, Cambridge University Press, Cambridge.

Plantinga, Carl (1998) 'Gender, Power and a Cucumber: Satirizing Masculinity in *This Is Spinal Tap*', in Barry Keith Grant and Jeannette Sloniowski (eds) (1998) *Documenting The Documentory Close Readings of Documentary Film and Video*, Wayne State University Press, Detroit, 318–32.

Prince, Stephen (1996) 'True Lies: Perceptual Realism, Digital Images, and Film Theory', *Film Quarterly*, Volume 49, Number 3, 27–37.

Punt, Michael (1995) '"Well, Who You Gonna Believe, Me or Your Own Eyes?": A Problem of Digital Photography', *The Velvet Light Trap*, Number 36, 3–20.

Pym, John (1983) 'Duke Ellington's Brother', *Sight and Sound*, Volume 52, Number 4, 283.

Pym, John (1986) 'Review of *Shoah*', *Sight and Sound*, Volume 55, Number 3, 187–9.

Reidelbach, Maria (1991) *Completely MAD: A History of the Comic Book and Magazine*, Little, Brown and Company, Boston.

Renov, Michael (1999) 'New Subjectivities: Documentary and Self-Representation in the Post-Vérité Age', in D. Waldman and J. Walker (eds), *Feminism and Documentary*, University of Minnesota Press, Minneapolis 84–94.

Romney, Jonathan (1994) 'In the Time of Earthquakes', *Sight and Sound*, Volume 4, Issue 3, March, 8–11.

Roscoe, J., H. Marshall and K. Gleeson (1995) 'The Television Audience: A Reconsideration of the "Taken-for-granted" Terms "active", "social" and "critical". *European Journal of Communication*, Volume 10, Number 1, 87–108.

Roscoe, Jane (1994) 'The Irish Conflict as Represented in two British Drama-Documentaries: An Analysis of the Encoding/Decoding Process.' Unpublished PhD thesis, University of East London.

Roscoe, Jane (1999) *Documentary in New Zealand: An Immigrant Nation*, Dunmore Press, Palmerston North.

Roscoe, Jane (2000) 'Mock-Documentary Goes Mainstream: The Blair Witch Project', *Jump Cut*, Volume 43, 3–8.

Roscoe, Jane, and Craig Hight (1996), 'Silver Magic: Colin McKenzie Takes his Place in New Zealand History', *Illusions*, Number 25, winter.

Roscoe, Jane and Craig Hight (1997), 'Mocking Silver: Re-Inventing the Documentary Project (or Grierson Lies Bleeding)', *Continuum*, Volume 11, Number 1.

Roscoe, Jane and Peter Hughes (1999) 'Die Vermittlung, von, "wahren Geschichten". Neue digitale Technologien und das Projekt des Dokumentarischen'. ['Communicating "True" Stories: New Digital Technologies and the Documentary Project'], *Montage*, Volume 8, Number 11, 34–154.

Rose, Margaret (1993) *Parody: Ancient, Modern and Postmodern*, Cambridge University Press, Cambridge.

Rosen, P. (1993) 'Document and Documentary: On the Persistence of Historical Concepts', in M. Renov (ed.), *Theorizing Documentary*, Routledge, London.

Rosenbaum, Jonathan (1975) 'Improvisations and Interactions in Altmanville', *Sight and Sound*, Volume 44, Number 2, 90–5.

Rosenthal, Alan (ed.) (1999) *Why Docudrama? Fact-Fiction on Film and TV*, Southern Illinois University Press, Carbondale.

Rothman, William (1998) 'The Filmmaker as Hunter', in B. K. Grant and J. Sloniowski (eds), *Documenting the Documentary: Close Readings of Documentary Film and Video*, Wayne State University Press, Detroit, 23–39.

Rubin, Martin (1992) 'The Grayness of Darkness: *The Honeymoon Killers* and its Impact on Psychokiller Cinema', *The Velvet Light Trap*, Number 30, 48–64.

Ryan, Susan and Richard Porton (1998) 'The Politics of Everyday Life: An Interview with Ken Loach', *Cineaste*, Volume 24, Number 1, 22–7.

Sanderson, Mark (1990) 'Shots in the Dark', *Time Out*, 30 May–6 June, 20–1.

Sarchett, Barry W. (1994) '"Rockumentary" as Metadocumentary: Martin Scorsese's *The Last Waltz*', *Literature/Film Quarterly*, Volume 22, Number 1, 28–35.

Schickel, Richard (1998) 'Reel War: Steven Spielberg peers at the Face of Battle as Hollywood Never Has Before', *Time*, 23 November, 78–81.

Seidman, Steven (1994) *Contested Knowledge: Social Theory in the Postmodern Era*, Blackwell, Oxford.

Self, Robert (1982) 'The Art Cinema and Robert Altman', *The Velvet Light Trap*, Number 19, 30–4.

Silvestone, R. (1985) *Framing Science: The Making of a BBC Documentary*, British Film Institute, London.

Slavin, John (1994) 'Witness to the Endtime: The Holocaust as Art', *Metro*, Number 98, 4–13.

Smith, Gavin (1994) 'Oliver Stone: Why Do I Have To Provoke?', *Sight and Sound*, Volume 4, Issue 12, 8–12.

Smith, Gavin and Richard T. Jameson (1992) '"The Movie You Saw is the Movie

We're Going to Make" ', *Film Comment*, Volume 28, Number 3, May–June, 20–30.

Sommerville, Margaret (1999) 'DocoEthics, Keynote Presentation', Australian International Documentary Conference, Adelaide, 2–6 November.

Stacey, Jackie (1993) 'Textual Obsession: Methodology, History and Researching Female Spectatorship', *Screen*, Volume 34, Number 3, 260–74.

Stalker, John (1989) *Stalker: Ireland, 'Shoot to Kill' and the 'Affair'*, Penguin, London.

Taubin, Amy (1991) 'Killing Men', *Sight and Sound*, Volume 1, Issue 1, 14–19.

Testa, Bart (1998) 'Seeing with Experimental Eyes', in B. K. Grant and J. Sloniowski (eds) *Documenting the Documentary: Close Readings of Documentary Film and Video*, Wayne State University Press, Detroit.

Thompson, David and Ian Christie (1990) *Scorsese on Scorsese*, Faber and Faber, London.

Thompson, Robert J. (1996) *Television's Second Golden Age: From Hill Street Blues to ER*, Syracuse University Press, New York.

Thomson, David (1994) 'The Best Interests of the Game', *Film Comment*, Volume 30, Number 5, 20–6.

Tulloch, John (1990) *Television Drama*, Routledge, London.

Van Lier, M. (1993) Editorial, *DOX*, Number 0, Winter.

Vaughan, Dai (1976) *Television Documentary Usage*, British Film Institute London.

Waldman, Diane and Janet Walker (eds) (1999) *Feminism and Documentary*, University of Minnesota Press, Minneapolis.

Walker, Alexander (1971) *Stanley Kubrick Directs*, Sphere Books Limited, London.

Walker, Martin (1994) 'Making Saccharine Taste Sour', Volume 4, Issue 10, 16–17.

Wasson, Haidee (1993) 'Assassinating an Image: The Strange Life of Kennedy's Image', *Cineaction*, Number 38, 4–11.

Weissberg, L. (1997) 'The Tale of a Good German: Reflections on the German Reception of *Schindler's List*' in Y. Loshitzky (ed.), *Spielberg's Holocaust: Critical Perspectives on* Schindler's List, Indiana University Press, Bloomington.

Weissman, G. (1995) 'A Fantasy of Witnessing', *Media, Culture and Society*, Volume 17, 293–307.

Wetherell, M. and J. Potter (1992) *Mapping the Language of Racism: Discourse and the Legitimation of Exploitation*, Harvester Wheatsheaf, London.

White, Les (1994) '*Schindler's List*: My Father Is a Schindler Jew', *Jump Cut*, Number 39, 3–6.

Williams, Linda (1993) 'Mirror Without Memories: Truth, History, and the New Documentary', *Film Quarterly*, Volume 46, Number 3, 9–21.

Williams, Raymond (1976) *Communications*, Penguin, Harmondsworth.

Williams, Sita (1999) 'The Making of *Hostages*', in A. Rosenthal (ed.), *Why Docudrama? Fact-Fiction on Film and TV*, Southern Illinois University Press, Carbondale, 324–32.

Wilmington, Michael (1992) 'Laughing and Killing', *Sight and Sound*, Volume 2, Issue 2, June, 10–15.

Wilson, David (1971) 'Politics and Pontecorvo', *Sight and Sound*, Volume 40, Number 3, 160–1.

Winston, Brian (1995) *Claiming the Real*, British Film Institute, London.

Winston, Brian (1996) *Technologies of Seeing: Photography, Cinematography and Television*, British Film Institute, London.

Winston, Brian (1999) 'The Primrose Path: Faking UK Television Documentary, "Docuglitz" and Docusoap', http://www.latrobe.edu.au/www/screeningthepast/firstrelease/fr1199/bwfr8b.htm, 12 November.

Wober, Mallory (1990) '*Who Bombed Birmingham?*', ITC Research Reference Paper, Independent Television Commission, London.

Wollen, Peter (1994), *Sight and Sound*, Volume 4, Issue 12, December, 18–21.

Woodhead, Leslie (1999) 'The Guardian Lecture: Dramtized Documentary', in A. Rosenthal (ed.), *Why Docudrama? Fact-Fiction on Film and TV*, Southern Illinois University Press, Carbondale, 101–10.

Index